READING
POVERTY

PATRICK SHANNON

Heinemann
Portsmouth, NH

Heinemann
A division of Reed Elsevier, Inc.
361 Hanover Street
Portsmouth, NH 03801–3912

Offices and agents throughout the world

Library of Congress Cataloging-in-Publication Data
Shannon, Patrick.
    Reading poverty / Patrick Shannon.
        p.   cm.
    Includes bibliographical references and index.
    ISBN 0-325-00017-4
    1. Poor—Education—Social aspects—United States.   2. Reading—
Social aspects—United States.   3. Literacy—Political aspects—
United States.   4. Poverty—United States.   I. Title.
LC4086.S53   1998
428.4'HQ071—dc21   97-46358
                                                                              CIP

Editor: Lois Bridges
Production: Elizabeth Valway
Cover design: Catherine Hawkes
Manufacturing: Louise Richardson

Printed in the United States of America on acid-free paper
02   01   00   99   DA   2   3   4   5

FOR ROBERT J. SMITH ◆
WHO TAUGHT ME TO READ

CONTENTS

PREFACE

I'll Tell Ya What I Want; What I Really Really Want

text, lies, & videotape, my last book with Heinemann (Shannon 1995), was designed to demonstrate how revisiting stories from our everyday lives could help us develop critical awareness of ourselves and our world. I analyzed the dress code of my former junior high school, a curricular project about folktales and Disney, our daughter's and son's first days of school, a cab ride in New York City, Wal Mart's opening in our community, a doll contest, and watching the film "Free Willy" with our children. In each "text,"I read new ways to think about our bodies, ownership, approximations and intentions, otherness, curriculum, competition and learning, and listening to children. Through these stories and my assigned morals, I tried to refocus the debate about schooling—currently mired in concerns about test scores and high-skill/high-wage jobs—to questions of how we wish to live together. My hope for that book was that readers would reexamine their daily experiences to see how culture and power are encoded in the texts they encounter in and out of schools.

I'm told that the book is successful in eliciting stories of schooling in which the social forms—rules, organizations, expectations, etc.—restrict rather than enhance the possibilities of learning, living, and freedom. Some have suggested that the concept of critical literacy—previously believed to be beyond their grasp—became clear to them for the first time as a practical possibility for teachers and students. A few have written to me about their own versions of the Wal Mart curriculum or how to watch children's films. I admit to a certain pleasure at these remarks, a joy of being read. But I also worry about the limits of my argument in *text, lies, & videotape*, which convey a maverick individualism at a time when collective action is needed.

Reading Poverty has a different feel than *text, lies, & videotape*, although I think it too is about the stories of our everyday lives. It is not a personal tale, although I am doing the telling. *Reading Poverty* seeks to embed the stories of our lives within the social construction of poverty in America. At first, teachers and educators may not find immediate connections between their lives and poverty. Several of my university and public-school colleagues have remarked that they find themselves removed from poverty—as if that admission had nothing to do with poverty and the poor. "I teach in a suburban school. All our students are middle class or higher." "University students have enough money to take time out from earning in order to study. They are not poor, by definition." In both these cases, the speakers suggest that the poor are out of their sight at work, and apparently out of their minds also.

Yet poverty has everything to do with schooling—how it is theorized, how it is organized, how it runs. For example, IQ tests, content of textbooks, national curricular standards and examinations, standardized tests, teacher expectations, compensatory instruction, struggles over best methods of teaching, tracking, school/business partnerships, and even materials available for students are directly connected to various political representations of poverty and how poverty might be overcome. There isn't a day at school or university that our lives are not substantially influenced by issues of poverty.

Reading Poverty offers this backdrop to our revisiting of the stories in our lives. I believe that most of what passes for concern for the poor is rather carefully camouflaged support for cultural and economic inequalities in America. In most cases, writers represent the poor as remarkably different and separate from the rest of us who are ascribed other class statuses. These views of poverty have us working against ourselves at school to the detriment of nearly three-quarters of the American population. By presenting the values and interests that underlie these various views—and the politics between them in and out of schools—I hope to demonstrate how the internal logic of these approaches to poverty, schooling, and reading education is illogical when we switch the reason for our work and country from the protection of property to the well-being of people.

Reading Poverty suggests some new tools of analysis for our stories and some new language to think and talk about our goals for our work and our lives. I attempt to convey the various political representations of poverty from their advocates' positions. I am not always successful as my distaste for some seeps through; for that I apologize. I believe that most representations are compelling only if readers start with the assumption that cultural and economic inequalities in classrooms, communities, and the nation are inevitable, permanent facts of our lives—something we'd better get used to. However, if you begin from a different starting point, as I do— one that is stated in the Constitution—that all Americans are created equal, that justice is possible, and that we all should have substantial opportunities to deliberate about our priorities and actions, then you can see that the currently popular views on poverty and the poor cannot help us read and overcome poverty. We need to think about poverty, our work, and ourselves differently.

Although I have been working toward this book for twenty years, I wasn't sure that I was ready or able to write it until Penny Oldfather asked me to write a Critical Issues piece on this subject for the *Journal of Literacy Research*. Since that request, many others have helped me form and polish my arguments. At Penn State, Ruth Lowery, Cathy Toll, Jackie Edmondson, Deborah Alviani, Elise Youth, and Carla Dueck read a selection of the primary sources, upon which the middle chapters are based, and offered helpful comments on how political ideologies and reading education overlap. At York University, Colette Drew, Julie Fellini, Ricci Haynes, Lisa Mensella-Bingi, Sherri Nishimuva, Andre Patterson, Hirfalin Scott, Inavet Siddigue, Daryl Sidial, and Johanna Zeeman helped me make my points more accessible to educators. Trish Crawford, Rich Gibson, Dan Marshall, Ron Miller, Sharon Murphy, and Sandra Wilde read the first complete draft of this book and made insightful comments. Judy Nastase prepared the final manuscript, charts and all. Lois Bridges was remarkably supportive in bringing this book to publication. As always, my family was involved in the project from the start. Kathleen Shannon provides the intellectual, moral, and emotional support that makes my work possible. Laura and Tim-Pat's emerging interest in popular music reminded me of the possibilities of music in our lives and hopes. All the chapter titles are lines from songs to which they listen.

INTRODUCTION

I Read the News Today, Oh Boy: Reading This Book

The idea for this book began while reading the *Metro* section of the November 28, 1996, *Washington Post.* Having written on the importance of educational experiences apart from school, I was attracted by the title, "Student Pizzeria Still Delivering Second Chances." In the article, Julie Goodman described trials, tribulations, and successes of Project Soar, a pizzeria that served as a forum for tutoring in both academic and life skills. Run by David Domenici, son of Senator Peter Domenici of New Mexico, this establishment employed teenagers who had been in trouble with the police. The Project's schedule left little time for participants to "be on the street": two hours of academic tutoring after school, followed immediately by several hours of making and delivering pizzas at night. The culmination and primary goal of the project appears to be set at high-school graduation, the point at which participants left the Project for the world of work. In a real sense, the pizzeria seems to be one of the thousand points of light that George Bush called for during his presidency, and Domenici exemplified the volunteerism that has become a mania during Bill Clinton's Administration.

As I began the article, I was excited to learn that the students were offered opportunities beyond making and delivering

◆◆

pizza. They were asked to be customer representatives, to develop client files, and to learn ways to advertise their services on the Internet. However, by the end of the article, I had the sinking feeling that the pizzeria, this light, and these volunteers could not deliver on the promises made to most teenagers in America. My doubts stemmed from three short paragraphs.

"This is like a big family here," said Domenici, 32, a lawyer at Wilmer, Cutler & Pickering in Washington. "The kids are doing better than we'd ever expected." (3)

Tayon Walker, 20, who graduated from high school and Project Soar last spring, has been an inspiration to his peers and Domenici. Walker, who lives with his grandmother in Southeast Washington, became a cook at the Union Station restaurant, B. Smith's, and now works at McDonald's and Blockbuster Video. (3)

"He's like another father she didn't have," Lamons said of Domenici. "He pushed, and that's what I didn't have time to do. I gave up on her. I put her in foster care. He grabbed her and gave her a life." (3)

The sincerity of all concerned in Project Soar may be beyond doubt. Domenici, these teenagers, and their parents have found ways to take greater control of their lives through this association, I am sure. However, these three statements triggered several questions about the assumptions that underlie such projects, the interests and needs they serve, and the possibilities they engender or preclude. First, I wondered why Mr. Domenici, and the others in his "we," expected these teenagers to do poorly? Why did he doubt that these youth would achieve the typical camaraderie of teenagers working together? Words and phrases such as "big family" and "better than we'd ever expected" imply some assumptions about youth, about their lives, and about poverty that bothered me.

Second, Mr. Walker stated that the project was a good bargain for him. He worked hard and, in exchange, he "got the new me out of it." Yet the prospects for that "new me" are startlingly clear in the description of his employment. He graduated from high school—assumed by the project to be a ticket to opportunity—and now he works part-time at McDonald's and Blockbuster Video. During the six months since graduation, he's already changed jobs at least once. McDonald's and Blockbuster Video may be fine corporations, and they may offer careers for some. However, they do not pay most of their employees more than the minimum wage, and they do not offer them full-time employment, health insurance, or other benefits. If Walker is lucky enough to work forty hours through both jobs, his income will be at the poverty line for a single individual. Although his efforts may well be inspiring, the opportunities available to him and other teenagers are not. Journalist Goodman, if not Domenici himself, implies that such inspiration is all that keeps America from full employment and prosperity for all. What are the real incentives to work hard in and out of schools? How do schools serve the economy and how does the economy serve school graduates?

Finally, Ms. Lamons is grateful to Mr. Domenici and the pizzeria. She appreciates the push, the structure, and the time. However, I wondered about the phrase "grabbed her and gave her a life." What does that mean? The phrase seems to suggest that Ms. Lamons and parents like her welcome Mr. Domenici and people like him to take charge of their children, structure their behaviors for them, and offer them work. In the photograph that accompanied Goodman's article, a young black man makes a pizza, while in the background, four well-dressed white individuals laugh with one another during a party for "workers and friends" at the pizzeria. The racial and class implications of this photograph and statement are troubling to me. Should the wealthy and the white take charge of the poor and people of color? What types of lives would they offer them? And what does this mean in a democracy when the wealthy and the white have, or at least are perceived to have, the power to give (and, by implication, to deny) a life?

What had started for me as a sympathetic look at a possible alternative to teenagers growing up absurd and dangerous, quickly became an act of frustration as I struggled to understand how Goodman, Domenici, and others might address my questions. What troubled me most at the time was the way Goodman created a gap between the two groups involved in the Project and, by extension, between the reader and the poor. In his essay, "Doing Time, Marking Race," Widemann (1995) wrote about politicians' enthusiasm for being tough on crime.

What bothered me most about the hysterical, bloodthirsty TV ads during the last election was the absolute certainty of the candidates that the prison cells they promised to construct, the draconian prison terms, and the prison conditions they would impose, if elected, would never confine them or those who voted for them . . .

the ones they were promising to lock up and punish, by design, would never be their people. (504)

By framing her article with Domenici's surprise at these teenagers doing so well, Walker's Mcjobs, which are expected to be inspirational, and the Projects' lives to give, Goodman conveyed a similar distinction of value among human beings. Of course, Project Soar is offered as a more humane alternative to prisons for troubling teenagers, but even when successful, it would confine them to lives in or near poverty just as effectively. Moreover, it would do so without government expense. Programs like Project Soar are for street kids, not for our kids.

Two months after reading Goodman's report, I found a different take on poverty and social responsibility in Harriet Brown's article on Brenda Eheart in the Women of the Year issue of *Ms.* magazine (January/February 1997). Eheart, a college professor at the University of Illinois, is the founder of Hope Meadows, a community planned to help poor teenagers "pouring into the Illinois foster-care system." Previously, her research demonstrated that foster and adoptive families struggled with this group because "they had no help. They needed tons of emotional support and tons of information" (46). With a grant from the Illinois Department of Children and Family Services, Eheart purchased twenty-two acres and thirty buildings on a closed Air Force base two hours south of Chicago and transformed it into a community of thirteen foster families and forty senior citizens. "Hope Meadows is the children's last chance to do what's left of their growing up in a safe, stable environment" (46).

Eheart believes that caring for these teenagers is full-time work, and her grant provides foster families with free rent and a salary of $18,000 a year so that one parent can remain available all day for the children. Each two-parent family agrees to raise (and hopefully adopt) four Hope children over a period of time. Single parents agree to raise three children. Brown noted that "[Eheart's] attitude flies in the face of the current wave of welfare reform, with its implicit notion that a parent who stays home and cares for children is not really working" (47). To complete the community, Eheart made Hope Meadows multigenerational by offering seniors low rent in exchange for volunteering with the foster children six hours a week. These

surrogate grandparents offer tutoring, supervision, and friendship for the teens.

Although there are certain similarities between Project
Soar and Hope Meadows—both are led by white professionals,
both target poor teenagers, and both include academic tutoring
—they differ in important ways. Eheart concentrates on the
present. Her community seeks to immediately make life better
for these children and offers only vague statements about the
future. Domenici's project is all about getting ready for some
other time. Hope Meadows takes Hillary Rodham Clinton's
book on children seriously—it takes a village to raise a child.
Project Soar offers specialized training for individuals. Finally,
Eheart has no doubts about the Hope teenagers; she knows they
will flourish within the proper environment, while Domenici
is surprised that Washington teens adapt so readily and well to
the regimen of the pizzeria. Clearly, Eheart intends Hope Meadows to be for all of us, not just the troubled teens, and she is
surprised that her liberal friends and associates from the university have not joined her community.

Yet as promising as Hope Meadows seems to be, Eheart's
utopian experiment raises some questions for me. Were the
Beatles correct? Is love all you need? Doesn't a community
also need some type of economy? Some political system?
Won't reliance on the regular economy offer many of the hardships that created the original problems for the caregivers?
While I understand the need to make the present safe and stable, I wondered what the future held for these teens outside
the protected environment. Most troubling to me was Eheart's
attempt to reproduce her old neighborhood as the solution for
the torrent of poor children in the foster-care system. "She
grew up on a small dairy farm in western New York, in the
archetypal 1950s family: mom, dad, twin brothers, and older
sister. Her grandparents lived next door" (47). "I loved that
block (in Madison, Wisconsin, during the 1970s). There were
two or three houses of young professors who were our age.
There were working-class families our age. And in between all
those houses were seniors. We were all having babies, and the
seniors loved us, loved our babies. And we loved them. I
thought every block in the country was like that. Whoa, was
I wrong" (48). Eheart defines herself as normal, so she
attempts to re-create her past to make a "normal" present for

foster teens. "Today the site of the old air base is a miracle of normalcy. Children who once had little hope but to be institutionalized now live with loving families in a tidy suburban neighborhood of winding roads and long, low split-levels, in a section of Illinois as flat as a piece of paper" (47). Are suburban neighborhoods with two-parent families the only normal environment for growing up? Is this the solution for poverty in this country—to make all neighborhoods like Eheart's?

In the March 3, 1997, issue of *The Nation*, Jay Walljasper describes the renaissance of Dudley Street, a section of the Roxbury district in Boston, Massachusetts. Approximately thirty-five percent of the Dudley Street families lived below the poverty line, twenty percent of the community's lots were vacant, and virtually all the major businesses had moved to the suburbs when the turnaround began during the middle 1980s. Currently, African Americans make up forty percent of the neighborhood's residents, thirty percent come from Latin America, twenty-four percent from the Cape Verdi Islands off the African coast, and six percent are whites, mostly elderly Irish and Italians. The revitalization began when La Alianza Hispana, a local service agency, interested a Boston trust foundation in investing in the neighborhood. During their first meeting of the trust executives, members of the Dudley Street community challenged the trust to treat the community as an equal partner in the project.

To the surprise of many, the trust executives decided to fund improvements in the Dudley Street neighborhood without maintaining direct control over planning or implementation of the projects. Robert Holmes, one of the executives, reported "some people thought we were crazy. They thought we were throwing away our grant money" (12). The Dudley Street Neighborhood Initiative (DSNI) became the deliberative and management body of the project, with an initial membership of residents and representatives from local social-service agencies, churches, and businesses. Emphasizing that the organization should be a political force rather than a clearinghouse for low-income housing or social services, the neighborhood boasts of many successes. The projects began small—opening a closed station for the commuter train, ridding the streets of abandoned cars, and stopping illegal dumping in vacant lots. Early successes brought increased membership in the organization; currently 2,500 residents are members and meetings are held in Spanish and Portuguese, as well as English.

Perhaps the biggest victory was DSNI's successful employment of eminent domain to force the sale of vacant land and abandoned buildings to the neighborhood group. Since that victory, more than three hundred units of housing have been rehabilitated. Moreover, two housing developments have been completed with units that can be purchased by families with incomes as low as $15,000. These developments have attracted young families to remain within the neighborhood even after they could afford to move. Because the DSNI was involved in the design of the projects, the neighborhood avoided high-rise units and "the usual cookie-cutter subdivision designs." Streets are narrow with sidewalks and houses that include front porches on which neighbors can visit. New residents have already pulled together several times to ward off traffic problems, crime, and noisy businesses. Walljasper concludes:

Dudley Street's significance as a symbol of hope for America's hard-hit urban neighborhoods is not that it represents a magic way to mend problems without spending taxpayers' money. Rather, it points to what can be done to make sure that both public and private money invested in low-income areas truly makes a difference in people's lives. . . . The most important message from Dudley Street is that conditions in inner-city neighborhoods can actually improve if revitalization efforts inspire the enthusiastic involvement of people who live there. (17)

The Dudley Street project differs from Project Soar and Hope Meadows in important ways. Foremost, it is based on trust in the competence of people in trouble to develop solutions for their own problems. In this way, Walljasper suggests that the poor migrants from the South, immigrants from the Caribbean and Atlantic, and whites who have lived there since the 1950s are just like us. While expertise and financing from outside was needed and used, leadership for the project came from within the community—not from universities, law firms, or other businesses. All ages of residents have participated in the revitalization, not just the young. Yet as Walljasper states, the Dudley Street project raises questions about interventions to alleviate the causes and consequences of poverty. Does Dudley Street's success imply that government money is not necessary in fighting poverty? Could such a model work in neighborhoods marked by stronger racial and ethnic identity divisions? In rural or suburban areas, where the geographic distances are greater, could a DSNI have such a singular impact? And what about the economy? Small businesses with minimum-wage jobs are a start, but like the graduates of Project Soar, Dudley Street residents will need better paying and more jobs to extend their renaissance.

The editors of the *Washington Post, Ms.,* and *The Nation* presented Goodman's, Brown's, and Walljasper's articles to readers as compelling stories with good photo opportunities. These "good news" items seem intended innocently to make readers feel good about themselves and their community. And I'll admit I started these stories with that in mind. Yet these articles are much more than that. When read, they teach us about poverty, its causes, its cures, and its heroes. That is, articles such as these present policy statements loudly and clearly to readers who might avoid such topics on the front or editorial pages. None of the articles seem written for the poor; rather, they instruct middle-class readers how to think about poverty and the poor, and tell us what we and the government should do. Goodman's piece instructs us to grab the poor, to mold them in our image of their proper place, and to forget about propriety because they can't help themselves. Brown's teaches us to invite the poor into our safe and stable neighborhoods, to care for them, and to make them just like us. Walljasper's tells us to assist the poor by sharing our wealth and expertise and by trusting them to develop solutions to their problems themselves. In this way, the articles and authors represent ideological positions, projecting different goals and values that point toward their vision of ideal ways of living together.

Moreover, these and other articles about poverty teach us about ourselves. They help us to locate, negotiate, revise, and reconfirm ourselves by describing the lives and values of others as the images and stories they evoke are woven together with our feelings and understandings of ourselves, our connections with others, and the world. The lessons of these articles come not only from their contents, but also in the ways they are presented to us—their allusions, metaphors, visual images, and organization. Our coming to understand poverty, its causes, and our responsibilities, then, is affected by what we

know *and* by how we know it. Our feelings and understandings are always relational, shifting, and vulnerable. Editors
and authors recognize this and assume a certain capacity
among their readers to engage these visions of the past,
present, and future as they attempt to make their visions
seem natural, obvious, and commonsensible. I share these
intentions to teach. I assume the readers of this book to consider themselves among the non-poor, to coin an awkward
phrase, a group who has explicit and implicit knowledge and
feelings based on actual and vicarious experiences with poverty and the poor. Because of the geographic, social, and political isolation of the poor in our society, I have assumed that
the vicarious lessons of film, television, radio, and newspapers
influenced our understandings considerably. These lessons,
which often come to us as stories, make our views of poverty
and the poor elastic as we stretch our understandings to
accommodate the examples presented to us.

This book is about particulars and extensions of these
popular media lessons. It's about poverty, policy, reading, and
human value and agency in our democracy. More precisely, it
attempts to identify the conditions under which the reading of
popular understandings of poverty enable or disable the exercise of critical awareness and action. Toward that end, I construct and engage representations of the poor that rub taken-
for-granted understandings of poverty, its causes, and its
solutions against the grain so as to revitalize and rearticulate
what we see as desirable and necessary for an open, just, and
life-sustaining future. Let me be clear, the central purpose of
this book is to challenge current social constructions of poverty, reading education, and the putative relationship between
the two. This requires an exploration of how official and popular representations of poverty are bound to specific historical, social, and economic conditions of their own production.
Advocates of these representations think in patterns that they
do not develop themselves. Rather, they project a social style
of thought that they adapt and transform. How are the texts
they produce situated within structures of affect and meaning
as they compete to influence our understanding and direct our
actions? In the end, I hope these explanations and inquiries
help us learn to read poverty in order to take responsibility
for self-production of our own identities, to know others, and

to insert ourselves forcefully into the open narratives of democracy.

To read poverty, we must employ a sociological imagination to push the definition and practices of reading education beyond traditional fascinations with decoding words, finding main ideas, and following someone else's meanings until they become means for understanding ourselves; our human, social, cultural, and historical connections with others; and social structures. "The sociological imagination enables us to grasp history and biography and the relations between the two within society" (Mills 1959, 6). By slowing the speed of "this age of facts" that comes to us too quickly for careful comprehension, and by stripping away the aura of naturalness of official and popular texts of poverty to reveal their social constructions, this type of reading can help us locate ourselves and others in the economic, social, and political relations of our times. Such readings highlight our agency, leading us to challenge social constructions of poverty that seek to separate us from the poor in ways that diminish democratic possibilities, and to envision alternatives to these constructions that will increase our chances for economic and social justice. By reading poverty and by helping others do so as well, we take important steps toward revitalizing the roles of literacy, schooling, and ourselves in civic life.

This book offers four stances of reading poverty. In the first, the official construction of poverty is interrogated to expose the lives behind government statistics. The second reading explains how various representations of the causes of poverty allow us to see the ideological positions of their proponents and their political intentions. The third pass reverses the connotation of the double-entendre in the book title to explore the poverty of reading practices in American schools, which, I argue, are largely based on the same ideological positions that underlie explanations of poverty. The fourth reading presents our need to retheorize poverty and school reading practices in our post-industrial democracy. In this way, every passage within the book is also a reading lesson, teaching us how to read the world differently.

This association of reading and poverty is not forced on my part. I am not the first to make this association. For example, during the late 1970s, the Ford Foundation commissioned Hunter and Harman (1979) to report on the connections between adult illiteracy and chronic poverty. Five years later, Kozol (1985) offered his critique of their report, and proposed a mobilization of university students and faculty to overcome the ravages of illiteracy in America. Most recently, Stuckey (1991) presented a more pessimistic view of literacy and its relationships to poverty. "The truth is that literacy and English instruction can hurt you, more clearly and forcefully and permanently than it can help you, and that schools, like other social institutions, are designed to replicate, or at least not to disturb social divisions and class privilege" (123). I share neither Stuckey's pessimism nor Hunter and Harman's or Kozol's belief that literacy is a natural lever for success. Although the latter critique past and present schooling of the poor, they echo a traditional rationale for public education.

Public investment in schooling in general and reading programs in particular has been connected directly to the prevention of poverty since at least the advent of common public schooling in this country. In 1848, Mann argued, "Education, then, beyond all other devices of human origin, is the great equalizer of the conditions of men—the balance-wheel of the social machinery" (87). In the following chapters, I take up various ways in which this association has been made and evaluate their consequences on poverty, policy, and reading instruction in light of current economic, social, and political conditions. My ultimate intent is to help readers to understand possibilities and limitations of current policies and practices in our efforts to construct a just democracy, to envision more just alternatives, and to act.

Democratic ideals—justice, common good, and citizenship—are socially constructed. Readers can be sure that writers representing different political groups will vary greatly in the meanings and intentions they assign to these words. Indeed, *democracy* is and has been a term struggled over since the beginning of this country. Sehr (1996) contends that these various positions fall somewhere along a continuum between private and public democracies. Conceptions of private democracy stem from the political philosophies of Thomas Hobbes and John Locke, in which the primary reason for government is to enhance and protect the accumulation of property—happiness and life as well as capital in its many forms. Toward that end, American "founding fathers" designed a government that protected individual rights, but that also placed several buffers against popular control. Framers feared the consequences of the "natural" differences among people to accumulate property. Through restrictions on eligibility for voting, representative government, and limits of state intervention in private (property) matters, a democratic ideal could be realized—one that places severe limits on our abilities to control political and economic decisions that affect our lives.

In contrast, advocates of public democracy see popular participation in public life as the essential ingredient in democracy government. Fundamental to this participation are the creation and maintenance of publics, which serve as forums in which individuals and groups can meet to discuss their desires, needs, and prospective actions. This process of communication and deliberation over collective goals makes a democracy public. Grounded in the work of Rousseau and certain Native American philosophies, public democracy is based on a collective spirit of caring and responsibility in which the work and benefits of society can be shared equitably for the common good. Accordingly, direct involvement in democratic government is a necessary safeguard against the separation of government affairs and the common interests of individuals and social groups. Without such involvement, the possibilities of a ruling aristocracy increase and the power of property in public matters grows. Thomas Jefferson offered three modest proposals for public democracy for Virginia after the American War of Independence: popular suffrage (for white males) would force representatives to declare and explain their positions on issues of the day, free mass public education (for white males) would prepare voters to judge candidates and understand the complexities of civic affairs, and limits on inheritance would slow the concentration of power among the wealthy. Since that time, many theorists and activists have worked to extend the possibilities of public democracy.

My hope for this book is that it can connect reading education and these public-democratic projects. Without a reconsideration of poverty and how it affects schooling and reading instruction, my fear is that we will help perpetuate the economic, cultural, and political inequalities of the past into the twenty-first century. Unless we can redirect our work to connect our lives more directly with those of others and to investigate the redistribution of power in our society, we will continue to lose control over our well-being. Poverty only appears to be about "the other." Reading education can help build and strengthen public-democratic values in which individuals can acknowledge the social roots of inequalities and the need to connect the personal with the political. Despite his sexist language, Mills can help us consider how reading and public democracy might be linked.

Whether or not they are aware of them, men in a mass society are gripped by personal troubles which they are not able to turn into social issues. They do not understand the interplay of these personal troubles of their milieu with problems of social structure. The knowledgeable man in a genuine public, on the other hand, is able to do just that. He understands that what he thinks and feels to be personal troubles are very often also problems shared by others, and more importantly, not capable of solution by any one individual but only by modifications of the structure of the groups in which he lives and sometimes the structure of the entire society. Men in masses have troubles, but they are not usually aware of their true meaning and source; men in publics confront issues, and they usually come to be aware of their public terms. (1959, 187)

A word about political labels. Although many eschew political labels as too narrow or confining to capture the nature of their thoughts and work, even the most nuanced thinkers are attracted to specific schools of thought, sets of values, and views of the world. Thinking is a social process, and although there are points of variation among individual thinkers, there are also points of similarity. Reading with political labels in mind helps us name and understand both differences and similarities that may not be self-evident on first glance. These labels are not meant as revelations of truth, but rather as products of convenience that help us read between and beyond the written lines.

Chapter 1 develops the connection between policy on poverty and reading instruction by looking closely at President Clinton's "America Reads" proposal to enact a volunteer system to teach every child to read by the end of second grade. Although Clinton makes reference to other policies for the poor during his first iteration of the proposal, he relegates these policies to secondary importance, asserting a neo-liberal position that development of human capital will enhance economic growth, which in turn will end poverty and address all other social concerns by enabling the poor to work their way into the middle class. According to Clinton, universal reading is the key enabler to the American dream. To address Clinton's proposal, his assumptions about poverty and literacy, and his style of presentation, I apply a form of critical policy analysis and briefly review other policy studies on the relationship between poverty and reading instruction.

Chapter 2 offers a look at the social construction of the official poverty line, a review of who is considered poor, and a description of current federal programs directed to help the poor. The U.S. government employs an absolute income-based rubric to draw a hard and fast line between the poor and rest of American society. The poor are a gendered, raced, and aged social category with ascribed characteristics based on various conceptions of who is and who is not worthy of federal support to alleviate the consequences of poverty. Aid to the poor comes in several forms, each with specific criteria to determine eligibility and explicit behavioral expectations to maintain support. Aid to Families with Dependent Children (AFDC) and Supplemental Security Income (SSI) programs are compared to demonstrate how different groups are treated differently in antipoverty programs. Finally, Taylor's work (1996) on "toxic literacies" is discussed as a weapon to crack official representations of the poor and as a tool to explore how literacy can be used to discover connections between our lives and those of people classified as being poor.

There are several versions of why the poor fall below the official poverty line, ranging from references to original sin to detailed analyses of the productive and distributive capacities of late twentieth-century capitalism. Working from representative public statements, Chapter 3 describes conservative, neo-conservative, liberal, and radical democratic attempts to explain both the causes and the cures for poverty in America. Contrasting personal responsibility with the harsh realities of the economy, advocates of these positions offer vivid portraits of who the poor are and who among them are worthy of support. It may not be startling to anyone that they agree on very little as they fit their readings of poverty into their broader idealized visions for America. Yet their differing views hold profound consequences for how we understand poverty, the poor, and ourselves.

Chapter 4 offers a reading of Herrnstein and Murray's (1994) *The Bell Curve*, which explains poverty as a consequence of individuals' and select social groups' low cognitive ability. This argument is set within a conservative political agenda to naturalize social, economic, and political inequalities. The authors marshal statistical evidence to argue that cognitive ability is heritable and generally fixed. Consequently, little if anything, short of genetic engineering, can be done to eliminate the basic cause of poverty. Attempts at social engineering have resulted in deepened problems of dependency, crime, and out-of-wedlock births. Herrnstein and Murray maintain that society must learn to live with these facts and return to a private democracy directed by a natural aristocracy in which everyone seeks and then enjoys their place of value in society commensurate with their mental endowment. Toward that end, they call for a reversal of federal aid to the poor through education to enhance the academic offerings to the cognitively gifted.

In Chapter 5, I present a neo-conservative argument for ending poverty through the development of moral literacy. Using hyperbolic rhetoric about the violence of superpredator, the economic drain of welfare cheats, and the political threat of special interests to scare the public, neo-conservatives reduce social, economic, and political issues to individual moral behaviors. Criminals, the poor, and teenage mothers suffer a moral poverty that prevents them from controlling their impulses and empathizing with others. The neo-conservative solution is education, a moral education that will enable individuals to live moral lives and to take advantage of currently available opportunities. I review and analyze Bennett's notions of reading education and moral literacy at considerable length because it forms the foundation of the neo-conservative solution to poverty and other social problems. By being explicitly taught to read the word and the world through a prescribed moral lens, the poor with their many threats to economic, social, and political status quo can become productive members of society and, therefore, end all social problems.

Liberals reject the conservative and neo-conservative explanations of the causes of poverty. Rather than character flaws, liberals name restricted opportunities for the poor to develop their human and economic capital as the cause of poverty. Chapter 6 offers a look at neo-liberal versions of the restricted-opportunity explanation for poverty through examination of the suggestions to improve institutional services to all citizens. Employing a crisis metaphor to describe the inability of American workers to meet the demands of global competition, neo-liberals seek to solve the "reading crisis" through national standards for curriculum and testing in public schools. I examine Hirsch's (1987) cultural literacy and the National Council of Teachers of English and the International Reading Associations Standards for English Language Arts as different versions of this solution. According to neo-liberal logic, improved school performance will increase students' skills, preparing all students—even the poor—to compete in the world economy to obtain high-wage employment. Once literate and gainfully employed, the poor will be able to work their way above the absolute poverty line.

Chapter 7 offers a stronger version of the restricted-opportunity explanation for poverty. A liberal position on poverty maintains that biases based on race, class, and gender are encoded within institutional policies, procedures, and practices that systematically reduce the opportunities available to minorities, women, and the poor. According to liberal logic, policies to bring about general improvements cannot reduce the economic gap between blacks and whites, women and men, and the poor and other economic classes because past discrimination has disadvantaged some social groups and privileged others. At best, general solutions maintain the status quo; at worst, they increase the gap because unequal access to the programs continues. Liberals call for programs targeted to decrease the gaps between rich and poor by ensuring that benefits are delivered to society's have-nots. Since the War on Poverty in the 1960s, liberals have developed Head Start, Elementary/Secondary Education Act (ESEA), and Even Start to compensate for the inability of regular schooling to reduce the academic-skills gap between the poor and other economic classes. If the reading test scores between these groups can be closed, liberals believe that the economic gap between classes will close soon also because there are ample well-paying jobs waiting for the poor to improve their skills and grab their opportunities.

I place the theoretical relationships between poverty and reading education within the current American economic contexts in Chapter 8. That placement brings the functionalist logic of these theories into question because the economy no longer seems able to deliver the high-wage, stable jobs that have served as the reward for learning to read at school. While the promise of a good job has long been problematic for women and minorities, during the 1990s it has become true for the majority of Americans. As a result of fewer jobs, declining wages, and government neglect, the lines between economic classes become blurred, making the social construction of class visible and new alliances and coalitions possible. The unwillingness of the economy to uphold its end of the functionalist equation, which relates poverty and reading education, requires new theories for both phenomena—that is, if we hope to live in a democratic future.

Chapter 9 considers the question of power in America—the ability of the bottom three-quarters of the American population to participate fully in the decisions that affect their lives. Toward that end, I reexamine the implicit models and policies in the articles on poverty with which I began this chapter. This time I analyze their potential to finesse the dilemma of cultural recognition and economic redistribution, which seems to splinter this majority into powerless subgroups. Conservative corrections for poverty make little attempt to empower this majority either culturally or economically. Liberal affirmative solutions to cultural and economic inequalities are generating perverse effects with intensive cultural antagonisms while failing to end poverty. Transformative remedies, however, challenge us to reconsider our systems for valuing cultural difference and distributing wealth, and force us to look at ourselves and our social alignments differently. From these analyses, new possibilities for public democracy arise and with them come new roles for reading education. Reading cannot make us rich, it cannot guarantee power, but it can help us struggle for justice, equality, and freedom.

Federal attempts to circumvent teachers with volunteers, IQ scores, moral literacy, national standards, what every American needs to know, compensatory programs, which method is best—all these alternatives for schooling and reading education stem directly from attempts to use schooling to overcome poverty without addressing standing inequalities. Reading poverty, then, becomes a way to place these seemingly disparate actions into a coherent whole. Moreover, it's a way to act on the world, in our homes, classrooms, and communities.

ONE

THIS TRAIN DON'T CARRY NO SHIRKERS . . .
Reading Bill Clinton

While traveling by train from West Virginia to Chicago to accept his party's 1996 nomination, President Clinton stopped frequently to speak to assembled audiences about his accomplishments and plans for our future. At 1:30 on August 27, he stepped from that train in Wyandotte, Michigan, to listen to Justin and Elizabeth, two third-graders from a local elementary school, read *The Little Engine That Could* (Piper 1984) on the steps of Bacon Memorial Public Library. With the stage set, President Clinton offered his solution to the political, social, and economic inequalities in America.

I sought the presidency because I wanted to make sure we were prepared for the twenty-first century, because I wanted us to go roaring and united into the next century with the American Dream alive for everyone, with every person in this country who's willing to work hard having the chance to live out their dreams and to live up to their God-given potential. And we are moving in the right direction to meet that goal.

I have followed a very simple strategy. I think it's the basic American bargain—opportunity for all/responsibility from all, and then telling every single person if you will be responsible, if you will seize your opportunity, if you believe in the Constitution, the Declaration of Independence, and the Bill of Rights, you don't have to tell us anything else. We don't care what your race is, we don't care what your religion is, we don't care where you started out in life. If you're willing to work hard and share our values, we'll join arm in arm with you and walk together into the future. You're a part of our America.

Yesterday in Ohio I talked mostly about responsibility and especially about our responsibility to make our streets, our schools, our neighborhoods safe for our children and to bring down the crime rate. Today we've been talking about opportunity. In Toledo we talked about how we work together and how management and unions work together to create hundreds of new jobs, and how America, after twenty years, is now number one again in the production and sales of automobiles because of what we've done. Now I come to this library with all these schoolchildren because their future is our future, and because we need to talk about another kind of opportunity—opportunity, without which America cannot triumph in the global economy, in the Information Age of the twenty-first century. . . .

Just last week, I signed a bill to raise the minimum wage for ten million Americans, including 325,000 here in Michigan. . . . That minimum-wage bill also contained a tax cut for small businesses that invest more in their businesses to create more jobs and income, and it contained provisions making it easier for small-business people and their employees to take their pensions when they change jobs, and that's very important. And there's a third thing that bill contained that I believe every single American, without regard for political party or conviction, can agree on—that bill did some dramatic things to encourage the adoption of children who do not have permanent homes. It gave a $5,000 tax credit to families who adopt a child, a bigger one if the child has a disability. . . .

I also signed the Kassebaum-Kennedy health bill to make twenty-five million Americans more eligible for health insurance by simply saying you can't be denied health insurance anymore if somebody in your family gets sick, and you can't lose it if you move from job to job. Now let's talk about education a minute. I have worked hard to increase the quality and the availability of education, to expand Head Start, to expand the Chapter One program so that it helps more poor children reach their full potential, to help school districts and local schools set high standards with grassroots reforms, to give more authority to principals and teachers and parents to basically chart their own course. . . .

But we have to do more. Not every child has access to the same information and learning every other child does. By the year 2000, I want to see every classroom in this country not simply have computers and teachers well-trained to teach how to use them, but connected to the Information Superhighway so that every child in the poorest inner-city school, the most remote rural district, the standard middle-class community, and the wealthiest school district—they all have access to the same unlimited store of information that is the key to our future. . . .

I want a $1,500 tax credit refundable to every family who needs it to go to a community college to pay for two years of education after high school. I want every college student, including the parents as well as the kids that are going back to college, to be able to deduct the cost of college tuition up to $13,000 a year. That will revolutionize the cause of education in America.

But before that, we must make sure that basic learning is taking place. I told you the good news. Now let me tell you some of the challenging news. Over the last decade, our country has worked hard to raise math and science scores, but reading scores have stayed flat. And it may be because a higher and higher percentage of our young people come from countries and families where English is not their first language. It may be because a lot of our young people live in homes where the parents are having to work two jobs, sometimes three jobs, and don't have enough time to spend with them reading. But for whatever reason, we know that our reading scores have not increased as much as our math and science scores, and we know that unless we can read, we will not be able to take advantage of the future or understand the past.

That's why Justin and Elizabeth were up here with *The Little Engine That Could*, pointing us the way to the future. That is what we have to have—a Justin and an Elizabeth in every single home in the United States of America. I have come here to this wonderful community to ask all of you to join me, without regard to your political party or your views on other issues, in a simple, straight-forward, critical national goal: All America's children should be able to read on their own by the third grade, every single one of them.

We know—look at what we know—we know that students who can't read as well as they should by the third grade are much less likely ever to graduate from high school. We know that without reading, the history books are closed, the Internet is turned off, the promise of America is much harder to reach. We know the children who can read learn from our founding fathers, explore the limits of the universe, and build the future of their dreams. If we're going to ensure that those are the children of America's future, they also need not only the best possible teaching in school, they need individualized tutoring; help with their homework before school, after school, and over the summer; and they need more parents involved in helping them learn to read and to keep reading.

To meet this challenge, we need one million tutors ready and able to give children the personal attention they need to catch up and get ahead. Today I propose a national literacy campaign to help our children learn to read by the third grade—a plan that offers thirty thousand reading specialists and volunteer coordinators to communities that are willing to do their part, people who will mobilize the citizen army of volunteer tutors we need, America's reading corps. We will only succeed, however, if the thirty thou-sand are joined by legions of volunteers—seniors and teenagers, business and civic groups, libraries and religious institutions, and above all, parents. We have to build on the groundwork we have been laying by AmeriCorps, our nation's national service program. Today I am giving AmeriCorps a new charge: Make reading central to your mission.

Let me tell you what they have done already. Let's just take one place—in Simpson County, Kentucky, a county in rural Ken-tucky, twenty-five of our young AmeriCorps volunteers helped 128 second-grade students make up almost three years of reading progress in just one school year. We can do that. We can do that.

All over America, efforts like this are working. And several places in America have organized to train, galvanize, and energize parents to make a difference. We worked hard on that when I was the Governor of Arkansas; I've seen the program work in Mis-souri.

Parents should be their children's first teachers and we should give them the support they need to be those first teachers. There are a lot of things you can do for your children, but nothing will do them much more good in the long run than reading to them every night. I can still remember as many of Chelsea's books as she can. Some of them I can almost remember by heart, because kids want to hear the same ones over and over again.

But when they grow and they learn to read on their own, and you see their imaginations fire, and you know their lives are going

to be richer because of it, then every single tired night a parent
spends reading a book to a child is a night well-worth it. Every dollar we spend bringing in people to help these kids after school
with personal tutoring is a dollar well worth it.

We know our children have to spend more time reading and
less time in front of the television set. We know—we know that if
every single parent would just spend half an hour a night reading to
their children, within a matter of years there would be no issue
about whether our third-graders could read as they should. We
know that. . . .

So let me leave you with this thought—we've got ten million
more jobs, a million and a half fewer people on welfare, the crime
rate is coming down, child-support collections are going up. America is growing together and going forward, wages are rising for the
first time in a decade. But the most important thing we have to do
is make sure that our children are ready for the twenty-first century. And I want you to join with me in saying one way we're going
to do that is to make sure every single boy and girl in America can
read on his or her own by the time they're in third grade. Will
you do it?

Already campaigning for the presidency in this speech,
Clinton listed the criteria to become part of "our America,"
an America preparing for the twenty-first century. Referring
to an unnamed group, he suggested that if they will be responsible, seize their opportunities, and share our values, then
they will have equal access to what America has to offer. The
list of American responsibilities is long and growing, from
working hard to preventing crime to volunteering to support
others. Shared values are circumscribed to the belief in the
formal documents of our government. Opportunities, of
course, are what Clinton's Administration has provided for all
Americans since 1992. Responsibility, opportunity, and
shared values keep the "American Dream" alive. (Clinton's
speechwriters capitalized *American Dream* as if it were an
easily identifiable trademark or a commodity.) During his
speech, Clinton presented his accomplishments in keeping
that dream alive for many Americans: a rise in the minimum
wage (along with tax cuts for business and dowries for
orphans), portable pensions and health insurance for workers
"when they change jobs" or "move from job to job," and
anticipated creation of jobs through the telecommunications
and other legislative bills.

According to Clinton, education is foremost among American opportunities, one that offers "a chance to live out their

dreams and to live up to their God-given potential." Without education, Clinton argued, "America cannot triumph in the global economy." Loans, tax cuts, computers, high academic standards, and safe and rebuilt schools will enable more Americans to seize this opportunity. "But before that, we must make sure that basic learning is taking place." Basic learning and, apparently, the basis for taking responsibility, seizing opportunities, and sharing values, is the ability to read a book on your own by the end of second grade. Those who cannot read cannot pursue the Dream and, therefore, waste their potential. They are doomed to live impoverished lives and hamper American efforts to go roaring and united into the twenty-first century. To eliminate poverty from our future lives and to prepare for the twenty-first century, America needs one million volunteers who will help children learn to read and do their homework. These efforts will produce "what we have to have—a Justin and an Elizabeth in every single home in the United States of America."

FUNCTIONALISM AND POLICY

Clinton's speech is an example of a formal relationship between poverty and reading education. Since the 1960s, federal policy on poverty has been tied directly to schooling, and often to reading instruction (Kaestle and Smith 1982; Kantor and Lowe 1994). Schools in general and reading instruction in particular have been charged with ameliorating the cause of poverty and, eventually, eradicating poverty in America altogether. For various reasons, American educators have accepted this challenge and have worked diligently to keep these charges in plain view of the taxpaying public. (Actually, preventing poverty has been a primary rationale for public schooling since the inception of the common school [Cremin 1988].) If schooling and reading instruction are expected to eliminate poverty, then they must be tailored theoretically and practically to prevent or overcome it. By looking closely at the policies that embody definitions of poverty and its causes, we gain new insight into rationales for the theories and practices of reading instruction over the last thirty years, and new ways to judge their adequacy and abilities to serve the majority of Americans now in what has been characterized as a post-industrial society.

The mediating role for policy in the relationship of poverty and reading instruction is based on functionalist social theory (Parsons 1959; Merton 1967). Functionalism says that society is like the human body, with its internal elements working with the goal of adaptation for survival. The natural state of society is homostasis, the status quo. If something threatens society's survival, then elements must adjust accordingly to bring a return to a previous balance. Since any society must continually face and solve such problems, policies are needed to direct social elements in order to reduce the hardships of the immediate threat and to facilitate the return to balance. In this case, federal policy on poverty directs educational policy (largely through reading instruction), which is expected to re-create a social balance, however that may be defined.

Most policy research concerned with reading instruction begins and ends with this functionalist assumption. That is, after a policy has been recommended or named to adjust reading programs in order to ameliorate a social concern, policy analysts study its process, content, and consequences to judge its adequacy on the prescribed terms. For example, Calfee and Drum (1979) edited descriptive reports on reading programs for which "many school districts receive some type of compensatory funding in order to improve the reading performance of children from low-income families" (vii). They conclude that "several models are equally workable, that present practice is by no means the best for many low-performance students, and that change is needed" (186). In an excellent discussion of how compensatory and special-education policy competes as remedial services for children experiencing difficulty learning to read, McGill-Franzen (1987) reported that "children experiencing reading failure may be defined quite differently depending on which school district they attend, in which state, and what financial constraints they are operating under" (487). She urged reading professionals to reengage in debates surrounding reading failure or else lose remedial services to special education altogether. Allington and Walmsley (1995) offered a series of essays that find current policies and practices inadequate and provide policymakers with better information that should lead to "not just a majority of children, but virtually all" (2) learning to read along with their peers.

In such studies, policy analysts accepted policymakers' definition of the problem and allow them to set the parameters of valid investigation. For instance, Calfee and Drum restrict their discussion to programs that already exist; they do not posit alternatives. McGill-Franzen refrains from a full-blown political analysis of the interests that underlie the struggle over remedial students among compensatory and special education. Allington and Walmsley confine their efforts to doing schooling better. While each study offers important insights into particular policies and how they might be changed, all stick closely to rearranging the elements within the status quo of schooling and its current role in society at large. Their functionalism turns policy analysis concerning reading instruction into a mechanical endeavor and neglects most possibilities that begin with different givens. Perhaps we need different goals, different elements, and different ways of considering their interactions to help children having difficulty learning to read? Most policy studies cannot help us with those issues.

Yet policy analysis need not be mechanical because, clearly, policy is more a matter of the "authoritative allocation of values" (Easton 1953) than a natural, rational, deliberative process. Anyone who has listened to the Congress debate the federal budget, the funding for the National Endowment for the Arts, or the Space Program can attest to this. Policies begin with their makers' images of an ideal society, and they are intended to bring those images, ideals, and values to life. Images, ideals, and values do not float independently from social context; they have histories and other social attachments. Policies cannot be divorced from interests, conflicts, or justice. Analyses of policy, then, require an examination of the values embedded within policy, images used to make the policy seem necessary and compelling, and its real, expected, and unanticipated social consequences. "The authoritative allocation of values draws our attention to the centrality of power and control in the concept of policy" (Prunty 1985, 136). We must ask: Whose values are being served by particular policies? What is ideal in this vision of ideal society? How have these values and ideas been institutionalized? To ask these questions is to engage in critical policy analysis (Ball 1990), which is (1) overtly political, (2) attentive to issues of power, (3) semiotic, (4) cognizant of human agency, and (5) committed to praxis—a unity of thought and action.

CLINTON AND THE NEW DEAL

Clinton's Wyandotte speech to propose the America Reads policy offers a good text for such an analysis because it encodes the values of several social groups about poverty and it represents much of the history of federal policy toward poverty and its relationship to reading instruction. By mentioning the minimum wage, pensions, and welfare, Clinton invokes the Roosevelt Administration's New Deal, a previous attempt to overcome American inequalities during the Great Depression of the 1930s. Faced with skyrocketing levels of unemployment and confronted with millions of hungry and homeless, New Deal policymakers mobilized federal resources to prevent destitution and the unraveling of state and federal authority. The minimum wage was part of the Fair Labor Standards Act of 1938, which also promised a forty-hour work week, "time and a half" for overtime, and an end to child labor. With a wage of twenty-five cents an hour, 750,000 workers received raises at that time. The Social Security Act of 1935 offered guaranteed federal pensions, aid to families with dependent children (now more often referred to as welfare), and financial support for state-level unemployment insurance and bailouts for state pension plans.

All three acts were part of the second New Deal, which extended the government's direct intervention of emergency aid to banks, farmers, and homeowners and jobs for unemployed workers (i.e., Civilian Conservation Corps, Public Works Administration, National Youth Administration, and Works Progress Administration). Policymakers in the Roosevelt Administration, and most Americans, deemed both New Deals necessary because they believed the American economy and the previous administration's market-based policies to be unable to provide adequately for too many Americans. In other words, minimum wage, pensions, and aid to families with dependent children represented contemporary American values about poverty and appropriate federal action. Although the New Deals were by no means completely successful government efforts to revitalize the American economy, such legislation did bring immediate relief to millions of citizens who were suffering apparently through no fault of their own. Although never quite as generous as those of other industrialized countries, these policies comprised a social safety net symbolizing the federal government's commitment to each citizen to guarantee his or her economic well-being within an economy that could produce material wealth, but that did not seem to care well for the majority of its participants. Schools and reading instruction, although important, could not alter the structure of the economy and, therefore, were not integral parts of the New Deal policies against poverty.

In his Wyandotte speech, Clinton employed the symbols of the minimum wage, portable pensions and health care, and welfare to give the impression that his administration shares the New Deal values and that it has been directly active in aiding the undeserving poor. However, the location of and the time Clinton spent on these values suggest that he considers these direct actions secondary, at best, to indirect methods of volunteers teaching children to read a book by themselves by the end of second grade. Moreover, the actual impact of Clinton's commitments to these direct acts suggests that he does not value them highly as remedies for poverty. For example, most employees who are paid a minimum wage provide second or third incomes in working- and middle-class families and are not the sole incomes for families living in poverty (Smith and Vavrichek 1987). Raising the minimum wage to $5.15 an hour does not provide an income that will lift a family out of poverty. Portable pensions and health insurance are default measures for Clinton's plans to privatize Social Security (Dreyfuss 1996) and his failure to secure national health insurance (Sklar 1995). Finally, during that same summer, Clinton signed a welfare-reform bill that absolved the federal government from responsibility to provide for the guaranteed economic well-being of all citizens (Cancian and Gordon 1996). His use of these symbols of the New Deal is misleading and conceals the fact that many of his policymakers and other current legislators have lost faith (or never had faith) in the federal government's obligation to minimize human suffering by aiding the poor directly and immediately.

CLINTON AND THE WAR ON POVERTY

As if he were providing a history of federal policy on poverty, Clinton also offers a few words about his administration's support for Head Start and Chapter One, two cornerstones of the Johnson Administration's War on Poverty. These policies have their roots in economic studies (e.g., Harrington 1962), which found that nearly fifty million Americans lived in poverty, sharply contradicting the widely held contemporary assumption that after the Korean War, the United States became an affluent society for all. Moreover, the civil rights movement of the 1950s and 1960s demanded that school desegregation progress with all deliberate speed to provide equal educational opportunity for all citizens. These actions resulted in the Civil Rights Act of 1964, which extended federal regulation in the areas of voting rights, public accommodations, education, and employment. Title VI of the Act gave the government the right to withhold funds from any school that would not comply with federal regulations.

Kennedy-Johnson Administration values toward poverty were captured in Heller's "The Problem of Poverty in America," which appeared as part of the 1964 *Annual Report of the Council of Economic Advisors.* "Equality of opportunity is the American dream, and universal education our noblest pledge to realize it. But for children of the poor, education is a handicap race; many are too ill-motivated at home to learn at school. It is difficult for children to find and follow avenues leading out of poverty in environments where education is deprecated and hope is smothered." In language pointing toward the eventual plans for Head Start and Title I, the *Report* continues, "This often means that schooling must start on a pre-school basis and include a broad range of more intensive services" and "the school must play a larger role in the development of poor youngsters if they are to have, in fact, equal opportunity." During the War on Poverty, schools were considered a primary social tool to bring about both racial integration and economic justice.

Head Start began as part of the Economic Opportunity Act (EOA) of 1964 which also included legal assistance, health care, loans for farmers, the Job Corps, and National Youth Corps. EOA's centerpiece was the authorization of community-action programs to encourage local communities to develop their own plans for the attack on poverty. "The singlemost popular creation of community action across the country was Head Start, a collection of programs for the preschool children of poor families" (Cremin 1988, 316). The first Head Start programs were introduced during the summer of 1965 with 500,000 children participating. Although programs varied widely in philosophy and applications (Spodek 1986), they each sought to prepare poor children to start school on equal footing with children from other economic classes. All Head Start curricula included strategies and activities that earlier studies (e.g., Deutsch 1963) found were undertaken as a matter of course in middle-class homes but were considered to be frequently lacking in lower-class homes (e.g., reading to children, conversing with them, and playing games with them). Competition among alternative ways of providing for these "deficiencies" in reading readiness continue to this day—most often pitting the academic focus of the Distar Model against more social-oriented curricula (Delpit 1995; McGill-Franzen 1993; Schweinhart, Weikart, and Larner 1986). In 1967, the Head Start programs were expanded into homes through Parent and Child Centers, which offered entire families strategies to prevent the need for Head Start, and into schools with Project Follow Through, which continued Head Start's remedial services until third grade.

On April 11, 1965, President Johnson signed the ESEA, which included Title I. (ESEA has been reauthorized eight times since then, with core elements and the name changed to Chapter One during the Reagan Administration, and then back again during the first Clinton Administration.) Title I services were to provide economically "disadvantaged" students who were behind in their schoolwork with additional instruction in reading and/or math programs. Because federal legislators doubted that school administrators would spend the ESEA funds on additional services for poor and African American students, they required a reporting system that would inform the public of the relative success of each funded project (McLaughlin 1975). The strict targeting of funds and the nature of the reporting system—standardized reading achievement test—promoted uniformity with Title I reading programs. Students left their classroom to work with a specialized teacher on word-recognition skills and paper-and-pencil comprehension exercises.

During Senate hearings on the bill, Secretary of Health, Education, and Welfare Anthony Celebreeze (1965) stated that the ESEA was "designed to break this cycle, which has been running on from generation to generation in this most affluent period in our history." More boldly, Commissioner of Education Francis Keppel (1965) remarked, "Archimedes told us many centuries ago: 'Give me a lever long enough and a fulcrum strong enough and I can move the world.' Today, at last, we have a prospect of a lever long enough and supported strongly enough to do something for our children of poverty. The lever is education, and the fulcrum is federal assistance."

Head Start and Title I of the ESEA connote shifting values from the New Deal concerning the definition of poverty, its causes, and possible federal roles in its elimination. Poverty was no longer characterized just by a lack of income. Rather, poverty also included a distinct set of attitudes, behaviors, and personality traits. Moreover, the problems in the economy did not cause poverty; rather, it was a range of characteristics of culture that poor parents and other community members passed on to children. Although Myrdal (1944) in *An American Dilemma* and Harrington (1962) in *The Other America* first used the concept of culture of poverty, Lewis is most often credited with coining the term. According to Lewis, the culture of poverty "perpetuated itself from generation to generation because of its effect on children. By the time slum children are six or seven, they have absorbed the values and attitudes of their subculture and are not psychologically geared to take advantage of changing conditions or increased opportunities that may occur" (1966, 191).

These shifting values also redirected the federal role in combating poverty. They are markedly different than the values expressed during the New Deal. Instead of direct policies to modify the economic system and to provide immediate relief for all poor citizens, the War on Poverty reduced the pool of the "undeserving" poor to children and designed educational policies to save them from their cultural fate. According to the logic of these policies, the literate poor would earn their way into the middle class and eliminate the antisocial tendencies of their culture—crime, delinquency, teenage pregnancy—along the way. In essence, the War on Poverty absolved the economy and middle and upper economic classes from blame, placed full responsibility for poverty and recovery on the shoulders of the poor, pitted children against their communities, and placed schooling and other educational programs in the middle.

The expectations for these policies were too high for Head Start or Title I programs to be completely successful. Clearly, they did not bring integration or end poverty. Nor have they produced lasting academic success for the majority of their participants (CSR 1985; Slavin 1991). Today, more modest goals are set for those programs. For example, Edward Zigler (1992), former Director of the U.S. Office of Child Development, argued that whatever its effects on achievement, Head Start has "improved the nutrition and health of thousands of low-income children" (Zigler and Muenchow 1992, xi). Mary Jean LeTendre (1991), Director of the U.S. Office of Compensatory Education, writes that while Chapter One may have failed to produce great gains in academic skills, it nonetheless has been a "success in helping to make kindergarten universal, increasing parent involvement, and bringing national attention to the needs of low-income learners" (331). Perhaps the most lasting outcomes of Head Start and Title I programs are the permanence of federal involvement in public schools (Kaestle and Smith 1982) and the prominence of standardized test scores as the measure of school and individual success (House 1978).

Clinton's use of Head Start and Chapter One as symbols in his Wyandotte speech attempted to align his administration with values of the War on Poverty, and this act demonstrates some political courage. After all, conservatives have attacked these programs stridently for twenty years. For example, Jendryka (1993) of the Heritage Foundation wrote that "If Chapter One were a business, it would be in Chapter 11" (79). Yet Clinton's commitments to the actual programs have proved modest indeed. His notion of expansion of Head Start amounts to restoring some Reagan Administration cuts to the program's funds. By its own admission (Smith and Scoll 1995), Head Start still serves only half the eligible students (a lower percentage than when the program began). Moreover, Clinton's reauthorization of the ESEA as the Improving America's Schools Act of 1994 shifts the responsibility of oversight of programs and funds to the states—much like his welfare reform. "The new ESEA programs focus on ensuring that all children, especially those in high poverty areas, the limited English-proficient, migrant children, and others in need of extra education supports, are taught to the same content and performance standards as all other children in the state" (Smith and Scoll 1995, 37–38). The attempt to "push resources and decision-making authority as far down as possible" (39) is the antithesis of the original ESEA, when school districts proved themselves reluctant to provide adequate education for poor children and tightly coupled federal oversight was required.

CLINTON AND THE AMERICA READS INITIATIVE

After invoking the conflicting values of both the New Deal and the War on Poverty, Clinton clouds the issue still further by outlining his America Reads policy, which is based on a different set of values than either Roosevelt's solidarity with or Johnson's altruism for the poor. Again, Clinton's choice of symbols conveys his vision of an ideal America and his values about poverty.

Why were Justin and Elizabeth asked to read *The Little Engine That Could* on this occasion? On the surface, it appears that Clinton's advisors wished to offer an example of what Clinton hopes to accomplish through his America Reads initiative. Simply, two seven-year-olds demonstrated that his goal is possible. A bit more abstractly, their act of reading symbolizes the future ("their future is our future"). These children seem to have seized the opportunity to acquire the skills that give them instant access to the past and future. The story they read is about an unappreciated locomotive that seizes its opportunities, and then perseveres through sheer determination to accomplish its dream. Perhaps President Clinton, who pundits discounted after the 1994 congressional election, identifies with that little engine. Or perhaps Clinton's advisors meant the reading to be just a good train story for a candidate traveling by train. Whatever the reason, the symbol of Justin and Elizabeth reading that story worked well because it is mentioned in every major and minor news account of the Wyandotte stop (e.g., the August 28, 1996, editions of the *New York Times, Washington Post, Palm Beach Post, Richmond Times Dispatch*, and *Wisconsin State Journal*).

Beneath that surface, however, Justin and Elizabeth reading *The Little Engine That Could* represents Clinton's criteria for being considered partners for "our America." By implication, the act identifies why some families "choose" to live outside "our" grace. Reading *The Little Engine That Could*, Justin and Elizabeth demonstrate that they, and apparently their parents, have been responsible. That is, they have seized the opportunities presented to all through schooling, and they share "our" values (which have expanded to include the obligation to make America triumphant in the global economy). Moreover, like the little engine, they accomplished the task on their own by thinking positively and working hard without any assistance from others. Getting over the mountain—like learning to read—will bring prospects for all. In contrast, those children who cannot read by third grade—and their parents by association—have been irresponsible, lazy, and valueless. They have chosen not to hitch themselves to the train of prosperity despite all requests. At the very least, they do not possess positive characteristics in the same quantities as Justin and Elizabeth and their families.

By stating the imperative, "have to have a Justin and Elizabeth in every single home in the United States of America," Clinton provides not only his account of the American ideal, but also his agenda for combating poverty. Each household must have all individuals ready, willing, and able to do whatever is necessary for America to be triumphant in the world economy of the twenty-first century. To reach this ideal, parents and volunteers must band together to clone Justin and Elizabeth as corrective agents in ill-prepared and ineffective households. Of course, it would be best if all households were already identical to Justin and Elizabeth's—"If every single parent would just spend half an hour a night reading to their children, within a matter of years there would be no issue about whether our third-graders could read as they should." However, under any circumstances, America Reads volunteers will serve as surrogate responsible parents for unfortunate children whose real caretakers are non-English-speaking, working two or three jobs to support their families, or just irresponsible. According to Clinton, America Reads will begin the chain of events that will enable every citizen to achieve the American Dream, if they work hard enough. Those who do not comply will be excluded as partners in "our America" and left without government support.

With his America Reads, Clinton pulls the federal government even farther back from direct and immediate help for the poor. The economy escapes blame, race is discounted, and culture is not mentioned. Rather, individual families with unpatriotic values prevent us from going "roaring and united into the next century with the American Dream alive for everyone who's willing to work hard." According to Clinton, federal responsibility is not to reduce the harsh realities of the economy by providing jobs and/or guaranteed services. In fact, Clinton assumes that economic growth is the primary way to overcome social problems and, for that reason, all his legislative successes that he mentioned in his Wyandotte speech include business incentives as well as social provisions. Nor will the federal government initiate bold new educational interventions that redirect institutional efforts to end the culture of poverty through special programs. School reform is limited to high academic standards for everyone, access to technology, and reductions in violence. In Clinton's mind, schools become tools to further economic growth, which is expected to raise all boats together. However, to prepare the poor to take advantage of these new schools, the Clinton Administration will rely on one million volunteers from the already responsible "our America," who will intervene in family life to teach young children to read. Once able to read, the poor ones will continue to follow Justin and Elizabeth in order to take equal advantage of the opportunities already available in schools and society.

By couching his America Reads policy proposal within the values of economic growth and national community, Clinton demonstrated a neo-liberal (rather than liberal) set of values about poverty (Fowler 1995). In this light, reading *The Little Engine That Could* represents more than confirmation that children can read or even Clinton's political triumph. The reading of that story represents Clinton's American ideal, an America poised to go "roaring and united into the next century, with the American Dream alive for everyone who's willing to work hard. . . ." The only barrier, he claims, is a lack of commitment and confidence that we can teach all children to read a book on their own by the time they enter third grade. A roaring economy will fuel the engine that pulls a train of united cars who "think they can" and share his plans to make society work again. Forget the economic justice sought in the liberalism during the New Deal. Forget the political justice sought in the War on Poverty. Through America Reads, Clinton seeks to rally Americans as troops to enhance our national chances for economic growth and market dominance.

With Clinton's election in November 1996, his little engine made it over the mountain, but who was left back at the station?

TWO

THEM THAT'S NOT SHALL LOSE

Reading Official Poverty in America?

During the autumn of 1996, the New York Stock Exchange surpassed six thousand points, and 1.2 million children were added to the official ranks of the poor because of welfare reform; former British princess Sarah Ferguson and the Artist Formerly Known as Prince discussed their sex lives during separate hour-long interviews on television, while the year-old strike against the return of the twelve-hour workday at the Staley Plant in Illinois went unmentioned by the mainstream national media; taxation and public security rights were granted to wealthy real-estate owners through the formation of business improvement districts in major and minor cities across the country; and the amount to be cut from Medicaid and the privatization of Social Security were debated in both houses of the federal legislature. Collectively, these events laid waste to the lingering nineteenth century rhetoric that America is a classless society, as our nation appeared in transition from a moderate war on poverty to an open war against the poor.

An application of Karl Marx's definition of class, based on the relationship of individuals to the means of production, would result in a simple bifurcation of Americans into owners and workers. Heilbronner and Thurow (1982) set limits of the owner class at the wealthiest five percent of the U.S. population. In 1990, according to the Internal Revenue Service (Kennickell and Shack-Marquez 1992), that meant that the owner class consisted of just under four million families and individuals who earned approximately $500 billion in wages and salaries. The remaining 105 million Americans who filed tax returns that year received a little over $2,200 billion. Although this might not seem to be an inequitable split, note that the owners received as much in salary and wages as the bottom half of the workers. The wealthiest five percent and the poorest fifty percent each received one-sixth of the salaries and wages in 1990, leaving two-thirds of the salary and wages to the upper half of the working class.

Some argue that Marx's analysis of social class is outdated and suggest that more can be learned by dividing a population into stratified income levels: (1) poor, (2) working class, (3) middle class, (4) upper middle class, and (5) the rich. The U.S. Census Bureau (1993) arranges those classes according to quintiles. (Income includes wages and salaries along with supplemental wages, rents, capital gains, and so on.) Table 2–1 offers the income distribution among social classes in 1993. In this second analysis, more members are added to the ranks of the rich—the wealthiest twenty percent of tax filers received nearly as much income as the remaining eighty percent of the U.S. population—returning to a two-class society.

Table 2–1 Income Distribution Among Social Classes in 1993

Class	Mean Income	Percent of Total Income
$0 to $16,952	$9,735	4.2
$16,953 to $29,999	$23,378	10.1
$30,000 to $45,000	$37,056	15.9
$45,001 to $66,794	$54,929	23.6
$66,795 and over	$107,471	46.2

U.S. Bureau of Census 1993. Household wealth and asset ownership, 34 (viii): 70.

Few people around the world associate poverty with America (Blackburn 1994). With only five percent of the world's population, Americans produce more than twenty-five percent of the world's output. Although more than half the world's population struggles along with less than $1,500 annually in per-capita income, the average American family seems to enjoy more than $30,000. In Indonesia, Kenya, Romania, Haiti, and Pakistan, many families do not have running water, indoor plumbing, or even kitchens—things Americans take for granted. We worry about a health-care crisis with one doctor for every five hundred people; in Ethiopia, there is one doctor for every eighty-eight thousand citizens. Although some Americans do indeed experience these conditions of world poverty (Harrington 1984; Kozol 1995), images of poverty presented in American popular media are typically ones of the distended bellies and living conditions of children in other countries.

Different images of poverty in America evoke different responses from citizens. Children playing between parked cars in a trailer park with a mother watching, two elderly women sitting and talking in a one-room apartment, three young black men on a street corner, a woman carrying lye to an outhouse, a homeless man asking for change—each image offers a partial picture of poverty in the United States. However, each elicits a certain amount of sympathy from viewers, a different mix of caring and judgment. While many Americans seem willing to assume some responsibilities toward children and the elderly poor, most now seem unwilling or unable to empathize with apparently able-bodied adults—both women and men—often referred to as "the underclass." All may be poor, but only some are deemed to be worthy of help. Diversity among the poor, coupled with the manipulation of images of the poor, makes it difficult to come to grips with the complexities of American poverty. This chapter lays the groundwork for understanding who the government considers poor and what actions governments have taken to help them.

Remember Ronald Reagan's stories about welfare cheats, Martin Luther King, Jr.'s remarks about sanitation workers in Memphis just before his assassination, or Charles Kuralt's stops in remote areas during his travels across America. Think about the ways in which Rush Limbaugh, Joseph Kennedy, and Bill Moyers talk about the poor in America today. Who was and is telling the truth? Because politicians and media reporters rely so heavily on emotional images and stories to convey their messages and points of view, many of us are uninformed about "the facts" of poverty in America. As a counterpoint, I offer those facts with modest interpretation about the adequacy of current governmental support for the poor and their declining condition in our country of great affluence. Without such information about official poverty, we are at the mercy of storytellers with tales to tell us, and we have little hope of entering the public debate about poverty that directly affects our lives and our work.

AN OFFICIAL DEFINITION OF POVERTY

American poverty is usually associated with an unequal distribution of America's abundance. The idea of poverty is a social construction. There is not a natural line that separates the poor from the non-poor. As a construction, our conceptions of poverty begin as the images and stories of poverty meet our feelings and understandings of ourselves, others, and the world.

The view of poverty as contagious, as having the stench of terminal illness, leads us to take sanctuary in the word *underclass*, which must mean someone else because it certainly doesn't refer to me. A voyage of discovery is always a voyage of the self: Columbus was unlikely to have known about his hostility to non-Europeans until he met some. They could be safely dealt with as "savages." Once I'm satisfied that those in this "underclass" are safely other than I am, I can afford to think about where they came from. (Davis 1995, 15)

Take, for example, the seemingly simple issue of whether American poverty is an absolute or relative condition. An absolute poverty suggests that there is, and we can determine, a set minimum of food, shelter, clothing, and the like that will keep an individual alive, if not well. Absolute poverty forms a hard separation and leaves those above the line remarkably untouched by those below. A relative poverty, however, emphasizes the distributive aspect of poverty. That is, poverty can be defined only in relationship to all other economic classes. A relative definition of poverty might set the poverty line as an income in the bottom quintile (under approximately $17,000 in 1993), as an income below half of the median (under $18,500), or as half the average and below (under $23,600). In each of these measures, all Americans are involved because poverty is directly related to the lives of all citizens. In both the absolute and relative cases, poverty is about the distribution of wealth. However, in the latter case, poverty can be overcome only when the wealth is distributed equally.

[The Saturday Group of the Council of Economic Advisors of 1963] would get into discussions about the definition of poverty. What kind of a concept and what kind of a numbers frame would you have in mind? Some people would say poverty obviously means lack of money income. That had the great merit of being something we had some numbers on. We could say how many people there were above and below some line and where they were and so on. But other people said that's really not what poverty means; poverty is more or sometimes less than money. It's a spiritual concept; or it's a participation-in-government concept; or it's a lack of some kind of self-esteem, sort of a psychological or image problem that people had. Or people would say, well, it really has to do with race; it has to do with sort of a near caste system in the United States. Still others would say it really has to do with lack of opportunity. It has to do with lack of facilities like schools and so on. That's what makes people really poor. . . . So there was a kind of sociological theory of poverty with its lack of remedies, and the economic theory with easy optimism that you could do something about it all. (Robert Lampman, Council of Economic Advisors from 1962 through 1964, as quoted in Gillette 1996, 6–7)

Perhaps it is not surprising, then, to learn that the U.S. government chose an absolute rubric for drawing the poverty line. In 1963, the President's Council of Economic Advisors (CEA) set an official poverty line for the first time. Using a U.S. Department of Agriculture (USDA) report written by Mollie Orshansky, which determined that a typical family of four could prepare three minimally adequate meals a day on exactly $2.736, the CEA established $3,000 in income as the poverty line ($2.736 × 365 days = $998.64 × 3 [because the average family in 1963 spent one-third of their income on food] = $2,995.92).

Because of inflationary effects on the Consumer Price Index, the 1995 poverty line was set at $15,660 for a family of four and $12,380 for a family with one parent and two children. Since 1963, no adjustments have been made in the official poverty equation to accommodate the many changes in Americans' standards of living. For example, although the average family now spends one-fifth of its income on food with housing, health care, utilities, and child care occupying significantly higher percentages of household budgets, the original food budget ratio is still used. The USDA's warnings have not been heeded that those original figures were meant only for "temporary or emergency use when funds were low" (Sherman 1994, 4). Apparently, the U.S. Office of Budget and Management, which now adjusts the poverty line annually, "still assumes families will bake daily and cook all their food from scratch, never buy fast food or eat out, use dried beans and no canned food, be experts in nutrition, and have a working refrigerator, freezer, and stove" (6). There have been no adjustments for differences in cost of living across geographic regions or between urban and rural areas. Despite these concerns, the official poverty line continues to be the primary criterion used to test an individual's eligibility for programs of public assistance.

Poverty is a family-based concept within the official guidelines. An individual is considered poor if his or her income is less than the official poverty line for that size family. Table 2–2 presents the income maximum for 1995. Family is defined as all related persons living together under one roof. A married couple living with one set of parents is considered one family. Two sisters living together with their children are considered one family. Yet two unrelated women living together with their respective children are considered separate families. This family-based concept assumes that relatives who live together share their incomes as one unit, while unrelated people will not share and, therefore, cannot be considered a single economic unit.

Table 2–2 Poverty Thresholds

Size of Family	Poverty Standard
one	$7,811
two	$9,987
three	$12,223
four	$15,662
five	$18,512
six	$20,919
seven	$23,746
eight	$26,351

Schiller 1995. *The economics of poverty and discrimination.* 17.

The official poverty count was 33.4 million in 1963 or about twenty percent of the population. By 1973, after the War on Poverty, the percentage dropped to a low of 11.1 percent (under 24 million people). In 1994, a total of 38.1 million people lived in poor families, which represents 14.5 percent of the population (Blank 1997). The more recent figures do not include any in-kind support for the poor (e.g., Medicare, food stamps, or housing subsidies), which varying percentages of the poor receive. Nor do the figures consider taxes or individuals who do not reside with a family in a permanent residence.

CONTESTING THE OFFICIAL DEFINITION

According to Vaughan (1993), public perceptions about the adequacy of poverty-level budgets were fairly close to the official poverty line in 1963. Since that time, Americans have changed their minds about their and the poor's standards of living. A national sample of Americans stated that they would need $25,000 (median response) in income in order for a family of four to "just get by." They'd need $40,000 to "live in reasonable comfort" and $102,200 a year "to fulfill all [their] dreams" (Roper 1994, 9). By these criteria, at least thirty percent of American citizens should classify themselves as living below the unofficial poverty line, while more than half should recognize that they live without reasonable comfort. Only five percent of Americans have enough income to fulfill all their and many poorer Americans' dreams. In their book on the working poor, Schwartz and Volgey (1992) show that a family of four needed an income of about 155 percent of the official poverty line to buy minimally sufficient food, housing, health care, transportation, clothing, and other personal and household items (even they do not include child care!). Using Schwartz and Volgey's formula, one person in four is living in poverty. Sam Fulwood, a journalist for the *Los Angeles Times*, estimates the number of working and nonworking poor to be between seventy and seventy-five million. "[The working poor] are the ones whose income places them at constant risk of falling into poverty. A divorce, loss of a job or home, illness or injury, or the death of a wage earner—any of these will destroy their fragile hold on the lower rungs of respectability and plunge them into desperate poverty." Even small changes can inflict considerable consequences.

When [Ernest Bartelle, a maintenance worker in a Denver High School who made $12,500 a year in sole support of a family of four] get my paycheck and my mortgage is due, after medical insurance and what the government takes, the whole thing doesn't cover my mortgage. The whole thing's gone. A couple of days ago, I just heard they want to raise the electricity rates another thirteen percent. If they raise the rates, we're going to eat less. The only place we can cut back on is places like the food budget. Sometimes we've gone for days just eating potatoes. When we buy food, sometimes, we don't have enough money to pay other bills. In other words, you rob Peter to pay Paul. You just juggle back and forth. We're always behind. (Schwartz and Volgey 1992, 27)

Others argue that it does not matter whether the line set is reasonable. An absolute definition of poverty simply masks the relative economic inequality among citizens. Remember that twenty percent of the American population enjoys nearly the same amount of wealth as the other eighty percent. For example, Bok (1993) questions the salaries and income of top executives in comparison with their workers. Gordon (1996)

suggests that corporate organizational and employment practices squeeze the American worker while recording record
profits. Phillips (1990) wrote that "the 1980s were the triumph of upper America" (10). These critics are not wild-eyed
radicals, but rather the former president of Harvard University, an endowed professor of economics, and a former strate-
gist for Richard Nixon. Each demonstrates that poverty is a
relative issue, with the wealthy top being directly responsible
for the impoverished bottom.

WHO IS POOR

Table 2–3 is a brief demographic breakdown of the American
poor. According to the U.S. Bureau of Census in 1993, race,
gender, and age figure prominently within the probabilities of
landing below the official poverty line.

Table 2–3 Poverty Rates for Select Demographic Variables

Group	U.S. Population	In Poverty	Rate
All	259,278,000	39,265,000	15.1
White	190,737,000	18,883,000	9.9
Black	32,910,000	10,877,000	33.3
Latino	26,559,000	8,126,000	30.6
Two-parent	103,956,000	9,470,000	9.1
Single-parent Male	5,596,000	1,237,000	22.1
Female	28,336,000	13,601,000	48.0
Over 65	30,779,000	3,755,000	12.0
Under 18	69,292,000	15,729,000	22.7

U.S. Bureau of Census 1993. Household wealth and asset ownership, 34 (vii): 70.

Among all age groups, races, and family types in America
today, a single mother with children has the highest probability of being poor. There is a forty percent chance of being poor
for white single women, and a nearly two-thirds chance for
black or Latina women with children. Although more than a
third of the poor live in families with two married adults, the
increasing rate of single-mother families (and their high li]
lihood of being poor) is a primary reason for the appallin;

high rates of child poverty. One in five children live in poverty in the United States. In fact, children under the age of six comprise the fastest growing poverty rate in America.

Young families, those headed by parents younger than thirty, have been hit the hardest. The median income of young families with children plummeted by one-third (thirty-two percent) from 1973 to 1990, after adjusting for inflation. In contrast, young families without children achieved a modest five percent gain in median income. Even those insulated from such crises in earlier times have been deeply affected: one-fifth of children in two-parent families, nearly one-third of children in young families headed by a high-school graduate, and more than one-quarter of children in white young families were poor in 1990. As a result, fully forty percent of the children in young families lived in poverty, up from twenty percent in 1973. The consequences of the young families' plight will affect the next generation profoundly, as most children spend part of their earliest and most developmentally vulnerable years in a young family. (Children's Defense Fund 1992b, 25)

If children's poverty rates have climbed steadily in recent years, poverty rates among the elderly have fallen. In 1993, elderly poverty rates were at an all-time low, while children's poverty rates again equaled those of the 1960s. The decline in poverty among the elderly is largely due to increases in retirement income—specifically Social Security and SSI, which have greatly increased during the last thirty years. The elderly who remain poor are older widowed or divorced women who accrued little pension or Social Security income on their own and who have found themselves destitute following a husband's death. Women's increased participation in the labor force should shrink the size of this group over time. However, the continued lower pay for most women may mean that this group will not disappear anytime soon.

[The 1990 Census] found that certain groups of the elderly were especially vulnerable to economic problems. Elderly women were nearly twice as likely as elderly men to be poor or near-poor (23.4 versus 12.8 percent, respectively). In addition, elderly minorities were two to three times as likely as elderly non-minorities to be poor or near-poor (Hispanics 33.5 and blacks 45.1 percent versus 16.4 percent for whites). Similarly, persons over the age of seventy-five were almost twice as likely as persons between sixty-five and seventy-four to be poor or near-poor (15.1 versus 24.9 percent, respectively). In fact, across all racial and ethnic groups, persons over the age of seventy-five were more likely than any other group of adults to be poor and near-poor. The additive effect of sex, race, and age was dramatic:

More than half of all black women over age of seventy-five were poor or near-poor in 1990. Such figures are disturbing and clearly demonstrate that some groups of older Americans have not enjoyed the general income improvements experienced by the elderly population as a whole. (York 1992, 72)

Members of racial and ethnic minorities are disproportionately more likely to be poor. While whites have a one-in-ten chance overall, African Americans and Latinos face one-in-three odds. Native Americans who live on reservations often have extremely high rates of poverty. Recent immigrants, like generations of immigrants before them, are also more likely to be poorer than the general public. Moreover, members of these groups are more likely to be poor at some time in their lives and to remain poor longer (Blank 1997). For example, seventy-five percent of whites have never been poor. In contrast, a little more than a third of African Americans can make that claim. Less than two percent of whites were poor for longer than ten years, while more than sixteen percent of African Americans experience poverty for that length of time.

Statistical analysis shows that African Americans and Latinos earn less that whites, even taking into account differences in education and labor-force experience. A recent study sent "testers" (carefully selected pairs of young black and white men matched closely in terms of education, work history, age, and height) to apply for entry-level jobs. The results: Blacks were three times more likely than whites to be rejected. A similar study using matched pairs of Latino and Anglo men found that Latinos were significantly less likely to be offered a job interview or a job. (Folbre 1995, 413)

Most Americans picture an urban ghetto when they think of poverty. Yet slightly less than ninety percent of all poor and more than seventy-five percent of the black poor live outside such places in mixed-income urban communities, suburbs, and rural areas. During the last twenty years, suburban communities have had the fastest growing rates of poverty. Poverty is shrinking in rural areas, where nearly half of the poor lived until the 1970s. Despite these changes, the poorest counties in the United States are still rural, where many families still live isolated lives without many prospects for full-time employment.

Because the economic resources and social conditions of different regions in the United States vary tremendously, it is important to know the geographic location of the poor. The South contains a disproportionate number of poor persons. Less than a third of the total U.S. population lives in the South, but forty percent of the poor reside there. This excess of poverty results not only from high concentrations of blacks in the South, but also from the fact that the South is simply poorer and less urban than any other region. A southern resident, regardless of race, is more likely to be poor than his or her northern counterpart. In both the North and the South, a black person is roughly three times as likely to be poor as a white person. (Schiller 1995, 50)

Like Ernest Bartelle's family, most poor families have at least one member working. Although the number of hours and the length of employment vary considerably from those of the non-poor, nearly two-thirds of poor families work for wages. Twenty percent of these families has one member who works full-time year-round. Employment does not necessarily guarantee that a family can work its way out of poverty. Two-parent families are more likely to have a full-time worker. Work among low-income single parents has increased over time, but among poor married couples, particularly among men, it has declined.

The view that anyone who works hard can get ahead is so widely held that there is a tendency to attribute the lower earnings of minorities to race-specific factors. However, slow growth and rising inequality of the 1980s had very similar effects on whites and minorities. The causes of this disappointing performance are *not* primarily due to behavioral differences among the races; they are due to changes in the economy. Large racial differences remain in any year, but the trends over time for the race/ethnic groups were quite similar. (Danziger and Gottschalk 1995, 75–76)

The poor are a diverse group. They are white and black and Latino. They are married and single. They are young and old. The largest single group among the poor is single mothers with children. The largest number in that group are white single mothers with children. They live in cities, suburbs, and rural counties. They work, mostly at part-time and low-paying jobs, and they don't. One reason most Americans don't see this diversity among the poor is that they often assume that poverty is synonymous with welfare recipient. However, in fact, welfare or AFDC is usually available only to single mothers and their children. Only sixty-five percent of eligible families receive these funds. Fully one-third of the eligible families choose not to accept AFDC. Overall, twenty-five percent of all poor families receive AFDC.

GOVERNMENTAL AID TO THE POOR

There are many federal programs to assist the poor. Cash-assistance programs (e.g., AFDC and SSI) offer direct cash transfers to individuals who meet means-testing requirements. In-kind assistance programs (e.g., Food Stamps, Medicaid, and housing) provide goods and services to eligible citizens. Earnings Subsidy programs (e.g., Minimum Wage Law, Earned-Income Tax Credits, and Employer Tax Credits) provide substantial supplemental income for the wage-earning poor through the establishment of a wage floor and tax reductions, incentives, and rebates. Job-training programs (e.g., Welfare to Work programs aimed at AFDC recipients, the Job Training Partnership Act, and the Job Corps) offer men and women instruction in specific skills for employment in the private sector of the economy. Child and youth programs (e.g., Head Start, School to Work, and Stay in School) provide preventive measures through education to ensure that poor children break the "cycle of poverty" by developing their job-related skills sufficiently to gain above-poverty-level employment. Finally, neighborhood economic-development programs (e.g., Enterprise Zones, Community Development Block Grants, and public housing funds) present tax incentives and funding to increase employment, rebuild housing, and encourage business and community growth. The shear number of these programs suggests that the government is preoccupied with the concerns of the poor.

Many misperceptions about the cost of poverty programs exist. For example, a recent CBS/*New York Times* (1995) poll indicated that half the U.S. population believes that more than twenty percent of the federal budget is devoted to programs to combat poverty. In fact, federal expenditures in 1995 were distributed at fifteen percent on interest on national debt, seventeen percent on defense, ten percent on Medicare, twenty-one percent on Social Security, twenty-one percent on a wide array of programs and expenses (e.g., education and foreign aid) labeled "other," and fourteen percent on public assistance. Of that fourteen percent, six percent is Medicaid and eight percent comprises AFDC (1.1 percent), food stamps (1.7 percent), and a host of other family-support programs. In fact, cash-assistance programs to single parents have decreased during the last twenty years and food stamps and other noncash transfers have changed little since 1980. Medicaid payments have continued to grow rapidly, but so have medical expenses for every citizen.

The costs of public-assistance programs are not always directly tied to the number of people served. For example, more than thirty million people participate in Medicaid at a cost of $3,821 per participant; twenty-eight million receive food stamps at $925 per individual. Head Start serves 714,000 children at nearly $4,000 per child, and fourteen million receive earned-income tax credits at a cost of $924 per tax filer. Although public-assistance programs for low-income elderly and disabled are less controversial, this relatively small group (i.e., about ten percent of the poor) receive nearly forty percent of federal funding. This imbalance is extended by such programs as Social Security, Medicare, veterans' benefits, and the like, which are not primarily antipoverty programs, but which supply additional income and benefits to these groups. AFDC, which serves twenty-five million individuals (two-thirds of whom are children), provides an average benefit of $1,785 per person, and SSI, which benefits primarily adults and the elderly (more than eighty-eight percent), offers more than $4,000 on average to each recipient.

A closer look at these last two programs demonstrates how different groups among the poor are treated differently. Both AFDC and SSI are cash-assistance programs, which means that eligible participants receive cash to spend in any way they deem appropriate. Up until this year, both have been guaranteed programs and benefits could not be denied based on the financial condition of the government. The 1996 "welfare reform" bill has ended the sixty-year guarantee for AFDC, and now state governments are to design their own programs based on modest national guidelines of family behavior (e.g., no benefits for children born while a family receives AFDC, adolescents' school attendance, and child immunization) and time limits on duration of benefits. In 1994, AFDC benefits varied considerably across states from a low of $120 per month for a family of three in Mississippi to a high of $680 for a similar family in Connecticut. Unlike SSI, AFDC benefits have not been adjusted for inflation. In constant dollars, an

AFDC payment was $792 per month for a mother with three children in 1970; by 1993, it fell to $435 per month.

Enacted in 1972, SSI provides assistance to elderly or disabled persons who are below certain income cutoffs. In comparison to AFDC, SSI remains a federal program with a national monthly average of $446 for an individual and $669 for a couple. This is substantially more generous than AFDC. In 1994, only thirteen states paid as much to a mother and two children as was available to a single individual on SSI. Benefits for AFDC and SSI are calculated in the same way. Those with no other income receive the maximum benefit, while those with other sources of income have their benefits reduced. Oddly, AFDC recipients lose one dollar in aid for each dollar they earn, but SSI recipients are taxed at a lower rate. Therefore, those we expect not to work have access to a program with greater work incentives than parents on AFDC, whom we have increasingly expected to be employed.

The differences in cash assistance and treatment under AFDC and SSI underscore the social construction of the definition of poverty in the United States. AFDC, originally enacted to aid widows and their children during the Great Depression, is represented as an inducement to some to choose a lifestyle of poverty and government support. SSI is viewed as aid to the "truly needy"—those who can't work because of factors (e.g., age or disability) beyond their control. These differences in perceived need and consequent support have substantial implications for the economic well-being among these two groups. "It is not too far from the truth to suggest that women and children tend to be poor in this country, in part because we choose to provide them only limited cash support. The elderly are among the least poor because we choose to provide them with generous cash supplements when they are in need" (Blank 1997, 104).

The controversy over AFDC does not end with a basic distrust of its recipients. Critics complain that the program has failed to reduce poverty and has increased poverty in some groups. Although AFDC has evolved into a bureaucratic rule-based program that often makes life difficult for recipients, it has accomplished several of its intended goals. AFDC cash assistance makes people less poor. For example, when President Reagan proposed welfare changes in 1981, the least poor families then eligible for AFDC were removed from the roles.

Primarily, these were two-parent families with both adults
working. All follow-up studies of these families reached the
same conclusion: Total family income declined by twelve to
twenty-six percent "even though many worked full time and
increased their earnings during this period" (U.S. General Accounting Office 1985, iv). If women are forced to work to remain eligible for "reformed" AFDC (Cancian and Gordon
1996), there is little evidence that they will be able to increase
their income sufficiently to work their way out of poverty. And
what about the cost of child care while they work? Without
AFDC or with drastic restrictions on eligibility, many more
women and children will find themselves destitute. If food
stamps, Medicaid, and other in-kind programs are reduced,
they will find themselves hungry, sick, and homeless as well.

READING GOVERNMENTAL RELATIONS WITH THE POOR

Not only does the government define poverty by setting the
official poverty line, through the many documents that regu-
late the distribution of government aid, they also define the
poor. Reading government and professional texts closely, Taylor (1996) offers a new glimpse of the government's involvement with poverty and reveals unacknowledged patterns of
biases—race, ethnicity, age, and gender—that increase an individual's probability of poverty. As she demonstrates, these
patterns of bias are often "papered over" in the language and
organization of the policies, laws, regulations, and forms that
separate the poor from the rest of society. In *Toxic Literacies:
Exposing the Injustice of Bureaucratic Texts*, Taylor offers a
reading of poverty that makes us present in the lives of the
poor, subjecting us to the ways in which language is used
against the poor. By gathering the official texts that construct
the legal identities of five individuals and comparing them
against the unofficial lived texts of their everyday lives, Taylor identifies our complicity in what she calls government-
sanctioned human-rights violations.

In America, who lives and who dies is controlled by the subtexts of
society. Official documentation hides the human-rights violations

that take place in this country. We enculturate members of our
communities into poverty. Men, women, and children are incapaci-
tated by legally sanctioned discriminatory practices that occur
through the use of bureaucratic texts. There is an official form to
deal with every situation. On paper, whatever action is taken
can be justified. It's all in the record. Through toxic forms of print
we abdicate responsibility—even though we are not always aware of
our duplicity. (14)

In a city that has just elected a Libertarian city council, Taylor
tracked the consequences of legal, medical, and government
texts on the lives of people that society "has pushed to the
margins." Repeatedly, she witnesses lawyers, judges, social
workers, doctors, nurses, welfare administrators, and police
who cannot or will not acknowledge the people they see before
them in need of help. Taylor records in excruciating detail the
inability of these social-support systems to provide compassion
as well as adequate care. For example, she offers the following
exchange between a welfare caseworker and a mother of three,
who is suffering from the after-effects of an overdose of radia-
tion she received during cancer treatment.

He takes one form and begins asking Laurie questions.

Does Laurie have a bank account?

"Yes," Laurie says, as she searches for it in the envelope that she
brought with her. She gives the caseworker her bankbook. "There
was three dollars in it, but that was about two years ago."

"Is there any money in it now?"

"I don't know if the three dollars is still in there." Laurie looks
quizzical, nervous. I'm caught up in the pathology of the questions,
the way they are asked, the assumption that she is cheating, that
she's a fraud.

"It's probably gone in bank charges," I interject and laugh.

Laurie smiles. The caseworker does not seem to think it's funny.

"Do you have a burial plot or an agreement with a funeral home?"

Laurie grimaces. "No."

"What if she did?" I ask.

"Assets." The caseworker gives me a sideways glance. "A burial
plot is counted as an asset." He looks straight at Laurie. "You
would have to declare it."

"I don't have one." Laurie's voice is barely audible. (187)

This is powerful work. Yet Taylor's book demonstrates both
the wonders and limitations of ethnography for the study of

poverty and literacy. Her careful descriptions of what happened to these five individuals enable readers to see what it's like to be poor. Her analyses of the texts that construct them as drug-pushers, hopeless drunks, welfare frauds, and punks provide a clear picture of how individuals are socially constructed within the public-assistance system. Her reading of the government's relationship to poverty is unique and generative. Her advocacy for these individuals is startling in its depth and overwhelming in its ferocity. However, she stops her study with these descriptions. In her conclusion, she offers only two lists of "observations." The first list considers bureaucratic institutions: their needs conflict with the needs of the poor; they reflect "dominant ideologies"; they work collusively; they are filled with waste, fraud, and abuse; administrators are highly paid, but caseworkers and public liaisons are often paid subsistence wages.

The second list contains observations about the lives of the poor: the notion of entitlement is a myth of dominant political ideologies; lives are reconstructed to fit the dominant ideologies of society; each time a person or family interacts with the public-assistance system, their lives are likely to deteriorate; difficulties compound when assistance is sought from multiple agencies; and the poor have little access to the texts that construct their lives and worthiness for assistance. Although the term *dominant ideologies* figures prominently in both lists, Taylor offers little information on what those ideologies might be, how those ideologies are realized in the texts she collects, why those texts are written and interpreted in the ways she describes, or why those ideologies are dominant in the first place within the United States. Taylor offers us a new way of thinking about reading and its relationship to poverty but, in the end, she leaves us only half-armed to struggle against the texts and ideologies that she rightly finds so deplorable.

THREE

IF IT WASN'T FOR BAD LUCK
Reading the Causes of Poverty

A government's social policy helps set the rules of the game—the stakes, the risks, the payoffs, the tradeoffs, and the strategies for making a living, raising a family, having fun, defining what "winning" and "success" mean. . . . The most compelling explanation for the marked drop in the fortunes of the poor is that they continued to respond, as they always had, to the world as they found it, but that we—meaning the not-poor and un-disadvantaged—had changed the rules of the world. Not of our world, just of theirs. The first effect of the new rules was to make it profitable for the poor to behave in the short term in ways that were destructive in the long term. Their second effect was to mask these long-term losses—to subsidize irretrievable mistakes. We tried to provide more for the poor and produced more poor instead. (Murray 1984, 9) ◆◆

> *Instead of nurturing virtue, popular culture celebrated intemperance—and intemperance, as Adam Smith pointed out two hundred years ago, may addle the rich, but it devastates the poor. (Klein 1993, 30).*

> *In the majority of cases, poverty starts for a person when the economic situation of his or her family changes, with no changes in family composition. Almost half of all poverty spells start when the earnings of the head or spouse fall, and another twelve percent start when other income sources are lost, such as a decline in child support, public assistance, or pension income. (Blank 1997, 25)*

> *It shouldn't be surprising that in the United States, black and Latino families—whether one-parent or two-parent families—have higher poverty rates than white families, since the wages and job opportunities of people of color reflect educational and employment discrimination. It shouldn't be surprising that single-parent families—male- or female-headed—have high rates of poverty since, with the fall in real wages, two or more incomes are increasingly needed to keep families out of poverty. Since single mothers of color experience both race and gender discrimination, their families are the most impoverished. (Sklar 1995, 91)*

Debates over the definition and number of citizens in poverty also are reflected in the struggle to identify its causes. Murray argues that governmental aid has actually increased the social problems among society's most vulnerable citizens. Without governmental supports, he argues, the poor would learn to overcome the blight of dependency and pull themselves up to social respectability by their bootstraps. Klein blames culturally induced moral weaknesses that prevent the poor from participating productively in either economic or social life. Blank states the obvious—that it's a lack of income that causes poverty. Neither the economy nor governmental programs provide enough aid to help the poor overcome their circumstances. Current policies do not help the poor to develop their human capital sufficiently to enable them to take advantage of available opportunities. Sklar finds those opportunities restricted based on biases of race, class, and gender. Poverty, then, is caused by deliberate and systemic discrimination in an economy that will not provide for all.

Each position in this debate represents a dialectical interpretation of the poor and non-poor, a certain self-interest, and a political agenda. In different but complementary ways, Murray and Klein detect personal flaws among the poor that prevent them from providing adequately for themselves and their families. Historically, these flaws had direct moral denotations; recently, they are more likely to be referred to as a lack of motivation or an absence of a work ethic. Murray understands the flaws as inherent within the poor, but active only under conducive circumstances. Klein sees them as correctable only under specific moral re-education. From both vantage points, each individual (poor and non-poor alike) is fully responsible for and is in complete control of his or her social class standing. By the choices each makes and the actions each takes, individuals determine their economic destiny. People choose to be poor or middle class or rich and, therefore, they deserve what they choose. Assisting the poor, then, is a choice that social and economic betters make to engage in acts of charity toward flawed individuals.

Blank and Sklar start from a different set of assumptions. They challenge the free-choice foundation of Klein and Murray's position. They argue, rather, that individuals' opportunities to develop their human capital and to work their way out of poverty are restricted in various ways. Blank emphasizes the lack of general opportunities for development and work, and Sklar begins her explanation from the unequal power and privilege among citizens at present. In either case, character flaws and poor judgment are assumed to be distributed randomly among individuals in all economic classes. Poverty is beyond an individual's control and is a natural consequence of a capitalist economic system. According to this logic, if the poor are disadvantaged, then the non-poor assume the role of socially advantaged at best, and economic oppressor at worst. Helping the poor becomes an issue of social, economic, and political justice within a democracy.

The debate over the causes of poverty provides much of the variety in past and current debates over what ought to be done in schools. Should schools be tailored to the inherent capabilities of individuals to help them be simply all that they can be, as Murray implies? Or do we think schools can enhance those inherent capacities so that individuals might become more than they seem? Should schools be honed according to a singular moral code to ensure "good" decisions as we currently define them, as Klein suggests? Remember that in the not-too-distant past, that moral code was interpreted to exclude women, minorities, and the poor from all substantive participation in decisions that influenced their lives. Who is excluded now? Should schools be about developing skills to overcome restricted opportunities and to ensure some income security? Which skills can make our lives secure any longer? Businesses are laying off employees in the Silicon Valley, the government is paying hospitals not to train more doctors, and the average income of lawyers is dropping. Finally, should schools reorganize to take up the struggles against discrimination in our society? Can schools be agents of social change? Do the poor choose to be poor? Do all A students stand on equal footing when they graduate from school or do some have more opportunities and choices available to them than others? By looking at the ideological explanations of poverty in America, we gain needed perspective on the debates over schooling in America. By exploring the values and interests encoded in these ideologies, we have opportunities to look carefully at ourselves as well as others.

VALUES ADDED

Before the twentieth century, it would have seemed preposterous to imagine the abolition of poverty. Resources were limited; productive capacities were unable to meet the needs of all. For most people, life would be a continuous struggle to survive. The question facing governments was to determine whether any level of hardship qualified an individual for help. Even for the most altruistic, scarcity required hierarchical classification of the poor. In Western societies, two criteria were established as early as the 1500s (Katz 1989). The first was to determine if the truly needy were neighbors or strangers. Neighbors were worthy of support; strangers were not. The second criterion was set to determine whether the individual was able or impotent. The able-bodied were expected to fend for themselves; the impotent deserved to be helped. Such classifications led to an ascription of social values to each rank.

In speaking of poverty, let us never forget that there is a distinction between this and pauperism. The former is an unavoidable evil, to which many are brought from necessity, and in the wise and gracious Providence of God. It is the result, not of our faults, but of our misfortunes. . . . Pauperism is the consequence of willful error, of shameful indolence, the pernicious work of man, the lamentable consequence of bad principles and morals. (Reverend Charles Burroughs 1834, as quoted in Katz 1989, 13)

Assessments based on these criteria influenced people's attitudes toward the needy and determined whether individuals received assistance. Poverty was thought to be in God's hands, since aging and illness were beyond individual control and choice. Pauperism, on the other hand, was a human endeavor, considered to be a personal choice—what might be called a "lifestyle" today. As such, the causes of pauperism were looked for and found within him or her who suffers it. Magnet (1994) offers a modern version of this valuing:

The key to the mystery of why, despite opportunity, the poorest poor don't work is that their poverty is less an economic matter than a cultural one. In many cases, the have-nots lack the inner resources to seize their chance and attitudes, along with an impoverished intellectual and emotional development, that generally imprison them in failure as well. (213)

According to Gans (1995), many labels have been associated with the undeserving poor over the last three centuries— pauper, defective, dependent, delinquent, debauched, ne'er-do-wells, dregs, residue, residuum, feebleminded, morons, white trash, school dropouts, culturally deprived or disadvantaged, rabble, mob, lumpenproletariat, underclass. "All of the labeled are inevitably charged with the failure to adhere to one or more mainstream values by their behavior, but this is why they are considered undeserving in the first place" (16). Even labels for the aid offered these groups received different labels. The deserving poor received social insurance, offered to prevent all citizens from ever becoming impoverished. Aid to the undeserving poor, when it was offered at all, was public assistance, designated only for those who would not help themselves.

A CONSERVATIVE POSITION

Conservatives blame government policies for the social problems that surround poverty. They argue that social-support policies create a "blight of dependency" and, in fact, have taught the poor to rely on others rather than themselves (Gilder 1981). Sowell (1993) offers a new version of the fable "The Grasshopper and the Ant" to make this point. As in the original, Sowell's ant works to store food for the winter, while the grasshopper "romped and played." Winter brought hunger for the grasshopper, who asks the ant for assistance. The ant denies the grasshopper's request because the grasshopper had told the ant during the summer that he "was one of those old-fashioned clods who had missed the whole point of the modern self-realization philosophy."

The ant and the grasshopper are joined by another ant, "Lefty," who argues that ants should share their natural bounty with all in need. The two ants discuss what Lefty had learned at college about unequally distributed incomes. Toward the end of their discussion, Lefty explains that he works for the government because he wants to make a difference. To which the first ant responds, "You really have been to college." Lefty leads the grasshopper to a government shelter to provide for his needs, while the first ant implores him to teach the grasshopper to work during the summer and to save something for the winter.

Lefty not only won the argument, he continued to expand his program of shelters for grasshoppers. As word spread, grasshoppers came from miles around. Eventually, some of the younger ants decided to adopt the grasshopper lifestyle. As the older generation of ants passed from the scene, more and more ants joined the grasshoppers, romping and playing in the fields. Finally, all the ants and all the grasshoppers spent all their time enjoying the carefree lifestyle and lived happily ever after—all summer long. Then the winter came. (6)

Sowell makes clear who is to blame for continued problems among the poor—government policies and the intellectuals who theorize about but do not create wealth. He and others state that they have the data to prove this point. For example, according to the Family Research Council (1994), AFDC makes marriage less attractive because a single mother already on AFDC would have her combined income reduced by thirty percent if she chose to marry a cohabiting partner. However, although her income would be higher in the short term, her less stable relationship means in all likelihood that this increase will be temporary. In this case as in others, government policy tampers with the natural order of things and creates problems worse than the original concerns.

Murray calls these policies "the rules of the game" that changed the lives of the poor "others," but left the lives of the intellectuals and rulemakers unchanged. In *Losing Ground*, Murray presents the basic conservative argument upon which Sowell rewrote the ant and grasshopper fable. According to Murray, during the Kennedy Administration, elite social scientists' discovery of structural poverty began a moral and economic decline of the poor, particularly the African American poor. Liberal discovery transferred responsibility for poverty from individuals to the economy, making the working, middle, and upper classes' success a direct consequence of the poor's economic failure. Theories of structural poverty stated that the poor were poor because of the way the system distributed income. Accordingly, the way to fix poverty was to alter the system in order to redistribute income. Murray criticizes, "If society were to blame for poverty itself among all races, and *if society's responsibility were not put right by enforcing a formalistic legal equality,* then a social program could hardly be constructed on grounds that simply guaranteed equality of opportunity. It must work toward equality of *outcome*" (1984, 33 [italics original]).

Conservatives maintain that the policies designed to overcome inequality of opportunity and outcome created disincentives among the poor to work, marry, or be responsible parents. Cash and in-kind assistance reduced the need for the poor to work in order to buy food or obtain shelter. Means-tested eligibility requirements offered poor women incentives to stay unmarried and to give birth to additional children while receiving AFDC. Their primary example of causality comes from governmental evaluations of the Negative Income Tax (NIT) policy, which started in 1968 and was canceled in 1980. NIT supplied payments to individuals whose income fell below a scaled floor. NIT reduced work efforts by nearly ten percent for married men and twenty percent for married women. The reduction was primarily due to men and women leaving the workforce altogether rather than a general decline in hours worked. The effects of NIT were even more pronounced for young men who were not married: For this group, work hours per week declined forty-three percent. Again, most of the decline was explained by individuals opting out of the workforce. The NIT had a negative impact on marriage also, with some sites reporting dissolution of marriage as high as eighty-four percent. Murray concludes, "The only time we have been able to put the question [whether government programs provide disincentive for work, marriage, and responsible parenting] to a controlled test, the causal effect was unambiguous and strong" (1984, 153).

According to Murray (1984), conservatives begin with three basic premises: (1) people respond to incentives and disincentives; (2) they are not inherently hard-working or moral; and (3) they must be held responsible for their actions. Their solutions to poverty are simple, and they return to criteria established well before the turn of the century. Only the local impotent deserve assistance, all others should fend for themselves. That means all federal assistance programs should stop for those able to work. No AFDC, no food stamps, no public housing—to the contrary, the need for income, food, and shelter are incentives to work and to act responsibly. At the very least, Mead (1992) argues assistance must be tied to work. However, these ties cannot be voluntary because most poor will not choose to work, if left to their own choice. Rather, granting agencies must force the poor to work more hours in the private sector of the economy in order to demonstrate their social value. This "workfare" is admittedly paternalistic: "It joins the benefits that poor persons need with requirements that they function in improving ways" (Mead 1996, 266). To improve, the poor must get married, become acclimated to work routines, and regularize their lives and the lives of their families outside of work. This return to natural order will do more than any government program. "To a child, to have functioning parents is worth twenty-five Head Start programs" (Mead 1996, 274).

A NEO-CONSERVATIVE POSITION

Klein's title for his *Newsweek* article, "How About a Swift Kick," suggests not only that the flawed-character argument still exists, but that pejorative language about the poor is still popular. In fact, during the last fifteen years, the moral basis of the flawed character of the poor has been offered frequently on both floors of Congress, in popular media, and at civic and religious meetings throughout the country. The rediscovery of the flawed-character position, as Klein puts it in his article, is directly related to the rise of neo-conservatism in federal and state politics. Klein's allusion to impropriety is a thinly veiled reference to the civil rights, women's liberation, and sexual freedom movements of the 1960s, which inserted different voices into conversations about social, political, and economic rights and values. These voices challenged the taken-for-granted moral superiority of white middle-class American virtues.

The sixties counterculture rejected traditional bourgeois culture as sick, repressive, and destructive. Bourgeois culture's sexual mores, based on guilt, marriage, and the perverse belief that present gratification should be deferred to achieve future goals, were symptoms of its pathology. Its sobriety and decorum were mere slavish, hypocritical conformism; its industriousness betokened an upside-down, materialistic value system; its family life was yet another arena of coercion and guilt. This culture went hand in hand with an inherently unjust capitalist economic order, and a political order whose murderousness was plainly revealed by "Amerika's" war in Vietnam. (Magnet 1993, 17)

Hedonistic, expressionist values of the 1960s offered a social climate that unleashed the characters of individuals of various classes. As Klein suggests, this was/is unfortunate for all, but it was/is devastating for the poor, whose character is, by definition, flawed. Bennett (1994b) states the stakes dramatically: "Unless those exploding social pathologies of the last thirty years are reversed, they will lead to the decline and perhaps even to the fall of the American republic" (8). The assumption that human character is basically acquired rather than natural is essential to a neo-conservative position and separates it from traditional conservative views. Because character is learned, social-intervention policies are warranted. However, those policies must be aimed at the cause of social problems, that is, at moral character. Before the turn of the century, character was considered a matter of divine intervention—a struggle between good and evil for the soul. Neo-conservatives augment this spiritualism with biological explanations.

In his book, *The Moral Sense,* Wilson (1993) marshals evidence from anthropological and psychological studies to demonstrate that a variety of cultures attaches importance to similar virtues (e.g., fairness, self-control, duty, and sympathy) and that children from a very early age express—and are eager to express—these sentiments. Citing Aristotle, David Hume, Adam Smith, and Charles Darwin, Wilson concludes that these similarities are the natural outcome of an innate sense of sociability among human beings. He argues that these similarities would not exist unless they had been selected for by evolution. Part of this evolutionary inheritance is affiliative behavior forming strong attachments for one another. Innate sociability and consequent affiliative behavior account for our moral sense of fairness, self-control, duty, and sympathy. Neo-conservatives begin with the assumptions that humans are by nature social and that social groupings aim at some form of mutual well-being. This "naturalism" explains the similarities of basic values among all cultures, and the goal of mutual well-being invites a preoccupation with social order. From this vantage point, neo-conservatives are prepared to judge whether behaviors and social organizations are good or bad for human beings.

The essential first step is to acknowledge that at root, in almost every area of important public concern, we are seeking to induce persons to act virtuously, whether as schoolchildren, applicants for public assistance, would-be lawbreakers, or voters and public officials. Not only is such conduct desirable in its own right, it appears now to be necessary if large improvements are to be made in those matters we consider problems: schooling, welfare, crime, and public finance. By virtue, I mean habits of moderate action; more specifically, acting with due restraint on one's impulses, due regard for the rights of others, and reasonable concern for distant consequences. (Wilson 1995, 22)

Accordingly, to correct these public concerns, we must undo the cultural consequences of the 1960s and reinstate social order based on a single moral code. The first task requires the quieting of diverse voices, to reinstate guilt over sexual freedom, and reinvoke blind patriotism. Over the last fifteen years, perhaps beginning with President Reagan's firing of striking air traffic controllers, the federal government appears to be actively engaged in this first task. Affirmative action is

severely compromised; women's control of their bodies is rhetorically challenged and physically assaulted with the armed
intrusions into abortion clinics; family values (two-parent
households with one parent at home) are promoted through
legislation; abstinence campaigns abound under the guise of
AIDS education; and the military is sent to Grenada, Panama,
Libya, Iraq, Lebanon, etc., in order to erase Vietnam from our
memories. This cleansed social climate prepares the way, and
highlights the need, for a "critical time-honored task: the
moral education of the young" (Bennett 1994a, 9). And this is
how neo-conservatives intend to help the poor—not with
cash, in-kind, or employment assistance, but with moral education to contain their flawed characters. "We are trying to
produce right behavior. We don't simply want to reduce poverty" (Wilson 1996, 371).

These debates over policy on social spending are no doubt important, but there is something sterile and superficial about them.
Ultimately, they fail to engage questions of personal morality, of
character and values, and of moral leadership in the public sphere
(116). . . . Although public policy should not reflect particular
religious doctrines under the U.S. form of government, this is no
reason to keep an understanding of the importance of spirituality out of public discussions of poverty. Everything worth talking
about in public need not result in a government program or a
federal statute! We should recognize the importance of the efforts
in many communities to reconstruct systems of beliefs and values
from which individuals derive meaning and around which people
can organize their lives. From such conceptions of ultimate meaning, good people derive their understanding of their fundamental
responsibilities and their sense of their own worthiness. (Lowery 1996, 117)

A LIBERAL POSITION

Blank argues that poverty is caused by a lack of income
sufficient to support a family in decent ways. For whatever
reasons, many American families just are not paid enough to
meet their needs. These insufficiencies vary in severity and
length for families, but during those times, families require
assistance from others in order to survive. That assistance
should ease or prevent suffering and prepare the poor to work

their way out of poverty when new opportunities arise. Contrary to conservative beliefs, Blank finds that the federal government is essential in providing that assistance.

Rather than creating dependence, governments provide the framework for family life. In her testimony before the House Select Committee on Children, Youth, and Families, Coontz (1992) offered the case that families exist always within some legislative, judicial, and social-support system provided by some form of government. Moreover, she maintained that there has never been a natural family structure that could fully provide for all the personal dependencies and changes of fortunes for its members. Since the inception of the United States, the government has never taken a "hands-off" approach to families. For example, in early settlements, governments created legal and political frameworks that required individuals, households, and institutions to care for one another within a community. Only after the Civil War, during rapid industrialization did the courts limit the family-like social responsibilities for communities. At the turn of the twentieth century, a family wage system sought to strengthen the male wage-earner's salary so that his wife and children did not have to work. At that time, eighty-five percent of industrial workers had incomes at or below the poverty line. Coontz cites the Homestead Act; subsidies for dams, irrigation, and electrical power; and GI benefits as federal government support for all, including the needy, in order to create family life as we now know it.

In conclusion, government has always taken responsibility for creating the material and legal conditions that allow families to coordinate their personal reproduction with the prevailing system of socioeconomic production. The historical debate over government policy toward families has never been over whether to intervene, but how: to rescue or to warehouse, to prevent or to punish, to mobilize resources to help families or to moralize? The historical record suggests that government action is more helpful to families when it provides a general and generous support system of infrastructure, allowing families to work out their own values and interpersonal arrangements, than when it tries to impose a unitary value system and set of gender roles inside the family. (Coontz 1992, 101).

The problem, according to Carville (1996), is that the government and the economy are not doing enough to support the poor. Since 1972, the value of an average monthly AFDC

check has decreased by forty percent. Funding for public housing has been virtually frozen. Medicaid eligibility requirements have become more strict, excluding many from assistance. Head Start accommodates fewer children now than
when it started. School nutrition programs during the 1980s
listed catsup as a vegetable. National child and health care are
rarely addressed seriously among legislators. The U.S. government ranks sixteenth among industrialized nations in the
amount of support provided for the poor. As a result, more
single women and children fall below the poverty line in the
United States than in any other industrialized country.

The economy has not been kind to the poor either. There
are now fewer jobs in manufacturing and industry that pay
working- and middle-class wages, and more than half of the
new jobs created are at or below minimum wage. Moreover,
many of the new jobs are not full-time employment and do
not provide health insurance or other fringe benefits. Thus,
the incentives are low for the poor to leave even the low government benefits. In a sense, the poor have not rejected the
economy; rather, the economy has rejected them. Most
"good" jobs that pay working- and middle-class wages require
skills that are beyond the reach of the poor.

It's simply not the case that most of today's welfare recipients
could obtain stable employment that would lift them and their
children out of poverty, if only they would try harder. Fear of destitution is a powerful incentive to survive; it will not, however,
guarantee that an unskilled worker who actively seeks work will be
able to earn enough to support her family. (Danziger and Lehman
1994, 10)

The liberal position, then, offers structural rather than personal
causes for poverty. The economy does not provide for all citizens, and the government must accommodate the needs of
those left behind. While liberals might agree that out-of-
wedlock births, divorce, and reluctance to enter the job market
are social concerns, they see them as consequences of poverty,
not causes. And clearly they do not blame the idea of government assistance for the creation of these concerns. Clinton,
Kennedy, and other liberals may carp about families, but they
do not act as if they believe that government policy on family
values will end poverty. However, there is a fundamental split
among liberals over what ought to be done about poverty. Neo-
liberals, like Clinton, see economic growth as the sole savior of

America; more traditional liberals, like Blank, are less optimistic about the powers of the market and are more comprehensive in their approach.

Neo-liberals see an American economy engaged in global competition, which has created an excess of high-skill, high-wage jobs for a population with too many low-skill workers. They propose a modest social safety net of cash and in-kind assistance for the poor to induce them to engage in the greatly expanded human-capital development programs. "The key to both productivity and competitiveness is the skills of our people and our capacity to use highly educated and trained people to maximum advantage in the workplace. In fact, however, the guiding principle on which our educational and industrial systems has been built is profoundly different; this guiding principle, for long highly successful, is now outmoded, and harmful, and the time has come to change it" (Marshall and Tucker 1992, xvi). Accordingly, industry should receive governmental incentives to reorganize its management toward more quality control, and educational programs (from preschool to postsecondary) should receive incentives to raise their curricular standards and outcomes. Results of both incentive packages would be a careful match between industrial needs and educational supply. The poor would be equally prepared to accept high-skill/high-wage employment and cross the poverty line by themselves and for the last time.

Traditional liberals question this economic and educational optimism: I think the greatest concern confronting us as a result of these inequality trends is the effect of worsening labor-market opportunities on low-skilled workers. In the midst of an eight-year expansion, people with high-school degrees have seen their real wages decline. This is an appalling fact for anyone who worries about incentives. For years we have tried to tell our children that there are certain things they ought to do: stay in school, get at least a high-school degree, and once you leave school, get a job. It is hard to give that advice with a straight face when you know that for the past decade people who have followed that advice have earned less and less each year. An effective functioning economy must provide the incentives for people to take school and work seriously, and the wage inequality trends of recent years threaten those incentives. (Blank 1997, 192)

In this economy and with the ascendance of conservative political power, most liberals doubt the possibility of ending poverty in the foreseeable future. Rather, they recommend

policies that will provide needed assistance, training, and freedom. Accommodating the recent "welfare reform," which put
AFDC assistance in the hands of state governments, Blank
recommends a three-tiered system that would provide temporary help between jobs, training and work-mandated aid for
those engaged in long-term job searches, and cash assistance
for those who are unable to work. Because "they work," food
stamp, Medicaid (with cost containments), and earned-income
tax credits would remain federally funded programs. For liberals, improved federal programs would remain targeted toward
the poor because neither individuals nor the economy can end
poverty in America.

A RADICAL DEMOCRATIC POSITION

Radical democrats do not accept the absolute definition of
poverty. Rather, they suggest that the poverty line is set too
low for a family to support itself. For example, Gordon (1996)
offers the case of Paul and Jane Lambert and their three children, a solid working-class family with an income of slightly
below $25,000. After housing, health insurance, child care
(because both parents work), food, clothing, and automobile
insurance, the Lamberts are left without enough money to pay
their bills. They are $2,000 in debt annually, which they
shuffle among credit cards. Far from living extravagantly, the
Lamberts haven't been out to eat at a restaurant, they
reported, "within living memory, not even to McDonald's or
anywhere else" (98). That a family earning over 133 percent of
the poverty line cannot meet a subsistence standard of living
leads radical democrats to interpret the official attempt to
underestimate the size of poverty in America as a conscious
effort to disguise economic inequality.

The Lamberts escape official poverty figures because the government's poverty line, first formulated in the 1960s, is ludicrously
inaccurate. In September 1992, the Census Bureau reported that in
1991 nearly thirty-six million Americans were living in poverty. Most
people think the government's poverty line refers to a specific idea
or concept of a minimal standard of living. It once did, but no longer.
Divorced from any real definition of poverty, the official measure
has fallen below economic reality, masking particularly the number
of working poor. The number of year-round, full-time American

workers who live in poverty is actually three times what official census figures would have us believe. (Schwartz and Volgy 1992, 58)

Radical democrats suggest that the determination of economic well-being should be judged on relative terms—how individuals and social groups stand in relation to one another within a given society. When such comparisons are made, it appears that it's more than the population under the poverty line who are getting the short end of the stick. In 1993, according to the U.S. Census Bureau, the top twenty percent of tax filers received nearly the same amount of total income as the bottom eighty percent (i.e., 46.2 percent for the top and 53.8 percent for the rest). The lowest quintile (the poor and near-poor) received only 4.2 percent of the total income and, when added to the working class (up to $30,000 in annual income), the bottom forty percent of American citizens received 14.3 percent of total income each year. In relative terms, radical democrats argue, two in five families in America struggle continuously to get by economically.

Moreover, radical democrats point out the fact that impoverished classes exist in all capitalist economies as an indication that the poor serve an important economic function. Speaking of public opinion, Gailbraith (1992) stated, "What is not accepted, and indeed is little mentioned, is that the underclass is integrally a part of a larger economic process and, more importantly, that it serves the living standard and the comfort of the more favored community. Economic progress would be far more uncertain and certainly far less rapid without it. The economically fortunate, not excluding those who speak with greatest regret of the existence of this class, are heavily dependent on its presence" (17). Although the ethnic, racial, and gender composition of the poor has changed over time during this century, as many members from Eastern European immigration, Appalachians, black migration north after the Second World War, and now immigrants from Latin America and the Caribbean worked their way through poverty, there always has been a class labeled the poor, who took the lowest paying, distasteful, and most dangerous jobs because of their living conditions.

Radical democrats maintain that causes of poverty are confounded by social and economic discrimination based on class, race, ethnicity, and gender. First, they refer to the continued segregation in housing, in which the poor are restricted to areas with crumbling buildings, a lack of public resources, and high rates of crime is akin to apartheid (Massey and Denton 1993). Second, they demonstrate reduced access to good schooling, stating that the unequal funding (Kozol 1991), tracking (Oakes 1985), and treatment in classes (Sapon-Shevin 1995) prevent minorities and females from prestigious academic coursework and degrees. Third, they show that restricted access to work in general and from well-paying employment in particular keeps women and minorities unemployed or under-employed (Shelton 1992; Verdugo 1992). Finally, they report that minorities and women are paid between two-thirds and four-fifths of the wages and salaries paid to white males (Schiller 1995). As Sklar stated in her remarks cited at the opening of this chapter, radical democrats believe that it should be no surprise that racial and ethnic minorities and women are over-represented among the poor—and, clearly, it is not by their choosing.

In this light, federal efforts to assist the poor look more like calculated attempts to keep a considerable portion of the population impoverished and compliant (Conniff 1997). While federal aid does not cause poverty as conservatives charge, it appears to maintain poverty in order to keep a reserve army of the unemployed available for business to use as it wishes (Piven and Cloward 1971). Even liberal efforts to upgrade the skills of the poor seem more like attempts to placate business rather than as an effective means to end poverty. Instead, radical democrats propose more insurgent government programs that are aimed to reduce the relative inequality of the American economy without reducing individual freedoms. They begin with an effective social safety net—all-age Social Security to ensure that no one lacks food and shelter, universal health care with price controls, and national child care so working parents need not worry about their children. Second, radical democrats offer a number of proposals to achieve full employment in which everyone has a job that pays them a living wage. These efforts would mean a shorter work week and little overtime in order to share the jobs; increased unionization, which increases workers' pay and rights in the workplace; and government investment in the infrastructure, cities, and rural areas. To pay for these changes, they call for a genuine graduated income tax, no loophole corporate taxes, and extension of capital-gains taxes to be implemented. To ensure that the increased benefits of these changes are spread across races and genders, the Fourteenth Amendment should be formally extended to include women and then rigorously enforced. To make all this happen, radical democrats propose massive educational projects that help American citizens to actively engage in public life, with the twin goals of achieving recognition of the great diversity among the disenfranchised and redistributing wealth.

The ideological positions on the causes of poverty present differing definitions of poverty and differing representations of the poor (see Table 3–1). Conservatives, neo-conservatives, neo-liberals, and liberals maintain a separation between the poor and the rest of American society. Despite their apparent differences, these positions work according to functionalist assumptions about the role of government and other institutions in efforts to overcome poverty. That is, the relative social standing among Americans should be preserved as elements of society are altered to raise the poor's income above the absolute poverty line. Each offers a different version of how to understand, maintain, and conduct a private democracy in the United States.

Radical democrats, on the other hand, present a qualitatively different version of poverty and the poor; they adopt a relative definition of poverty that places all Americans within intimate economic relationships. Moreover, they argue that current economic and political organizations require and maintain the poor for the benefit of the upper classes. Radical democrats abandon functionalist logic because they seek to transform the structures of the economic and political systems to achieve greater cultural and economic justice. In the process, they seek the establishment and expansion of publics for popular deliberation of national priorities and action.

SOME WORDS ABOUT THE TERM *UNDERCLASS*

I have purposefully avoided the word *underclass* within this chapter. Some might see this decision as a weakness in my argument. I find the word useless and, frankly, distasteful. First, my intentions for Chapters 2 and 3 were to convey the demographics of poverty across America. Gans (1995) suggests that the term *underclass* is restrictive and vindictive.

Table 3–1 Political Ideological Perspectives on Poverty

| | PRIVATE DEMOCRACY | | | | PUBLIC DEMOCRACY |
	CONSERVATIVE	NEO-CONSERVATIVE	NEO-LIBERAL	LIBERAL	RADICAL DEMOCRATS
What is poverty?	Low income without achieving personal satisfaction through civic involvement.	Inability to be responsible for self or family. Poor life choices lead to low incomes.	Income below the poverty line and lack of job-related skills.	Income below the poverty line and social and psychological malaise.	Lack of control and security of well-being. Subject to loss of jobs, health care, housing, etc., without much recourse or governmental support.
What is its cause?	Low intelligence because of poor genetic endowment inhibits ability to compete for adequate income. Government policy to ameliorate problems exacerbate them.	Lack of moral character prevents poor from making good (middle-class) choices for behavior. Without appropriate morals, can't compete for jobs with sufficient incomes.	Lack of opportunity to acquire well-paying job because general institutional structure is inadequate to meet demands of global economy. Too many people compete for poor-paying jobs.	Institutional, social, and private discrimination based on race, class, and gender restricts the poor's life opportunities	Imbalance of power favoring the wealthiest 20% of the American population. Inability of the poor to recognize their multiple identities and to form conditions to address mutual goals.
Who advocates this stance?	Charles Murray Thomas Sowell Lawrence Mead	Joe Klein James Q. Wilson Glenn Lowery	Bill & Hillary Clinton Mark Tucker E. D. Hirsch	Rebecca Blank William Julius Wilson Linda Darling-Hammond	Holly Sklar Frances Fox Divens Herbert Gans

I write of a behavioral term invented by journalists and social scientists to describe poor people who are accused, rightly or wrongly, of failing to behave in the "mainstream" ways of the numerically or culturally dominant American middle class. This behavioral definition dominates poor people who drop out of school, do not work and, if they are young women, have babies without benefit of marriage and go on welfare. (2)

Because *underclass* is a code word that places some of the poor *under* society and implies that they are not or should not be *in* society, users of the term can, therefore, favor excluding them from the rest of society without saying so. . . . Because *underclass* is also used as a racial and even ethnic code word, it is a convenient device for hiding anti-black or anti-Latino feelings. (59)

To use the term *underclass*, then, is to accept the conservative or neo-conservative flawed-character position that behavior is a key determinate of poverty. Murray (1996) goes so far as to suggest that poverty is an easy problem to address, but the underclass is nearly a permanent social blight. In *Body Count: Moral Poverty and How to Win America's War Against Crime and Drugs*, Bennett (1996) calls for a national campaign to control the underclasses, by force if necessary. Wilson, whose book *The Truly Disadvantaged: The Inner City, the Underclass, and Public Policy* gave liberal legitimacy to the term in 1987, declared in 1990 that he would no longer use the term because of its ascribed values. Wilson stated that he would be and everyone else should be more precise about the population of concern. In his case, he'll use the term *the ghetto poor*. Radical democrat Holly Sklar writes: "Scapegoating labels like 'underclass' and myths like the 'culture of poverty' mask undermining and impoverishing economics" (1995, 70).

Nothing is gained by using the label and much is to be lost. At this point, the term *underclass* is a marker identifying the speaker's or writer's conservative or neo-conservative ideological position on poverty. That is, the use of the term should alert listeners or readers to the web of ideas, values, and behaviors that direct the speaker's or writer's views of the world. Identification of ideological webs, which also underlie the positions that do not condone the use of the term *underclass*, can help listeners and readers understand why people act, believe, and think in particular ways. Reading poverty, then, becomes not only a way of being with the poor and understanding their lives, as Taylor (1996) so ably demonstrates in *Toxic Literacies*.

It also becomes a way of understanding why institutions, laws, and social norms are constructed as they are; why bureaucrats, police, hospital personnel, and others understand and act toward the poor the way they do; and why these constructions, understandings, and actions all seem so natural to most Americans.

The ubiquity of the term *underclass* in public discourse provides some indication of the political terrain in which the poor struggle for survival. When coupled with the 1996 welfare reform and the 1997 discussion to privatize Social Security, it is clear that conservative ideologies now prevail over liberal agendas. Ridiculed in the 1960s, statements about how family structure causes poverty are now the foundational premise of most new social programs. Accordingly, the public's views of poverty have been directed by conservative, neo-conservative or neo-liberal constructions, making it more difficult to see the diversity among the poor, as Harrington did during the early 1960s and again in the 1980s. In our current political climate, we are much more likely to see only the menacing young black male or teenage mother as often portrayed in film or on television.

These ascendant political constructions of poverty project an idealized society in which the poor and non-poor need not connect. At best, the non-poor should provide assistance so that the poor can seize the ample economic opportunities available to all hardworking and virtuous citizens. At worst, the non-poor need only instruct the poor on their moral responsibilities and secure the social order. In the policies implied and implemented from these ideals, a mixture of conservative, neo-conservative, and neo-liberal values have been authorized through laws, policies, and institutions. The new state welfare programs predicated on reduced service is just the tip of this political, economic, social, and cultural iceberg. In all cases, the dual task is to correct the flawed behavior of poor as they work their way just over the absolute poverty line. And in good functionalist logic, reading instruction is offered as a primary means to reach these political ideals, educating the children of the poor to improve their human capital and to see, act, and value in particular ways.

Some last words—no one wants an irresponsible, immoral society, but how we will determine what our responsibilities are and to whom we should be responsible are less clearly delineated than conservatives would have us believe. Should our responsibilities at work obligate our employers to be responsible toward us and our communities? Clearly, American business leaders no longer think so. Are moral codes simple and consistent? The divorces of family-values advocates such as George Will, Bob Dole, and Newt Gingrich suggest that even conservatives and neo-conservatives apply their morals selectively. Most damaging to progress or poverty is the illusion of the self-made individual. We all need and have had others to support our life and development across our lifetime. As Coontz so aptly explained, all families—not just the poor's—have enjoyed governmental support throughout the twentieth century. Within these contexts—responsibility, morals, and individualism—our conceptions of personal choices and how they affect our lives become much more complex than they appear on the surface.

F O U R

AND THERE AIN'T NOTHIN' YOU CAN DO ABOUT IT
Reading *The Bell Curve*

Inequality of endowments, including intelligence, is a reality. Trying to pretend the inequality does not really exist has led to disaster. Trying to eradicate inequality with artificially manufactured outcomes has led to disaster. It is time for America once again to try living with inequality, as life is lived: understanding that each human being has strengths and weaknesses, qualities we admire and qualities we do not admire, competencies and incompetencies, assets and debits; that the success of each human life is not measured externally but internally; that of all the rewards we can confer on each other, the most precious is a place as a valued fellow citizen. (Herrnstein and Murray 1994, 551–552)

◆◆

So ends the text of *The Bell Curve: Intelligence and Class Structure in American Life*, and so began its controversial social life. Herrnstein and Murray offer an analysis of the impacts of intelligence on social behavior. The publication of their study in an 845-page book provoked a storm of commentary from psychologists, social scientists, government officials, journalists, media pundits, and educators of all political types. The book or its authors appeared on the cover of *Newsweek*, *Harpers*, and *Time*, and on the front pages of the *New York Times*, *Washington Post*, *USA Today*, and many other newspapers. The *Christian Science Monitor* called it "limited and skewed." The *Boston Globe* suggested that it "violates a basic tenet of democracy." The *Wall Street Journal* labeled its authors "brave and forthright." Immediately after the book's release, *The National Review* and *The New Republic* published entire issues devoted to lengthy examinations of Herrnstein and Murray's study and conclusions. Within two years, several anthologies of responses to *The Bell Curve* (e.g., Fraser 1995; Jacoby and Glauberman 1994), and at least one original book-length scholarly analysis (Kincheloe, Steinberg, and Gresson 1996) were published. To understate the case, Herrnstein and Murray's book was and continues to be controversial.

The Bell Curve is a logical extension of both Herrnstein and Murray's separate work. In 1971, Herrnstein published a spirited defense of Jensen's 1969 essay in the *Harvard Educational Review*, arguing that compensatory educational programs for blacks were useless because blacks were intellectually inferior to whites for largely genetic reasons. Herrnstein argued "because IQ is substantially heritable, because economic success in life depends in part on the talents measured by IQ tests, and because social standing depends in part on economic success, it follows that social standing is bound to be based to some extent on inherited differences" (Herrnstein 1971). Murray is the author of *Losing Ground: American Social Policy 1950–1980* (1984), in which he charged that governmental policies exacerbate the social problems they were intended to solve. In particular, policies during the 1960s and 1970s decreased the poor's and minority members' chances for economic, social, and even political advancement. He offered three laws of social programs:

1. **The law of imperfect selection,** which maintains that the task of rule-writing for eligibility cannot accommodate

individual circumstance and, therefore, some worthy people will always be excluded and some undeserving will always be included.

2. **The law of unintended rewards,** which claims that any social transfer will increase the condition that prompted the concern.

3. **The law of net harm,** which suggests that "the less likely it is that the unwanted behavior will change voluntarily, the more likely it is that a program to induce change will cause net harm." (216)

Together, their previous work predicts the conclusions of *The Bell Curve*. People of low intelligence will suffer economic and social disadvantage because their intellectual endowments are insufficient to handle the demands of public life. The disadvantage will be most severe for those at the lowest end of the intelligence continuum. Because their endowment is inherited, and therefore unchangeable, social policy will not be effective in attempting to better their situation. On the contrary, attempts to intervene to help them will only deepen their problems. Herrnstein and Murray conclude that all Americans must learn to live with these facts. They, of course, provide a classically conservative justification for the social inequalities. Differences in social outcomes are natural, therefore justified, and governmental attempts to bring about some sort of artificial leveling through genetic engineering are repugnant and, by social engineering, infringe on individuals' rights and freedoms.

These conclusions are no surprise to conservatives, as the opening story in Besharov's response to *The Bell Curve* attests:

It seemed like a simple enough project. Christmas was coming and the local mall had jobs for gift-wrappers. What better way for mothers on welfare to earn a few extra dollars? So a local job-training program decided to give a group of welfare mothers a quick course in gift-wrapping before sending them off to apply for a job. It wasn't that easy. The first lesson was bows. The instructor asked the mothers to cut pieces of ribbon, each five inches long. The mothers quickly became confused—they did not know how to measure off the ribbon for cutting. There would be no jobs at the mall that season, because the mothers lacked the basic cognitive skills to wrap packages. (1995, 358)

Although Herrnstein and Murray do not include this story from Murray's colleague at the American Enterprise Institute in their book, they offer similar assessments about the mental capabilities of the poor.

If the conclusions are predictable from previous work, then why publish a new volume of old conclusions? Herrnstein and Murray answer that they are simply telling the facts to reconvene the conversation about intelligence because they worry about the tyranny of the cognitive elite and its new alliance with America's economic elite. They write that they fear for "the way we are headed," which they believe could take a fascist turn to a custodial state if America is not careful. They call for a deepening of a private democracy in which a natural aristocracy looks out for the welfare of "the rubble" (Jefferson's term). Herrnstein and Murray seek a place for everyone. They quote Burke's *A Vindication of Natural Society* to suggest that they search for truth.

Literally none of the published respondents take Herrnstein and Murray at their word on this matter. Rather, respondents suggest that the argument and the way it is put together suggests that Herrnstein and Murray have other intentions for the book, the poor, and society. Their intentions are profoundly conservative because they attempt to reduce all social problems to matters of individual intellect and to eliminate all social programs aimed at broadening the opportunities of the poor, minorities, or any other group. In the process, they intend to justify their own social privilege and positions of power through their genetic endowments. To make their arguments appear natural, they push our lives under a statistical bell curve formed by scores on intelligence tests. At best, it is an imperfect fit that apologizes for continued discrimination based on race, class, and gender; at worst, it is a ploy to further consolidate the social control of the poor, minorities, and women within the hands of the already wealthy.

THE BOOK

The Bell Curve begins with a note to the reader to direct passage through the book. The authors report that the book was designed to be read at several levels. The quick read is a thirty-page precis of major findings distributed across the beginnings of most of the twenty-three chapters. The style used in these pages is informal and conducive to sound bites. For example, readers are told, "Low IQ continues to be a much stronger precursor of poverty than the socioeconomic circumstances in which people grow up" (127). Later, Herrnstein and Murray write, "A culture of poverty seems to have influence primarily among women who are of low intelligence" (191). The main text includes technical material, statistical analyses, and "boxes that add more detail" (xix). Here the style bogs down, not necessarily from nuance, but rather from the shear weight of information. Endnotes are reserved for scholarly references and digressions on details. A final level of reading is presented through appendices that offer a basic review of descriptive statistics and an elaborate, but selective, literature review on the topic of cultural bias in intelligence tests and testing. The last two reading levels seem designed to convey scientific integrity within the study. The "Note to the Reader" and the organization of the book suggest that Herrnstein, Murray, and their publisher were motivated to capture public sentiment rather than academic acclaim. For example, by placing the summaries before (rather than after) the chapters, they direct readers' attention away from the evidence and toward their conclusions and policy statements, limiting the possible meanings readers might make of *The Bell Curve.*

Although they argue that their conclusions are not necessarily based on IQ test scores because there are obvious differences in mental capabilities among individuals and groups, Herrnstein and Murray begin their book with a statement of six principles "now beyond significant technical dispute" (22):

1. There is a general factor of cognitive ability on which human beings differ.
2. IQ tests are the most accurate tests of that ability.
3. IQ is what ordinary people mean when they use the words *intelligent* or *smart.*
4. IQ is stable over much of a person's life.
5. Properly administered IQ tests are not biased against social, economic, ethnic, or racial groups.
6. Cognitive ability is substantially heritable.

Herrnstein and Murray acknowledge that these principles are unpopular because they contradict utopian views of egalitarianism, but the authors maintain that they are scientific facts.

With those principles as their unquestioned assumptions in the book, Herrnstein and Murray turn to the natural development of a cognitive elite. At its base, their argument suggests that the openness of capitalism with its demand for growth and efficiency created, and continues to create at ever-increasing rates of speed, conditions for individuals with high intelligence to gain access to positions of power and control in economic, social, and political spheres. The first condition was the availability of higher education and its connection to better-paying jobs. As demand for higher education became greater, colleges and professional schools were able to become more selective in the criteria they used for selection. Herrnstein and Murray argue that this selectivity took place primarily on grounds of intelligence, which yielded an intelligence hierarchy. Elite colleges attracted and segregated the highest IQs, other colleges confined people with above-average intelligence, high schools graduated primarily people of average intelligence, and those with below-average intelligence dropped out of grammar or secondary school. Occupations were generally partitioned accordingly. Better-paying jobs were reserved for the cognitive elites. Lower-paying jobs with fewer cognitive demands were available to the less intellectually capable.

Although the magnitude of these correlations has increased steadily over the course of the twentieth century, Herrnstein and Murray predict they will reach completion in post-industrial capitalism. As governments strive to equalize opportunity among citizens, "success and failure in the American economy, and all that goes with it, are increasingly a matter of the genes that people inherit" (91). The educational and occupational segregation of intelligence, they argue, leads to residential—even matrimonial—segregation. Matrimonial segregation has profound effects on gene pools. Selective breeding for intelligence is a defacto trend of American life at the turn of the twenty-first century. Herrnstein and Murray consider this a problem because birth rates for the poor are far greater than for the cognitive elite.

If the United States did as much to encourage high-IQ women to have babies as it now does to encourage low-IQ women, it would rightly be described as engaging in aggressive manipulation of fertility. The technically precise description of America's fertility policy is that it subsidizes births among poor women, who are also disproportionately at the low end of the intelligence distribution. We urge generally that these policies, represented by the extensive network of cash and services for low-income women who have babies, be ended. (Herrnstein and Murray 1994, 548)

LOW IQ

After finding natural justification for their own social standing, income, and procreation in just over one hundred pages, Herrnstein and Murray turn their gaze toward the other end of the intelligence spectrum. Using data from the National Longitudinal Survey of Labor Market Experience of Youth (NLSY), they analyzed possible statistical relationships between intelligence and "America's most pressing problems" (117). The periodic survey of 12,686 young people (ages fourteen to twenty-two when the study began in 1979) included questions to elicit detailed information about childhood environment, parental socioeconomic status, educational and occupational achievements, work histories, family formation, and an IQ test (compliments of the Department of Defense). These data, Herrnstein and Murray argue, allow for the first scientific analysis of the effects of intelligence on social life. Because of the proportional sampling designs for collection, the data also afford statistically stable comparisons based on race, class, and gender. However, Herrnstein and Murray are quick to point out that "cognitive ability affects social behavior without regard to race or ethnicity" (125). To demonstrate their fact, they load only the data from non-Hispanic whites into their initial analyses.

They begin with poverty, which they define as income below the official poverty line. Following a conservative line of thinking, and without an economic analysis, they offer a chart to demonstrate that steady progress against poverty ended during the late 1960s when the War on Poverty took effect. The three-decade drop from more than fifty percent living in poverty to nearly ten percent leveled off and even began to rise again during the 1970s and 1980s. "We will not reopen here the continuing debate about why progress came to an end when it did" (129). They conclude that IQ is directly correlated with income. Higher IQs bring higher incomes; lower IQs bring lower incomes. According to their analyses, this correlation holds true when parental socioeconomic status is considered or when educational experience is factored in. Cynically, they state, "if a white child of the next generation could be given a choice between being disadvantaged in socio-economic status or disadvantaged in intelligence, there is no question about the right choice" (135).

Gender matters in the relationships between IQ and poverty. Women with any IQ score are more likely to be poor than men; however, women with low scores, Herrnstein and Murray report, are highly likely to be among the poor for several reasons. First, they are more likely to be separated, divorced, or never married, and "marriage is a powerful poverty preventative" (138). Second, they are more likely to have children with men of below-average IQs. "The disquieting finding is that the worst environment for raising children, of the kind that not even the most resilient children can easily overcome, are concentrated in the homes in which the mothers are at the low end of the intelligence distribution" (203–4). Third, "nonmarriage," child dependency, and cognitive limitations reduce their abilities to find jobs that pay above poverty-level wages. Of course, Herrnstein and Murray are only worried because the children of these women are more likely to remain in poverty throughout their lives.

Like many other disabilities, low intelligence is not the fault of the individual. Everything we know about the causes of cognitive ability, genetic and environmental, tells us that by the time people grow to an age at which they can be considered responsible moral agents, their IQ is fairly well set. Many readers will find that, before writing another word, we have already made the case for sweeping policy changes meant to rectify what can only be interpreted as a palpably unfair result. (142)

Low IQ is directly and highly correlated with dropping out of school, unemployment, idleness, injury on the job, illegitimacy, welfare dependency, poor parenting, crime, and lack of

civility. In each case, IQ has a greater impact than environmental experiences, parental socioeconomic status, or gender.
Again, early- and mid-century successes in combating these
social problems leveled off and diminished after the 1960s.
Readers get a glimpse of Herrnstein and Murray's political
agenda during their discussion of IQ and civility. After dis-
missing any social science finding that is not supported by the
NLSY data, they write, "The NLSY does not permit us to
extend this discussion directly. . . . [about how] middle-class
values are related to civility" (263). Yet they continue their
analyses unabated, cobbling together a set of questions from
the NLSY that they label the Middle Class Values (MCV)
index. Lo and behold, there is a direct and pronounced correlation between IQ and the score on the MCV index. "A
smarter population is more likely to be, and more capable of
being made into, a civil citizenry. For a nation predicated on a
high level of individual autonomy, this is a fact worth know-
ing" (266).

RACE

Herrnstein and Murray are aware of the controversies that
accompany cross-race comparisons. To avoid the controversies, they reject the term *race* because "race is such a difficult
concept to employ in the American context" (271). They do
not consider the social construction of race as a tool of oppression (Goldberg 1990). Rather, they refer to ethnic differences
when making their case and reserve race for their commentary on liberal opinion and policy. This decision immediately
causes problems for them as they attempt to sort out groups
in terms of IQ and social life. Herrnstein and Murray spend
most of their energy in comparisons of non-Hispanic whites
and blacks (their term for African Americans); however, they
do make reference to Ashenazi Jews of European origin, Latinos, and East Asians. Latinos cause the most concern because
the term includes "highly disparate cultural heritages and a
wide range of racial stocks" (275).

Herrnstein and Murray begin matter-of-factly, "ethnic differences in cognitive ability are neither surprising nor in
doubt" (269), and then immediately go on the offensive:

Nothing seems more fearsome to many commentators than the possibility that ethnic and race differences have any genetic component at all. This belief is a fundamental error. Even if the differences between races were entirely genetic (which they surely are not), it should make no practical difference in how individuals deal with each other. The real danger is that the elite wisdom on ethnic differences—that such differences cannot exist—will shift to opposite and equally unjustified extremes. (270)

Although they score Jews and East Asians above whites on IQ tests, Herrnstein and Murray devote about forty pages to explain a fifteen-point difference between average scores for whites and blacks. Although "it should make no practical difference in how individuals deal with each other," they apparently found it of considerable practical significance to identify gaps between groups concerning IQ. Moreover, Herrnstein and Murray thought it important to attempt to account for this gap primarily through genetic inheritance. They pretend that statements such as "the average white person tests higher than about eighty-four percent of the population of blacks and that the average black person tests higher than about sixteen percent of the population of whites" (269) will have no practical consequence in everyday life.

When comparing how race and IQ affect social life, Herrnstein and Murray's conservative political agenda again becomes visible. Contrary to popular opinion, they report, blacks of equal IQ have an advantage over whites concerning educational attainment and access to higher paying jobs. According to Herrnstein and Murray's analyses of individuals with IQ scores of 114 or higher, blacks have a probability of 0.68 of "holding" a bachelor's degree and 0.26 of "being in" a high-income occupation, while whites have 0.5 and 0.1 probabilities, respectively. They write that there are only a few hundred dollars separating white and black incomes when controlling for IQ. Although these apparent advantages could be attributed to the successes of affirmative-action policies that seek to increase racial and gender diversity in higher education, employment, and income, Herrnstein and Murray suggest that the lack of attention to IQ in affirmative-action programs ensures the over-representation of unqualified blacks in higher education and high-wage occupations. They call for affirmative action to be returned to its original goal—to compare all candidates for admission or employment on all criteria (but particularly on

IQ)—and then to give preference to under-represented groups only if the individual is comparable to the white male candidate with the highest credentials. Given their data on race and IQ, this seems to be a disingenuous policy reform.

Comparisons within a section labeled "ethnic differences on indicators of social problems" (317) end with the statement, "Some ethnic differences are not washed away by controlling either for intelligence or for other variables that we examined" (340). Even when IQ is controlled in comparisons, blacks are more likely to be unemployed, bear children out-of-wedlock, be on welfare, give birth to a baby with low birth weight and low IQ, and be incarcerated. They are less likely to be married by age twenty-nine or to profess middle-class values. Herrnstein and Murray state that these differences provide "reason to avoid flamboyant rhetoric about ethnic oppression" (340). And they leave it to others to explain these differences. After hundreds of pages of explaining that genetic inheritance determines much of social behavior, their silence on this matter speaks loudly.

AND THERE AIN'T NOTHIN' YOU CAN DO ABOUT IT

Putting aside the issue of whether intelligence causes social problems, Herrnstein and Murray call for solutions based on their findings that people who have these problems "are heavily concentrated in the lower portion of the cognitive ability distribution" (369). Any solution must consider this correlation; that is, people with low intelligence must be able to comply. The obvious solution is to raise people's IQs. However, they report that "the story of attempts to raise intelligence is one of high hopes, flamboyant claims, and disappointing results. For the foreseeable future, the problems of low cognitive ability are not going to be solved by outside interventions to make children smarter" (389). If their original goals are considered, then Head Start, compensatory literacy programs, and intelligence training are all money poorly spent.

According to Herrnstein and Murray, public schools favor children of low and average intelligence over "gifted" students. School officials have "dumbed down" curricula to enable students with average IQs to master it. Ninety-two percent of all federal aid to schools is directed toward programs for "disadvantaged" students. College admission standards have been lowered to fill college classrooms built during the 1960s and 1970s. Together these conditions offer poor service to students with high IQs. However, Herrnstein and Murray conclude that this may be the best that public schools can do. They caution that "critics of American education must come to terms with the reality that in a universal education system, many students will not reach the level of education that most people view as basic" (436). Even given the economic, technical, and political constraints on schools and the distribution of intelligence across the population, "an American youth with average IQ is probably better prepared academically now than ever before" (417).

Herrnstein and Murray offer several policy initiatives, primarily to aid students with above-average intelligence. First, the federal government should support programs that enable all parents, not just affluent ones, to choose the school their children attend. With admissions standards, this program could enable the intellectual cream to rise to the top in a manner similar to the one proposed by Thomas Jefferson in 1779. Second, some portion of the federal funds designated for the disadvantaged should be reallocated to programs for the gifted. Such a policy is warranted because currently funded programs are not reaching intended goals and alternatives would meet with similar failure. In Herrnstein and Murray's cruel words, "For many people, there is nothing they can learn that will repay the cost of the teaching" (520). Finally, they call for an elevated status for the "educated person" by enforcing the idea that "at every stage of learning, some people reach their limits" (444).

The nation has been unwilling to accept in recent decades that the same phenomenon of individual limitations applies at every level of education. Given the constraints of time and educational resources, some students cannot be taught statistical theory; a smaller fraction of students cannot be taught the role of mercantilism in European history; for even a smaller fraction, writing a coherent essay may be out of reach. Each level of accomplishment deserves respect on its own merits, but the ideal of the educated person is in itself an ideal that must be embraced openly. By abandoning it, America has been falling short both in educating its most gifted and in inculcating, across the entire cognitive distribution, the values we would want in an educated citizenry. (444)

POLITICS OF SUBTRACTION

Herrnstein and Murray argue that unequal natural endowments of intelligence drive social life. These endowments account for the meritocracy within our private democracy that ensures individual freedom to participate in the economic and political life. Some enjoy plenty because they are smarter; others suffer want because they are not. This is nature, and "the egalitarian ideal of contemporary political theory under-estimates the importance of the differences that separate human beings. It fails to come to grips with human variation" (532). Herrnstein and Murray offer the French Revolution, the Soviet Union, and concern for the welfare state in Scandinavia as examples of that failure. Yet, they maintain that the federal government and the national media continue to express the ideology of equality, leading America toward decline, if not its end.

Since intelligence is not changeable and interventions toward equality are mistaken, Herrnstein and Murray ask us to embrace inequality. Toward that end, they suggest that everyone should seek a valued place in society warranted by their intellectual endowment. Once we have found our spot, we should be happy with our lives. "You occupy a valued place if other people would miss you if you were gone" (535). Both quality and quantity matter in this equation. If one person would miss you, then you "have a fragile hold on your place in society, no matter how much that one person cares for you" (535). Policy reform, then, should help individuals extend the number of others who would miss them in different parts of their lives and at different levels of intensity if they were gone.

This means that the federal government should do everything in its power to strengthen families, neighborhoods, and middle-class values. According to Herrnstein and Murray, not only will strong family ties deepen the quality of valued places for individuals, but they also will provide the foundation for increasing quantity. They advocate returning marriage to its formerly unique legal status and out-of-wedlock birth to its moral stigma. These actions would mean the end of no-fault divorce, AFDC for additional children for family already receiving assistance, and child visitation rights for nonmarried fathers, but not increased wages to support a family, national child care, or sex education in schools.

"Most adults need something to do with their lives other than going to work, and that something consists of being stitched into a fabric of family and community" (539). Yet according to Herrnstein and Murray, the federal government has removed most of the "stuff of life" out of neighborhoods. They include control over caring for the poor, feeding the hungry, and housing the homeless as three areas in which federal policy has reduced the numbers of ways in which individuals can be valued among their neighbors. Neighbors, they assert, can provide such services more humanely, effectively, and cheaply. "Government policy can do much to foster the vitality of neighborhoods by trying to do less for them" (540).

Beyond marriage, abstinence, and community service, Herrnstein and Murray define middle-class values as deciding right from wrong. Variability of intelligence means variation in the levels of sophistication with which individuals make such decisions. They argue that the federal government has complicated decisions on right and wrong through overly detailed and safeguarded laws and punishments. These complications lead people with low IQs to misunderstand what is at stake in daily decision-making about how to live one's life. To help these individuals, the authors suggest that legal codes be simplified. Although they avoid calling for the return of a legal system based on the ten commandments, they find few arguments with the ones of the 1950s. "The policy prescription is that the criminal justice system should be made simpler. The meaning of criminal offenses used to be clear and objective, and so were the consequences. It is worth trying to make them so again" (544).

Herrnstein and Murray conclude that at the heart of their call for policy reform is a quest for human dignity. Ultimately, individuals must make this quest alone. Governments cannot give dignity, although Herrnstein and Murray are adamant that governments can and do take it away. Paradoxically, this dignity comes from within, but is predicated on finding a valued place in the world. Value is assigned to individuals by others who would miss them if they were gone. Herrnstein and Murray draw all these conclusions from a body of evidence that reports little, if any, analysis of individuals. After readers are told that the rich are smarter than the poor, that whites are smarter than blacks, that these differences are genetic, and that they have grave social consequences, the authors ask us to treat each other as individuals. To carry out this request, of course, we must disregard all that the book has to offer.

CONSERVATIVE LITERACY

Politically speaking, there are many ways to read *The Bell Curve.* Clearly, Herrnstein and Murray display a conservative agenda in the questions they ask, the design of their study, the interpretation of the data someone else collected, and the conclusions they drew about what should be done. They assume that the poor are different from and inferior to the rest of society, and they conclude that this difference is based on genetic endowment resulting in intellectual inferiority, and that nothing can be done about economic and cultural inequalities. As expected, radical democrats (e.g., Gould 1994; Reed 1994; Willis 1994) and liberals (Gardner 1994) attack the premise and reality of the study. Neo-conservatives, while acknowledging that IQ probably does direct social behavior in important ways, seek to establish some distance between Herrnstein and Murray's position and their own (e.g., Glazer 1994; Loury 1994). Often this distance is created through positions on race and the prospects for social intervention (but not necessarily governmental interference). Yet, many conservatives welcome *The Bell Curve* (Jensen 1994; Brimelow 1994). For example, Harry F. Weyher, head of the Pioneer Fund, which funded similar studies for J. Philippe Rushton and William Shockley, regretted his lack of involvement in *The Bell Curve* study. "We'd have funded him at the drop of a hat, but he never asked" (as quoted in Sedgwick 1994).

Many conservatives welcome the book because it furthers their efforts to justify the "natural" order of society. Although theirs is certainly not the equivalent of divine right to rule sought by classical conservatives, Herrnstein and Murray provide an objective reason for inequalities. Call it social Darwinism or God's will, some power beyond human artifice ordained these differences, and the originators of the U.S. Constitution were wise enough to not only recognize these facts, but also to encode them in the rules of a private democracy. This allows the natural aristocracy to rise to the top in order to provide civic, economic, and political leadership. Fear that some might seek to disrupt the natural order of society to establish some egalitarian plan led several of the "founding fathers" to write *The Federalist Papers*, leading to our current privatized democracy (Sehr 1996) based on individual property rights and social order.

Following functionalist logic, schooling and literacy become a conduit through which individuals learn to sort themselves within the natural order. Before federal intervention brought the misguided utopian promises that education could improve on nature, schools and literacy education were used in conservative ways. That is, students attended and studied only until they reached their capacity, and then dropped out. To restore the natural order of things, federal intervention of this sort should stop. Head Start and Chapter One programs targeted to improve the intellectual capabilities of disadvantaged children should face the reality of genetic endowments and cut back their operations. That money would be better spent "smartening up" the academic programs for students with high IQs. In fact, because genetics are fixed, all school funding can be reexamined, reallocated, and reduced. Conservative reexaminations suggest low correlations between school funding and students' achievement or between funding and adult success (Burtless 1996).

Conservative literacy, then, has levels that correspond to an individual's valued place in the world. Equating these levels with academic tracking is reasonable but ultimately simplistic. Tracking seeks to sort according to academic talents in order to make instruction more efficient and curricula more appropriate. In theory, each track, each level, receives the proper instruction and knowledge to prepare students to be satisfied with their later social station. Yet the connections between the levels of literacy offered in these tracks and the levels of social practices are seldom tight. The literacy demands of a wide variety of ways through which individuals can seek to find multiple-valued places are rarely considered in the often mechanical designs of school tracking systems (Oakes 1985).

Conservatives devote little attention to educating people with low IQs because, in Herrnstein and Murray's words, they are not worth the instruction. Because of their limited intellect, they are simply unable to take advantage of sophisticated literacies of schooling; rather, they must learn the literacies of their lives through living them. Limited possibilities await them, and the laws will be written clearly so that they can lead virtuous lives. The vast middle range of IQs is served quite well by schools. Although certainly the average students would find advantage from the elevation of the image of the educated person, the literacies of schooling—both the skill and the requisite attitudes—are sufficient for the valued places these students might find. If the local schools do not, cannot, or will not provide for these groups, then conservatives argue that families ought to be able to take their state education allotment and attend the school of their choice.

For the gifted, current public-school curricula are woefully inadequate. Misguided attempts to educate all students to the same level and to include all cultures as if they were of the same value have reduced the utility of public schools in the development of the natural aristocracy. To remedy this situation, conservatives call for the celebration of the intellect and the challenge of rigorous academic programs that not only accelerate math and science curricula, but that also teach the wonders of Western Civilization. Most often, the works of Hirsch (1987), Adler (1982), and Bloom (1987) are associated with conservative literacy at this level. However, Hirsch calls for all American students to master basic factual information that "every American should know." He labels this *cultural literacy*. Adler suggests that *paideia* (Greek for learning and knowledge) of great books is for all students. Both maintain that all students can succeed in their programs and that no expense should be spared to ensure that they do. Although the content of their curricula may be nostalgic, poor and rich, low and high IQs, and minorities and majorities should learn to be culturally literate and wise.

◆◆

Only Bloom offers a truly conservative model for literacy. He gazes backward toward ancient Greece as the foundation of learning what is important to govern and manage our lives, and he assumes that only the intellectually gifted can benefit from this type of schooling. Bloom begins and ends his concern for education with four years of college, "a space between the intellectual wasteland he has left behind and the inevitable dreary professional training that awaits him after the baccalaureate" (336). Because more than seventy percent of American youth do not attend university and those who do tend to have above-average IQs, conservative literacy is directed only toward the cognitive elite. The problem remains what the gifted should learn at college to find their valued places in society.

> The only serious solution is the one that is almost universally rejected: the good old Great Books approach, in which a liberal education means reading certain generally recognized classic texts, just reading them, letting them dictate what the questions are and the method of approaching them—not forcing them into categories we make up, not treating them as historical products, but trying to read them as their authors wished them to be read. . . . The advantage they get is an awareness of the classic—particularly important for our innocents; an acquaintance with what big questions were when there were still big questions; models, at the very least, of how to go about answering them; and perhaps most important of all, a fund of shared experiences and thoughts on which to ground their friendships with one another. (Bloom 1987, 344)

Conservative literacy follows the same trickle-down logic that drove economic thought during much of the 1980s and raised the federal deficit to its highest point in history. By priming the intellectual capital of those already well endowed, the rest of society will benefit when they reinvest their enhanced knowledge publicly by assuming valued places of business, governmental, or social leadership (see Table 4-1). With a downward gaze, these benefits include clearer textual presentations of (1) what is right and wrong, and the consequences of doing wrong for the poor, blacks, and others with low IQs; (2) why poverty, unemployment, and lack of economic mobility are no one's fault and that nothing can be done about them; and (3) how everyone can find happiness in their natural place in the existing social order. Should we stop worrying and be happy?

**Table 4–1 Conservatives on Poverty: Definition,
Causes, Commentators, and Reading Solution**

CONSERVATIVE
Low income without achieving personal satisfaction through civic involvement.
Low intelligence because poor genetic endowment inhibits ability to compete for adequate income. Government policy to ameliorate problems exacerbates them.
Richard Herrnstein Charles Murray Thomas Sowell Lawrence Mead Allan Bloom
By tracking reading education to IQ of individual, all can be prepared properly to perform role consonant with genetic endowment. Content of texts will teach to value ascribed stations in life.

Conservatives challenge our democratic commitments. They suggest there is nothing to be done about inequalities in genetic endowments, income levels, and life's opportunities. They drive wedges between us and them—poor and non-poor, whites and blacks, men and women—and make us worry about them taking what we have away from us. They do this with little regard for the continuous human effort involved in making good on the notion that Americans are born equal with certain inalienable rights. Even if that phrase is limited to equality in the eyes of the law, the conservative gaze on poverty and literacy falls short of providing needed support. Without equal education, without adequate income or financial support to secure one's well-being, without equal opportunities to participate substantially in civic life, the poor are denied basic human rights and are relegated to second-class citizenship, regardless of what explanation conservatives can concoct. "Let them go," say conservatives, "they are not worth the expense." But make sure that they obey the laws and show up to clean the streets on time. Is that what America is all about?

FIVE

BAD TO THE BONE
Reading Moral Literacy

It's March fourth. On the front page of my local newspaper this morning were articles on sexual assault, heterosexual rights groups, a new state welfare system, a murder in a local trailer park, alcohol abuse, a robbery of a local convenience store, and an international study that shows that Americans are using more cocaine, marijuana, and LSD. Although each topic is not tied directly to poverty or the poor, in some way, all are offered as symbols of the moral decline in America. These articles report an absence of self-discipline, compassion, honesty, responsibility, work, and courage among the population. Together they project the notion that our society may be out of control. Perhaps it is not surprising, then, that several of the advertisements in the front section of the newspaper offered security services, door locks, and cellular telephones, or that the daily editorial was about the lack of participation in local governance.

Neo-conservatives offer an indirect link between crime and poverty—one that stops with immorality. They begin by acknowledging that most crimes are committed in impoverished communities, that crimes often involve the poor, and that a few antipoverty programs have made modest reductions on crime rates in particular areas. However, they do not accept these correlations as causal links between crime and poverty because poverty rates are often inversely correlated with crime rates. In particular, neo-conservatives wonder why crime rates rose during the relatively affluent 1960s. They speculate that the rapid increases in births during the 1960s overwhelmed the capacities of families and other social institutions to teach moral behavior and maintain order. The result was a yearly stream of youth who had not been civilized at home or in school. Because the goals and practices of those institutions also were being questioned at that time, society became unable to cope with the "perennial invasions of barbarians" and crime rates soared. Wilson states this case succinctly:

There is, perhaps, a "critical mass" of young persons such that, when that number is reached, or when an increase is sudden and large, a self-sustaining chain reaction is set off that creates an explosive increase in the amount of crime, addiction, and welfare dependency. What had once been relatively isolated and furtive acts (copping a fix, stealing a TV) became widespread and group-supported activities. (1983, 24)

Neo-conservatives follow a similar route to keep racism at a safe distance when looking for causal factors of crime. Again they concede that minorities, particularly African Americans, are more likely to be the victims of crime and that communities with disproportionate numbers of minority inhabitants are much more likely to experience crime. Moreover, they acknowledge that young black men stand a one-in-three chance of being placed under some sort of correctional supervision. However, they argue that racism does little to explain why approximately twelve percent of the population constitutes approximately fifty percent of the arrests for homicide, forcible rape, robbery, and aggravated assault. If the minority populations are committing crimes, neo-conservatives reason, then it cannot be considered racism if they are arrested and punished for their actions.

For neo-conservatives, crime is not about poverty or race. Rather, it's about how the poor and minorities lack the social and cultural capital to live law-abiding lives. Bennett names the cause as moral poverty, and he affixes the cause of moral poverty within the family.

Moral poverty is the poverty of being without loving, capable, responsible adults who teach you right from wrong; the poverty of being without parents and other authorities who habituate you to feel joy at others' joy, pain at others' pain, satisfaction when you do right, remorse when you do wrong; the poverty of growing up in the virtual absence of people who teach morality by their own everyday example and who insist that you follow suit. In the extreme, moral poverty is the poverty of growing up severely abused and neglected at the hands of deviant, delinquent, or criminal adults. (1996, 56)

According to Bennett, moral poverty breeds a lack of impulse control and a lack of empathy which, in turn, lead to "crime, addiction, and welfare dependency." These character flaws are passed on to children both genetically and socially. Despite some modest rhetoric to the contrary, neo-conservatives believe that these flaws are concentrated among the poor and minority elements in society. If this were not true, then the correlations among poverty, race, and crime would not be so strong. Although the logic seems tautological, it has been convincing to many. For some unexplained reason (but not because of class or race), criminals and their families were pushed aside when the population exploded and overwhelmed social institutions during the 1960s, and they failed to develop sufficient moral wealth among their young. The results of these failures have been staggering.

America's beleaguered cities are about to be victimized anew by a paradigm-shattering wave of ultra-violent, morally vacuous young people some call "the super-predators." At least that is the consensus emerging within precinct houses, university think tanks, and living rooms across the country. Indeed, some of those who have become experts against their will can testify that in some places the super-predators have already arrived. The trend should concern all Americans, wherever they live. Pathologies first sighted in cities rarely stay there for long. (*Boston Sunday Globe*, May 19, 1996)

Without mentioning poverty or race, the *Globe* manages to make the neo-conservative link clearly. For the moment, society will need more police, mandatory sentencing, and no-frills prisons to defend itself against poor and minority youth. These measures will deter the lost generation long enough to implement a permanent solution—one that protects the rest of society well into the next century. That cure, of course, is to provide poor and minority children with "a maximum dosage of moral tutelage from parents, teachers, coaches, clergy, and other responsible adults" (Bennett 1996, 57). The proper medicine will teach the young to control their impulses, which should reduce criminal behavior, as well as other social pathologies such as out-of-wedlock births, drug use, and welfare dependency.

MORAL LITERACY

Although there are many others involved in the neo-conservative moral intervention among the poor (e.g., William Kilpatrick and Thomas Lackona), the most well-known advocate is William J. Bennett. He lists his credentials for such a project as former Secretary of Education and Chairman of the National Endowment for the Humanities during the Reagan Administration, former Director of the Office of National Drug Control under President Bush, and currently Distinguished Fellow in Cultural Policy Studies at the Heritage

Foundation and senior editor of *The National Review*. He holds graduate degrees in political philosophy and law. He is the bestselling author of *The Book of Virtue: A Treasure of Great Moral Stories* and *The Moral Compass*. The Public Broadcasting System began a television series in 1996 based on the stories from these two anthologies. Since 1984, he has been the leading voice in the neo-conservative call to combat poverty and crime through moral literacy.

Bennett's ideas about moral literacy derive from Aristotle's writing. (Bennett is fond of tossing in quotations from ancient Greeks and American Federalists.) Aristotle argued that good moral character is developed through habits of mind. To develop a moral society, Aristotle called for education that would develop intelligent patterns of moral choice guided by attachment and love. These patterns were to be learned through moral apprenticeships within families and civilized communities. These apprenticeships required loving environments and social interactions that displayed and rewarded good moral choices. To carry good moral principles beyond the boundaries of family and community, great moral tales were composed, shared, and memorized. In this way, good moral habits of mind would lead to good moral habits of behavior.

Bennett's first efforts on behalf of moral education were directed at schooling. While Secretary of Education, he set his agenda "to get clear answers to the fundamental questions about education: What should children know? And how can they learn it?" (1984, 2). Standing in the way of clear thinking on these matters was an "infusion of diversity in schools" and a "surfeit of confusion, bureaucratic thinking, and community apathy" (3). According to Bennett, diversity became a concern for public schooling only after minorities and women began to question the Western European focus of school traditions and inequalities of academic outcomes during the 1960s. Although Bennett declared that diversity was not an "insuperable obstacle" for school success, he pondered the impact of socioeconomic class in rather ominous terms.

Our diversity is socioeconomic. We are rich and poor and most of us are somewhere in between. Yet the persistence of a socioeconomic "underclass" in America looms as one of the largest challenges to our nation in general and to our educational system in particular. Lack of money is only one aspect of the problem

and, perhaps, not even the most serious. Dependency, crime, ill
health, joblessness, drug addiction—these are not, of course,
confined to the poor nor do most low-income individuals experience them. But when they intersect within that burst of poverty that sociologists often refer to as the underclass, we have an
authentic and sizable problem for which the term *diversity* is not
nearly expressive enough—a challenge increasingly troubling for our
elementary schools. (1984, 8)

To clarify thinking about schooling, Bennett published *First
Lessons* (1986), *What Works* (1984), and *James Madison Elementary School* (1988) during his three years as Secretary of
Education. *First Lessons* offered a report card on elementary
schools, in which he wrote that "Although most teachers seek
to reinforce good character in their students by teaching honesty, industry, loyalty, self-respect, and other virtues, their
presentation of certain issues may yet be clouded by foolish
'value-free' educational theories and by their perceptions of
conflict among value systems represented in their students'
diverse backgrounds" (14). In *What Works*, Bennett selected
research findings about teaching that he boiled down to the
idea that the "belief in the value of hard work, the importance
of personal responsibility, and the importance of education
itself contributes to greater academic success" (17). *James
Madison* provided explicit elementary-school curricula that
"prove that despair over disadvantaged and minority school
children is fruitless and false—that there is, in fact, no broad
class of American students for whom the time-tested principles of good education do not and cannot apply" (9).

　　These time-tested principles included what Bennett called
the explicit and implicit curriculum. For Bennett, the explicit
curriculum ought to include specific statements about what
should be learned and when that should happen. The foundation of any school curriculum is the ability to read. Bennett
has definite ideas about how that foundation should be laid:

Phonics improves the ability of children both to identify words and
sound out new ones. Sounding out the letters in a word is like the
first tentative steps of a toddler; it helps children gain a secure ver-
bal footing and expand their vocabularies beyond the limits of basic
readers. (Bennett 1984, 21)

Good teachers begin the day's reading lesson by preparing children
for the story to be read—introducing the new words and concepts
they encounter. . . . Such preparation is like a road map. (22)

Storytelling also introduces them to cultural values and literacy traditions before they can read, write, and talk about stories by themselves. (25)

Students read more fluently and with greater understanding if they have background knowledge of the past and present. Such knowledge and understanding is called cultural literacy. (53)

Memorizing can help students absorb and retain the factual information on which understanding and critical thought are based. (37)

In these principles, the explicit curriculum is clear. Readers ought to focus their attention on accuracy in decoding and getting the author's intended message. They should look for the facts and cultural values that will enable them to understand and engage in critical thought later. Although a start, Bennett acknowledges that the explicit curriculum is not sufficient to produce good citizens. "Through science and history, through math and geography, students pursue the explicit goals of schooling. But schools also have another powerful 'curricula,' the implicit lessons they deliver concerning the development of character and morality" (1986, 39). Bennett believes that the implicit lessons for reading should be just as powerful as the explicit. For example, teaching phonics first means that students must defer the gratification of experiencing whole texts. Phonics instruction requires students to isolate their attention on meaningless symbols and to produce corresponding sounds. Accordingly, beneath the development of auditory and visual strategies to learn symbol/sound correspondences are lessons about instant gratification, perseverance, and work. Following the teacher's road maps to meaning, listening to stories to ingest cultural values, and memorizing facts as the basis for later critical thought offer similar powerful lessons of character.

Bennett uses Chall's research on the "fourth-grade slump" to aim these explicit and implicit lessons at the poor and minorities. Chall, Jacobs, and Baldwin (1990) concluded that "currently, cultural and political theories are offered as reasons for the low achievement of poor children and for the lag between mainstream and at-risk children. Although cultural and political explanations may help us understand the broader picture, in the end they must be translated, in practical terms, into what can be done in schools and in homes. Such translation ought to consider the historical findings of educational research—that good teaching improves achievement and thereby can empower *all* children and especially those at risk" (xi). That practical translation provides Bennett's clear answer concerning how children can learn. A steady diet of skill-based instruction will develop the minds and characters of poor and minority students sufficiently to overcome the fourth-grade slump like mainstream children. But Bennett's moral education is much more than academic exercises.

BOOKS OF VIRTUE

Leaving nothing to chance, Bennett offers three anthologies of consummate moral examples from "the corpus of Western Civilization, that American schoolchildren once upon a time, knew by heart" (1994a, 15) to direct the content of reading at school and at home. His first, *The Book of Virtues*, contains stories, essays, and poems selected for their "moral moorings and anchors that have never been more necessary" (12). *The Moral Compass* presents stories "aimed at clear concepts of good and bad without hesitation or apology. They treat life as a moral endeavor" (1995a, 12). The third volume, a picture-book entitled *The Children's Book of Virtues*, includes a few of the stories from *The Book of Virtues* that "speak to morality and virtue not as something to have but as something to be, the most important thing to be" (1995b, 6). Together these books are designed to "continue the task of preserving the principles, the ideals, and notions of goodness and greatness we hold dear" (1994a, 12).

Bennett does not equivocate on these principles, ideals, and notions; he names them as self-discipline, compassion, responsibility, friendship, work, courage, perseverance, honesty, loyalty, and faith. These virtues are encoded in "great moral stories" of the past and are organized into sections. For example, in *The Book of Virtues*, there are forty-five separate texts (i.e., poems, fables, letters, diary entries, and vignettes) on self-discipline, thirty-six on compassion, and so on. An odd assortment of authors are assigned to each virtue: George Washington to civility, Martin Luther King, Jr. to perseverance, Dolley Madison to courage, Oscar Wilde to friendship, and Watergate conspirator, Chuck Colson, to faith. For his second volume, he "decided to take a close look at some of the books American children were reading in their homes and schools around the turn of the twentieth century. The wealth of material was astounding, and it comprises a large part of this volume" (1995b, 14).

The books are expected to show what virtues look like, what they are in practice, how to recognize them, and how they work. Although each text and virtue might be discussed, they are not to be debated. True to his belief in basic skills, Bennett seeks rote learning of his interpretation of each.

> The reader scanning this book may notice that it does not discuss issues like nuclear war, abortion, creationism, or euthanasia. . . . But the fact is that the formation of character in young people is educationally a different task from, and a prior task to, the discussion of the great, difficult ethical controversies of the day. First things first. And planting the ideas of virtue, of good traits in the young, comes first. . . . This is a book of basics. The tough issues can, if teachers and parents wish, be taken up later. And I would add, a person who is morally literate will be immeasurably better equipped than a morally illiterate person to reach a reasoned and ethically defensible position on these tough issues. (1994a, 12–13)

Using his clear thinking about how children can learn from texts, Bennett starts each section with a two-page introduction to instruct readers on the meaning of that virtue. Each page has a section header to remind readers which virtue is being addressed. Each text has an introduction to act as a mindset for how to comprehend the moral message that the "author" intended to convey. Bennett even offers instructions on how to read. "This volume is not intended to be a book one reads from cover to cover. It is, rather, a book for browsing, for marking favorite passages, for reading aloud to family, for memorizing pieces here and there" (1994a, 15). Finally, readers are told to overlook any historical inaccuracies and to focus only on the designated moral.

For example, on page 177 under the heading "Compassion," Bennett presents and interprets a letter from Abraham Lincoln to a Mrs. Bixby, consoling her on the loss of five sons who fought for the Union Army. In his introduction to the letter, Bennett quotes Carl Sandburg, "the letter wore its awful implication that human freedom so often was paid for with agony," to direct readers' interpretation. Lincoln wrote:

I feel how weak and fruitless must be any word of mine which
should attempt to beguile you from grief of a loss so overwhelming.
But I cannot refrain from tendering you the consolations that may
be found in the thanks of the republic they died to save. I . . . leave
you . . . the solemn pride that must be yours to have laid so costly a
sacrifice upon the altar of freedom. (177)

Lincoln may be compassionate in his letter to Mrs. Bixby, but
other readings of the letter are possible. She lost sons to a war
that Lincoln declared to prevent the southern states from se-
ceding during his administration—a war that required the service of only those who could not buy their way out of the draft
and in which over six hundred thousand working class and poor
men and boys were killed. Without Bennett's prompt, readers
might place the letter under the category of responsibility. Yet
there's more here. In Bennett's efforts to demonstrate the pet-
tiness of those who have challenged the historical accuracy of
many of the documents he included in his book, he reports that
Lincoln had been misinformed about the Bixby boys. Two were
killed, one was taken prisoner, and two deserted. Clinging to
his agenda, however, Bennett writes, "Mrs. Bixby's loss and
sacrifice hardly could have been greater."

What virtuous lessons are readers expected to learn and
memorize from this letter? Compassion does not seem to be
the primary reason Bennett chose Lincoln's letter. Rather than
responsibility, courage, loyalty, or any other virtue he or others might name, his real purpose seems to be to prepare children and their parents for the next war that Congress declares
or for the many conflicts to which our presidents send our
sons and daughters. Bennett frames the Lincoln letter to tell
readers to forget those deserters and think about the glory of
the "sacrifice upon the altar of freedom." This is more than an
historical quibble that Bennett tries to circumvent ("Some of
the history that is recounted here may not meet the standards
of exacting historians," 1994a, 14). Through this and the other
texts within The Book of Virtues and The Moral Compass,
Bennett seeks to simplify ethics to serve his neo-conservative
agenda. Even his allies seem able and willing to raise this
point:

In modern times, the greatest challenge to any conception of virtue
is to find a basis for the proper recognition and treatment of
strangers. . . . The effort to do this has been largely based on providing a new interpretation of the idea of justice. . . . To judge from

the stories gathered in Bennett's book, it is not a task for which we can get much help among the tales, poems, legends, and homilies of our or any other culture. In fact, Bennett does not even have a section entitled "Justice," though he includes some important accounts of it such as the excerpt from Plato's *Republic*. (Wilson 1994, 33)

Bennett's book, as I say, is essentially torn between these poles. Thus, the reader may be going along reading the Tolstoy-approved folktales and hymn lyrics and suddenly find herself in the middle of Whitman or Shakespeare or Donne. Here are texts that testify to a simple, uniting type of faith, and there is Jefferson's instruction to his nephew that he examine the stories of the miracles in the Bible exactly as he would scrutinize similar tales in the histories of Livy and Tacitus. And this tension in Bennett is closely linked to another one, between political quietism and a prophetic demand for justice. (Nussbaum 1994, 41)

Wilson and Nussbaum identify the politicized nature of Bennett's agenda. First, his selection of virtues is skewed in favor of his neo-conservative politics. Although he quotes Plato frequently and he declares that his virtues reflect the best of Western Civilization, Bennett does not follow Plato's lead. Plato distinguished four cardinal virtues: wisdom, courage, temperance, and justice. While Bennett includes courage and temperance (labeled self-discipline), he ignores Plato's intellectual virtue, wisdom, and omits his political virtue, justice. Of course, as Wilson and Nussbaum suggest, other readers might interpret some of the text differently than Bennett. For example, he suggests that Frederick Douglass' 1852 Fourth of July speech on the hypocrisy of celebrating Independence Day in a slave nation is about responsibility; he selects courage as the virtue of Susan B. Anthony's symbolic vote in the 1872 presidential election; and he characterizes Mary Wollstonecraft's *A Vindication of the Rights of Women* as a demonstration of faith. These are more than poor historical interpretations. Bennett's representation of these and other texts steers readers away from thinking about justice. After reading his interpretations of these texts, readers are less likely to see the calls for justice in the next texts about apartheid, democracy, or women's rights they encounter.

This intention to repackage justice as other virtues provides another way of understanding Bennett's somewhat surprising decision to include several texts about minority and women's rights. In this light, those are the texts that must be neutralized, if virtue is to be kept straightforward and uncontroversial. By first arguing that those texts describe a closed chapter in American history and then by reinterpreting their intention as something other than cries for economic, social, and political justice, Bennett directs everyone's moral education toward moral conservatism and a simple optimism about possibilities. Moreover, this repackaging of those texts teaches the very ones who are most likely to meet injustice to forget about earning less than two-thirds of white men's salaries, about being the last hired and the first fired, and about those two Bixby boys who deserted the Union Army. Rather, they should turn the other cheek and have faith.

NEO-CONSERVATIVE LITERACY

Neo-conservatives work from a set of principles that overlap both conservative and liberal thinking to some extent. From conservatives, they accept the notion that life is infinitely complex and that the human predicament must be analyzed with a critical eye and a humble mind. Neo-conservatives believe that because so little is known about how the social world works, efforts to change it will bring limited results. Therefore, they view sweeping policy programs and blueprints to remake society with suspicion. In the end, the social institutions that placed them in favorable social and political positions are to be respected for their longevity and the service they provide to the majority. From liberals, neo-conservatives "assume without question the need for a minimal welfare state, the legitimacy of labor unions, and the justice of civil rights" (Gerson 1996, 20). They do not, of course, accept all liberal thoughts on the poor, workers, and minorities.

Neo-conservatives strain both conservative and liberal ideas through three propositions of their own. First, they see the world as a struggle between good and evil, and they worry that evil might be winning. Second, they seek community—its claim on individual autonomy and its responsibility to inculcate virtue among all members, but particularly within the young. Finally, they believe that ideas matter, that their principles are universal and, therefore, direct social life. Following functionalist logic, these principles direct neo-conservatives to work for programs to help the poor and others through locally controlled educational programs based on their ideas of virtue, which will prepare them to live the good life both in private and public life.

For neo-conservatives, this means that the American social order is based on personal moral conduct and that social problems are matters of individual moral lapses or an absence of moral capital with American subcultures. Crime, then, is caused by criminals' lack of self-discipline, compassion, and honesty. Drug addiction results from the absence of self-discipline, courage, and faith among individuals. The poor need a better sense of self-discipline, responsibility, work, and perseverance. Social problems persist because too many individuals lack compassion, friendship, and loyalty to others to band together in order to induce universal adherence to these neo-conservative virtues.

For neo-conservatives, solution is moral literacy—the ability to read alphabetic texts and live according to a proscribed set of virtues, to write virtuous lives in order to bring civility to public life, and to provide correct texts for others to read. Families, educators, and the virtuous public have equally important functions to perform in this solution. Two-parent families must begin the process of developing virtuous youth, setting higher expectations for their children, teaching by example, and providing discipline and love. Educators must reinforce and extend the right moral lessons learned at home and should correct any wrong lessons that children might bring to school or other institutions (e.g., YMCA, Girl Scouts, and Big Brother/Big Sisters). These lessons are to be encoded in the explicit and implicit curricula, and taught directly to the poor, minorities, and children from single-parent families. Without families and educators providing the basics of moral literacy, society cannot develop enough support programs, build enough prisons, or boost the economy enough to stem the tide of drugs, teen pregnancy, crime, or poverty. In the end, all virtuous citizens must play their part in their own and poor communities.

Bourgeois America can also help poor children in the inner city by providing role models, properly understood. I say "properly understood" because the idea of role models is so often grossly misconstrued. . . . Michael Jordan could spend every hour of the off-season preaching to kids the virtues of hard work, discipline, and abstinence from drugs and sex, but he would probably not change the behavior of one inner-city kid. . . . Inner-city kids will behave

like famous role models only when they regard the bourgeois virtues not as an idea but as a code, a code followed every day by lots
of people they know. It is not enough for kids to know that they
should stay away from drugs and irresponsible sex and that
they should work hard and go to church. They need to know, love,
and be loved by people who do all of these things—and more.
(Gerson 1997, 250)

Neo-conservative rhetoric on these matters has been so per-
suasive that civility and virtue have become central points of
other political discourses. President Clinton made family values a central tenet of his 1996 reelection campaign and convened a forum on civility at his alma mater, Yale University.
Colin Greer, President of the New World Foundation, and
Herbert Kohl, a radical democratic educator and author, edited
A Call to Character (1995), an acknowledged liberal alternative to Bennett's *The Book of Virtues*. Rev. Jim Wallis, a liberal active clergyman, published "A Crisis of Civility" in
Sojourners (1996). These texts offer barely a word about possible dialectical relationships between and among social problems and violations of neo-conservative versions of morality.
In the end, these attempts to co-opt moral literacy for different political goals cede considerable ground to neo-
conservatives in the struggle over reading poverty, and play
directly into the hands of advocates of private democracy.
    According to neo-conservatives, every American should be-
come morally literate and strive to be self-disciplined, responsible, honest, loyal, and faithful, and to work and persevere. In
return, they offer a safer, easier, and quieter future. They im-
plore us to read life and all we encounter through these moral
lenses. And who can object to the development of faith, courage, responsibility, and the like in our youth? Who will challenge idyllic representations of our past when all American
schoolchildren knew these virtues by heart? Who can reject
moral literacy? Yet when we stop and think about it, neo-
conservatives seek to reify morality into a set code of beliefs
and behaviors that prepares children and their parents to work
hard to protect a private democracy, the current states of the
economic, social, and political life. Remember, wisdom and
justice are not conservative virtues. As projected by Bennett, a
neo-conservative code of virtues repackages women's and minorities' questions about double standards and inequalities as
uncivil, even immoral, behavior. Rather than negotiating some
common cultural understanding, values, and meaning, neo-

conservative literacy requires the unconditional surrender of groups that read the texts of social life differently. They end all conversation and deliberation in public over the decisions that direct our lives. Neo-conservatives narrow the gap between them and us only through moral conquest.

Table 5–1 Neo-Conservatives on Poverty: Definition, Causes, Commentators, and Reading Solution

NEO-CONSERVATIVE
Inability to be responsible for self or family. Poor life choices leads to low incomes.
Lack of moral character prevents poor from making good (middle-class) choices for behavior. With inappropriate morals, can't compete for jobs with sufficient incomes.
Joe Klein James Q. Wilson Glenn Loury William Bennett Mark Gerson
Reading education for moral literacy will correct moral poverty in America, which in turn will end all social problems and correct economic poverty.

Is neo-conservative literacy what we want for our future? Are we so frightened by the present and each other that we wish to silence women, people of color, and the poor again? Are their naming of injustices in our society just figments of their immoral imagination? Can we reduce all social issues to moral conduct? Will poverty end when each member of the poor develops his or her moral capital through moral literacy?

SIX

THE WORLD IS IN AN UPROAR/ THE DANGER ZONE IS EVERYWHERE

Reading the Reading Crisis

To varying degrees, liberals reject the conservative and neo-conservative assumptions that individual characteristics and character flaws cause poverty. Rather, liberals argue that poverty results from forces beyond the control of individuals. Although President Clinton and other neo-liberals echo conservative concerns about long-term welfare recipients' unwillingness to work, most liberals act as if they still believe that the poor are poor because they have not had and do not have adequate access to good schools, jobs, and income. Lack of access supplants the conservative premise that the poor choose to be poor. According to liberals, the system makes that choice for the poor by denying them chances to participate equally in the material conditions from which middle- and upper-class citizens build their lives. In a weaker, neo-liberal version of this "restricted opportunity" perspective on poverty, advocates argue that, in general, governmental services are inadequate to all citizens, enabling only those who already possess economic and cultural capital to thrive. Neo-liberals seek ways in which the government can improve those general services.

Neo-liberals often employ a rhetoric of crisis and public policy when considering social problems. For example, teenage pregnancy is a crisis caused by poor sex education, inadequate access to birth control, or restricted abortions. Health care is a crisis caused by absence of national health insurance, reluctance to set prices within Medicaid and Medicare, or regulations of the Food and Drug Administration. Adequate public housing is a crisis caused by reduction in federal funds, neglect of inner-city economies, or high interest rates from the Federal Reserve Board. Teenage pregnancy, health care, and housing are issues for everyone. In each case, the crisis threatening the general welfare of American citizens overrides the specific problems of the poor. Although they are often most closely associated with the poor, general solutions—free birth control, national health insurance, and enterprise zones—help all citizens in their efforts to live better lives and, along the way, they should help the poor to do the same. Poverty, then, is never the real target of neo-liberal reform. Rather, the poor are expected to be carried along with the general rise of all other citizens who are expected to mobilize to overcome whatever crisis is at hand.

For neo-liberals, the major crisis facing the United States is the readiness of the American workforce to meet the demands of a global economy in the twenty-first century (Fowler 1995). The needs of business, then, become the primary criteria in public policy decisions. Remember the rhetoric of crisis that Bill Clinton used in his campaign speech in Wyandotte, Michigan, which I discussed in Chapter 1. Because neo-liberals see the global economy based on flexible production and specialization, they conclude that too few Americans are ready to meet and master the challenge of open, worldwide economic competition. And they can easily point their finger at the culprit for this lack of readiness within the workforce. Ray Marshall (former Secretary of Labor in the Reagan Administration and current trustee for the Carnegie Foundation) and Mark Tucker (President of the Center for the Economy and Education) state:

In the first part of this century, we adopted the principle of mass-producing low-quality education to create a low-skill workforce for mass-production industry. Building on this principle, our education and business systems became very tightly linked, evolving into a single system that brilliantly capitalized on our advantages and enabled us to create the most powerful economy and the largest middle class the world has ever seen. The education system, modeled on industrial organization, was crafted to supply the workforce that the industrial economy needed. America's systems of school organization and industrial organization were beautifully matched, each highly dependent on the other for its success, each the envy of the world. But most of the competitive advantages enjoyed at the beginning of the century had faded by mid-century, and advances in technology during and after the war slowly altered the structure of the domestic and world economy in ways that turned these principles of American business and school organization into liabilities rather than assets. (Marshall and Tucker 1992, 17)

According to neo-liberals, an out-of-date school system is causing an economic crisis and threatening the existence of the American middle class. Logically, then, they believe that policies to update our school system in order to meet the current demands of businesses will reverse our diminishing economic fortunes in the next century. As President Clinton reported in his Wyandotte speech, the basic educational concern is learning to read—too many adults and too many children are unable to read sufficiently well to perform their duties at work and at school. Richard Riley, Secretary of Education, states that "the most urgent task facing schools is to improve how they teach that subject" (as quoted in Sanchez 1996, 3). To begin, neo-liberals define the reading crisis and then offer general solutions of higher academic standards in reading for all. In the end, however, they appear to be manufacturing crises in order to pursue a business agenda.

THE READING CRISIS

This reading crisis is news to many Americans. During the 1990s, newspaper editors from all over the country have devoted numerous column inches to report the proportions, severity, and meager response to the crisis. Headlines on front-page articles decry the state of literacy in the United States: "Reading the Signs of a Crisis" (Meisler 1990, in the *Los Angeles Times*), "The Crisis at Hand" (Walt 1996, in the *Houston Chronicle*), "The ABCs of Illiteracy" (Trausch 1993, in the *Boston Globe*). Beneath the headlines, reporters offer terrifying commentary.

Experts say perhaps three to four million Americans cannot read or write at all—between twenty and thirty million Americans lack so many basic educational skills that they cannot read, write, calculate, solve problems, or communicate well enough to function effectively on the job or in their everyday lives. (Meisler 1990, 1)

According to an alarming federal report issued last week, about half of all American adults—90 million in all—struggle with basic reading, math, and reasoning skills. (Olszewski 1993, 1)

Although the literacy problem is national in scope, the majority of programs for teaching people how to read are small, unconnected, grassroots, each with its own agenda, teaching methods, and selection of materials. (Proulx 1993, 21)

I [the First Lady of Georgia] don't think that anybody actually knows how many can't read at all. I know there are pockets where you have teenaged mothers or women who became mothers in their teens who cannot read directions on medication for children. Whether those people can read the average children's book, I don't know. Being a banker, I've always been real concerned about the math level. Learning math is a big part of becoming literate. (Loupe 1997, Section C, 4)

Many of the facts amid the hyperbolic speculation in these newspaper articles come from two surveys: National Adult Literacy Survey (NALS) of 1993 (National Center for Education Statistics, 1993) and the National Assessment of Educational Progress (NAEP) conducted every other year (1996). In total, the NALS surveyed more than twenty-six thousand Americans aged sixteen and older, selected randomly to match U.S. demographics. The survey required respondents to perform a variety of reading and quantitative tasks of varying sophistication during a one-hour interview. In addition, a series of questions were asked to gauge relationships between literacy and social and economic variables such as voting, economic status, weeks worked, and income. According to statistical inference to the entire population, forty to forty-four million of the 191 million adults in this country have considerable difficulty with the most basic literacy tasks, such as totaling deposit slips, recognizing the time and place of a meeting, following a newspaper article. About fifty million others can perform those tasks but cannot make low-level inferences using printed materials or integrate easily identifiable pieces of information. These ninety-four million Americans are the ones referred to in the newspaper articles about the reading crisis.

Just under twenty percent of Americans, approximately thirty-eight million adults, demonstrated proficiencies with the most challenging tasks that the test-makers suggest are required for the high-wage/high-skill jobs of the global economy. The demographic profile of the lower eighty and the top twenty percentiles for the NALS results resembles American economic demographics. An individual is more likely to score among the lowest levels on the survey if they are older, have fewer years of schooling, are a member of a racial or linguistic minority, work less than thirty weeks during the year, and receive food stamps. Also similar to economic profiles, most of these individuals did not consider themselves to be "at risk" because of their literacy. Rather, seventy-five percent of the adults in the lowest level and ninety-seven percent in the second lowest level "described themselves as being able to read or write English well or very well" (National Center for Education Statistics 1993, 4). Apparently, most Americans consider themselves to be middle class in terms of literacy as well as economically. That is, most Americans do not experience a

reading crisis in their own lives; they do not consider themselves unable to perform the literacy demands made upon them
at work or at home. Daniel Wagner, Director of the National
Center on Adult Literacy, explains how these two perceptions
of reading ability can coexist:

In the 1960s, the United States was widely considered to be one of
the most literate countries in the world, with a United Nations-
listed "literacy rate" of nearly ninety-nine percent—this in contrast
to many developing countries with rates of fifty percent or lower.
Yet in 1993, the first report from the federally funded National
Adult Literacy Survey, the most comprehensive study of its kind,
painted a different picture. The so-called good news was that nearly
ninety-five percent of adult Americans could read at a fourth-grade
level or better, showing that illiteracy in its most basic form was
relatively low. The bad news was that nearly half of all adult Americans scored in the lowest two levels of literacy, levels that the
National Educational Goals Panel has stated are well below what
American workers need to be competitive in the global economy. (Wagner 1995, 23)

The NAEP test is conducted in participating schools across
the country as a biannual national assessment of the reading
proficiency of fourth-, eighth-, and twelfth-grade students.
The survey requires respondents to read for literary experience, to gain information, and to perform a task. The results
are assigned to achievement levels "based on collective judgment about what students should know and be able to do in
reading" (National Assessment of Educational Progress 1996,
1). The basic level denotes partial mastery of prerequisite
knowledge and skills that are fundamental for proficient work
at each grade level. The proficient level represents solid academic performance and demonstrated competence over challenging subject matter. The advanced level signifies superior
performance. The Executive Summary of the *NAEP 1994
Reading Report Card* states results of the survey in a curious
manner. "In 1994, thirty percent of fourth-graders, thirty percent of eighth-graders, and thirty-six percent of twelfth-
graders attained the proficient level in reading. Across the
three grades, three to seven percent reached the advanced
level" (4). Translated, this means sixty-seven percent of
fourth-graders have only "partial mastery" of skills needed to
read at a fourth-grade level. Slightly less than sixty percent of
twelfth-grade students are deemed somewhat prepared to read

the required material to graduate from high school. In his April 27, 1995, press release regarding the 1994 NAEP Reading Assessment, Secretary of Education Richard Riley exclaimed, "I am disappointed with the lack of improvement in this NAEP assessment. These preliminary findings indicate we have a long way to go to equip our students with the tools they will need for success in the next century."

The federal government has fourteen separate programs, with total budgets in the billions of dollars, that are designed to address the reading crisis. Targeting literacy directly are the Educational State Grants ($345.3 million budget), Educational National Programs for Evaluation ($5 million), Even Start for family literacy ($102 million), Reading Is Fundamental book-distribution programs ($10.3 million), Literacy Programs for Prisoners ($4.7 million), National Institutes for Literacy ($4.5 million), and National Writing Projects ($3.1 million). Several educational programs with broader goals also address literacy: Title I Compensatory in School Support ($7.2 billion), Individuals with Disabilities ($3.1 billion), Bilingual Education ($156.7 million), Immigrant Education ($100 million), Educational Research and Development Centers ($72.8 million), AmeriCorp Volunteer Programs ($402.5 million), and Head Start ($4 billion). Despite these programs and billions of dollars spent, Americans are still deemed unprepared to triumph in the twenty-first century.

GENERAL SOLUTIONS TO THE READING CRISIS

According to Hirsch, the reading crisis continues because Americans do not know enough about the word or the world to make reading automatic. Automatic reading would enable readers to devote most of their attention to the problem-solving task at hand and less to puzzling over the letters and facts. Currently, Americans do not have enough background knowledge to recognize facts automatically, nor do they recognize letter patterns quickly enough to free mental capacity to think. The remedy for the reading crisis, then, requires a uniform attention to facts and letter-pattern recognition at an early age. Such attention is possible only if consensus on content and pedagogy is achieved; Hirsch's answer to consensus building is to articulate the particulars of such a reading curriculum and to call for a national adoption of his plans.

Often Hirsch's critics label his approach to the reading crisis conservative or, at best, neo-conservative (Aronowitz and Giroux 1985; Knoblauch and Brannon 1993). They justify that label primarily by reference to Hirsch's ardent defense of traditional curricula and pedagogy and equally tenacious critique of progressive education. He is unapologetically nationalist and Eurocentric. Yet Hirsch calls himself "a political liberal and an educational conservative or, perhaps more accurately, an educational pragmatist" (Hirsch 1996, 4). He argues that literacy itself is conservative because it records and communicates traditions, and yet it is also liberal because it enables all to use, interpret, and extend those traditions. He states, "Thus, the inherent conservatism of literacy leads to an unavoidable paradox: the social goals of liberalism *require* educational conservatism."

Recently, Delpit (1995), Postman (1996), and others have prodded educators to acknowledge the possibility of this apparent contradiction. Delpit argues that progressive educators misunderstand the academic needs of African Americans and calls for explicit instruction in the codes of power that help middle- and upper-class individuals gain economic and social success. Postman maintains that progressive education privileges the worst of popular culture and materialism, which subvert efforts to achieve racial and class equity. By splitting liberal political goals from progressive pedagogy, Delpit and Postman offer theoretical invitations and rationales for Hirsch's self-description, significantly broadening the educational spectrum within the liberal political position.

Hirsch leaps over Delpit and Postman when he invokes the words of Antonio Gramsci, the Communist intellectual of the 1930s, to make his point. Turning the progressives' argument on its head, Gramsci warned that naturalistic learning would solidify class ranks within society, because the oppressed would be denied access to the knowledge, the cultural capital, that oppressors use against them in struggles to acquire and maintain economic capital. Through conservative education, the oppressed gain access to what Gramsci called hegemonic knowledge, and Delpit labels codes of power, with the ultimate goal of using that knowledge (or those codes) to subvert the inequalities that it masks. Although legitimate questions might be raised about Hirsch's commitment to that ultimate goal, he is clear that he intends his core curricula to be a way to raise all boats, especially those of the poor and minority groups. Hirsch summarizes Gramsci's position:

> The oppressed class should be taught to master the tools of power and authority—the ability to read, write, and communicate—and to gain enough traditional knowledge to understand the worlds of nature and culture surrounding them. Children, particularly the children of the poor, should not be encouraged to flourish "naturally," which would keep them ignorant and make them slaves of emotion. They should learn the value of hard work, gain the knowledge that leads to understanding, and master the traditional culture in order to command its rhetoric, as Gramsci himself had learned to do. (Hirsch 1996, 6)

Despite what he reports as a consensus among experts on how to solve the reading crisis, Hirsch points to a lack of conviction on the federal government's part and among school personnel for its continuation. Without a national curriculum of basic information that every American needs to know, a standardization of teaching methods across the country, or a commitment to a national culture, Hirsch argues that schools actually have facilitated the separation of racial groups and economic classes from one another. He maintains that the separation has reached a point at which these groups have difficulty communicating with one another. While such isolation enables the groups to learn about themselves, it systematically denies them access to the global skills and information they will need to prosper in the future. Because schools are the only public sphere that still reaches all groups, they are the first sites in which the change to a standard national agenda must occur. And to Hirsch's way of thinking, it is the elementary schools that must change the most.

For Hirsch, the main barrier to ending the reading crisis is the "formalistic principle that specific information is irrelevant to language-arts skills" (1987, 111). Up until the age of six, he argues, all children achieve similar scores on standardized reading tests. Yet only a few years later, by fourth grade, scores are separated primarily along race and class lines. Hirsch interprets that this variability happens "chiefly because low-income pupils lack elementary cultural knowledge" (111). To remedy this situation, he organized a panel of experts to list in detail everything that every elementary schoolchild ought to know. This curriculum is so elaborate that it appears in seven volumes, a separate book for each school grade from kindergarten to sixth grade.

Hirsch's curriculum is organized according to traditional academic disciplines of elementary schools: language arts, mathematics, science, history, and the arts. For each subject area, his curricula supply the basic information that students need to know in order to perform school tasks proficiently and to enable them to communicate with all others in continuously more sophisticated ways. To ensure that the sequencing of information was appropriate in his "Fundamentals of a Good Education" series, his core curricula was field-tested in Three Oaks Elementary School in Lee County, Florida. In comparison with other commercial textbooks, the content of each subject strand is academically demanding. For example, second-grade students are asked to consider Longfellow's "The Midnight Ride of Paul Revere"; a list of Greek gods and goddesses; the meaning of a number of idioms; blurbs on ancient and world civilizations; details of American history from the War of 1812 to Teddy Roosevelt; facts of basic music theory, art, and architecture; mathematical place value; some geometry; and science concepts from reproduction to astronomy. Accordingly, Hirsch expects that each lesson will be read to children, discussed with them through recitation, and repeated often until mastery is achieved.

Hirsch defines the mastery of such basic information as the acquisition of cultural literacy. Once culturally literate, all Americans automatically become prepared to handle the increasingly sophisticated demands in current workplaces and their everyday life. A critically literate workforce would boost the productive prospects of the American economy. Moreover, cultural literacy would make it an American workforce, one that was willing and able to communicate nationally. "It enables grandparents to communicate with grandchildren, Southerners with Midwesterners, whites with blacks, Asians with Hispanics, and Republicans with Democrats" (1993, xv). According to Hirsch, once everyone can communicate and think without undue attention to facts or text, then everything is possible. "True literacy has always opened doors—not just to deep knowledge and economic success, but also to other people and other cultures" (1996, xv). In this way, Hirsch invokes the

rhetoric of public democracy to reinforce the values and knowledge base that support the status quo of private democracy.

NATIONAL STANDARDS IN ENGLISH LANGUAGE ARTS

Although a commercial success, Hirsch's cultural-literacy curriculum has not found general acceptance among professional
organizations or with the federal government. However, the
argument that national answers are required for the reading
crisis and that those answers must determine what every
American needs to know has become common among liberals.
The history of the English Language Arts standards demonstrates how power works within the educational community as
the desires of business to employ a differently prepared workforce became the active agenda of English teachers across
America (McCollum-Clark 1995). In some ways, this history
requires that we do nothing more than what Deep Throat told
the Watergate investigators, Woodward and Bernstein, to do;
that is, "to follow the money." However, in the end, it demonstrates how politically naive attempts to "do good" for the
poor and minorities can cancel themselves out (Shannon 1996).

The call for national standards in all subjects started well
before President Bush and the National Board of Governors
offered their report on the state of education in 1989 at Char-
lottesville, Virginia. During the early 1980s, the Education
Commission of the States (founded by the Ford and Carnegie
foundations) convened a Task Force on Education and Economic Growth, including eleven governors and thirteen chief
executive officers from large corporations (e.g., Xerox, Ford Mo-
tor, Dow Chemical, and Control Data); the Carnegie Corporation brought together fifty national leaders in government,
business, labor and foundations; and the federal government
assembled representatives of business, governmental officials,
and university professors to comprise the National Commission on Excellence in Education (1983). Funded primarily by
philanthropic foundations with considerable overlap between
their boards and group memberships, these working groups or
policy networks sought to align schooling more closely with
the needs of business through excellence in schooling.

In one way or another, each broached the subject of national curricula. For example, the Twentieth Century Fund Task Force on Federal and Elementary and Secondary Education Policy stated, "While we strongly favor maintaining the diversity in educational practices that results from decentralization of the schools, we think that schools across the nation must, at a minimum, provide the same core components to all students" (1983, 3). In 1986, the Carnegie Forum on Education and the Economy published *A Nation Prepared: Teachers for the Twenty-first Century*, which called for demanding educational standards and a teaching force prepared to redesign schools in order to deliver those standards. This call for action led the Carnegie Foundation to fund two projects at the University of Pittsburgh—the New Standards Project to find new means for testing student competence, and the National Board for Professional Teaching Standards to develop criteria for national certification of teachers. Moreover, the forum was transformed into the National Center on Education and the Economy, which became the driving force behind much of the national-standards movement.

The year after *A Nation Prepared* appeared, Tucker established the independent National Center on Education and the Economy in Rochester, New York, with funds from the Carnegie Corporation, Rockefeller Brothers Fund, and New York State, to carry on the Forum's agenda. The National Center quickly became a strategic focus of national education reform, brokering and promoting consensus among elite corporate and political leaders. Among the luminaries on the Center's board were Ray Marshall, David Rockefeller, Jr., Governors James Hunt and Thomas Kern, the CEOs of Kodak and Xerox, Hillary Rodham Clinton, as chair, and John Sculley, the then CEO of Apple Computers. Through such contacts, the National Center has strongly influenced federal initiatives in education, first within the National Governors' Association and the Bush Administration, and more recently and far more directly within the Clinton Administration. (Noble 1994, 16–17)

In essence, the National Center for Education and the Economy wrote the subtext, if not the text, of the AMERICA 2000 educational initiative the Bush Administration announced during the State of the Union Address in 1991. Among the six national goals for education were two addressed directly at the reading crisis. After ensuring that all children would be ready for school by the year 2000 and that ninety percent of those students would graduate from high school, the third goal states that "All students will leave grades four, eight, and twelve having demonstrated competency over challenging subject matter, including English, mathematics, science, history, and geography; and every school in America will ensure that all students learn to use their minds well, so that they may be prepared for responsible citizenship, further learning, and productive employment in our modern economy." Along with goals for drug- and violence-free schools and for becoming first in the world in mathematics and science achievement, the fifth national goal stated, "Every adult will be literate and possess the skills necessary to compete in a global economy and to exercise the rights and responsibilities of citizenship."

Beyond those goals, AMERICA 2000 called for "world-class" standards with complementary "voluntary national tests" to demonstrate student mastery. To oversee progress toward these goals, the Bush Administration convened the National Council of Education Standards and Testing in 1991. Council members included many of the members of the Carnegie excellence groups, including several corporate executives. The Council's report recommended standards with "specification of content—what students should know and be able to do—and the level of performance that students are expected to attain—how good is good enough" (1991, 3). Although some members favored high-stakes testing at the announced grade levels, several questioned the technical possibilities of producing fair tests and the logistics of their implementation (Baker 1994).

The overlap of memberships between philanthropic and governmental councils on educational reform and the influence of the National Center for Education and the Economy helps explain the continuation of the AMERICA 2000 agenda into the Clinton Administration in 1992. Although at first national tests were dropped from conversations about academic standards, the national goals remained essentially the same. Within six months of assuming office, the new administration was accepting proposals from professional and other private organizations to write national standards. In October 1993, the U.S. Department of Education announced the award of a $1.8-million grant to the Center for the Study of Reading at the University of Illinois (CSR), the International Reading Association (IRA), and the National Council of

Teachers of English (NCTE) to develop standards for English language arts. In a matter of a decade, the desires of business executives to employ a differently skilled workforce had been transferred from boardrooms to classrooms with the help of the Carnegie and other philanthropic foundations and the federal government. Miles Myers, Executive Director of the NCTE, stated this simply, "The point of public schools is to give children power in English so they can be productive workers. There isn't any doubt about our goal" (as quoted in Woo 1996, 17).

ONE STEP FORWARD, TWO STEPS BACK

In rallying the English and elementary schoolteachers to participate in writing the standards, the leaderships of the three groups offered different sets of reasons. P. David Pearson, Director of the CSR, suggested that the standards project would afford a conversation about what teachers value, an opportunity to expose and evaluate teachers' implicit standards, a chance to influence the allotment and use of public and professional resources, and a way to ensure a changing, supportive, thoughtful curriculum for all students (1993). Clearly, Pearson believed that the profession could manipulate the writing of national standards and direct them toward its own ends. Myers offered a more politically sober rationale for participation. Compliance would increase federal funds to public schools, thereby ensuring their survival in states experiencing economic hardships, keep the professional organization at the center of debates about their field of expertise, supplant an English-language-arts curriculum that was no longer adequate to meet the needs of contemporary citizens and workers, and provide a means for civil-rights activists to pursue equity in schooling in new ways (1995). "The standards documents may be used to launch a new kind of civil-rights movements focused on educational opportunity and, as a result, the present standards movement may begin to have a federal and national character quite different from past standards movements" (Myers 1994, 151). By writing opportunity-to-learn standards, which specify which resources are necessary to teach and learn English language arts, the IRA and

NCTE could supply minority groups with ammunition to fight for equitable schooling through the courts.

During the NCTE's annual conventions in 1993 and 1994, the membership was told in open forums that having federal funding, as well as the membership's mandate, gave the standards project both political and professional legitimacy. The NCTE leadership explained that the U.S. Department of Education, the funding agency, placed no contingencies on the funding. In Louisville, Kentucky, Myers reported, "We are free to write the standards as we see fit, and if the membership doesn't like the standards, we can reject them" (1993, 24). Janet Emig, Chair of the English Language Arts Standards Joint Project, stated, "No federal body can legislate our success or failure" (40). Yet four months after the second public forum, the Department of Education rejected the interim report from the CSR, IRA, and NCTE joint project, citing that the group was not making "expected progress" toward promised goals (Diegmueller 1994). The government withheld half of the $1.8 million. At the time of the government's announcement, Pearson was quoted as responding, "I thought we were developing these standards for kids, their parents, and their teachers" (Diegmueller 1994, 9). Firing the standards developers was unprecedented among the federally funded standards projects. For example, although the first version of the national history standards was labeled a national disgrace by popular media (e.g., Elson 1994) and denounced in the *Congressional Record* (1995), the National Center for History in Schools at UCLA received their full $1.5 million from the government and an additional stipend to write a second version.

Embarrassed but unwilling to quit, the IRA and NCTE boards voted to fund the second half of the English-language-arts standards with $1 million from their own coffers ("NCTE/IRA Say Standards Effort Will Continue," 1994). Forgetting their rhetoric about the need for federal support, IRA and NCTE leadership explained their dismissal on the basis that they were writing content and opportunity-to-learn standards when the government sought performance standards. Content and delivery standards specify what should be presented and what resources are necessary to make that presentation to all students in all schools. Performance standards specify what should be learned, when, and at what level of competence. Politically, the Department of Education had rendered moot whatever standards the IRA/NCTE might create. Making public its rejection of their first draft, the government neutralized any criticism these professional organizations might make about the appropriateness of high-stakes testing of students' competence in English language arts. And two years later, when the IRA/NCTE professional standards were published, they were indeed dead on arrival, at least with the federal government.

Michael Cohen, senior advisor to Education Secretary Richard Riley, presented the official response to the English-language-arts standards. "The report contains very vague and very general statements that don't tell parents or students what is important to learn and don't tell teachers what is important to teach and by when" (as quoted in the *New York Times*, Tabor 1996, A12). "They don't appear to have made much progress" (as quoted in the *Washington Post*, Sanchez 1996, A3). "It doesn't result in anything that is clearly measurable" (as quoted in the *Los Angeles Times*, Woo 1996, A17). Reports in the nation's newspapers and news magazines were not much kinder.

They are vague. The whole point of standards is to define clearly what students should be able to do. This falls well short of providing useful guidance to teachers and parents. (Sanchez, *Washington Post* 1996, A3)

With our SAT scores so low and our public schools in deep trouble, this is not a very good time to convince students that reading comic books is just as good as traditional schoolwork. The good news is that the publication of the English standards is exposing this awful stuff to a broad public for the first time. It has hummed along in the background without much opposition, mostly because few of us noticed it and fewer still were inclined to demand an English-language version. Now it's out in the open, and we all can throw mudpies. (Leo, *U.S. News and World Report* 1996, 38).

A curriculum guide for teaching English has just been released in a tongue barely recognizable as English. . . . Nowhere in their twelve rules will you find the prescriptive verbs "should" or "ought." Simple declarative sentences are equally hard to find. . . . The only plausible reason one can think of for such circumlocutions is that the writers were paralyzed by caution. (Editors of the *New York Times* 1996, A22)

[The federal government] objected to the group's theme of multiculturalism in literature and it said the group should not have included "opportunity-to-learn" standards, which spell out what resources and expertise every classroom should provide instead of what skills or knowledge should result. In the end, the group issued twelve simple standards. None specifies what "opportunity-to-learn" resources a classroom should have. (White, *Atlanta Constitution* 1996, C3)

IRA/NCTE Standards for English Language Arts

1. Students read a wide range of print and nonprint texts to build an understanding of texts, of themselves, and of the cultures of the United States and the world; to acquire new information; to respond to the needs and demands of society and the workplace; and for personal fulfillment. Among these texts are fiction and nonfiction, classic, and contemporary works.

2. Students read a wide range of literature from many periods in many genres to build an understanding of the many dimensions (e.g., philosophical, ethical, and aesthetic) of human experience.

3. Students apply a wide range of strategies to comprehend, interpret, evaluate, and appreciate texts. They draw on their prior experience, their interactions with other readers and writers, their knowledge of word meaning and of other texts, their word-identification strategies, and their understanding of textual features (e.g., sound/letter correspondence, sentence structure, context, and graphics).

4. Students adjust their use of spoken, written, and visual language (e.g., conventions, style, and vocabulary) to communicate effectively with a wide variety of audiences and for different purposes.

5. Students employ a wide range of strategies as they write and use different writing process elements appropriately to communicate with different audiences for a variety of purposes.

6. Students apply knowledge of language structure, language conventions (e.g., spelling and punctuation), media techniques, figurative language, and genre to create, critique, and discuss print and nonprint texts.

7. Students conduct research on issues and interests by generating ideas and questions and by posing problems. They gather, evaluate, and synthesize data from a variety of

sources (e.g., print and nonprint texts, artifacts, and people) to communicate their discoveries in ways that suit their purpose and audience.

8. Students use a variety of technological and informational resources (e.g., libraries, databases, computer networks, and video) to gather and synthesize information and to create and communicate knowledge.

9. Students develop an understanding of and respect for diversity in language use, patterns, and dialects across cultures, ethnic groups, geographic regions, and social roles.

10. Students whose first language is not English make use of their first language to develop competency in the English language arts and to develop understanding of content across the curriculum.

11. Students participate as knowledgeable, reflective, creative, and critical members of a variety of literacy communities.

12. Students use spoken, written, and visual language to accomplish their own purposes (e.g., for learning, enjoyment, persuasion, and the exchange of information). (National Council of Teachers of English and International Reading Association 1996, 3)

NEO-LIBERAL LITERACY

Advocates of weaker versions of restricted-opportunity explanations of poverty identify the failures of social institutions to serve the general public adequately. Under such conditions, only those individuals who already possess cultural and economic capital can spend it wisely in order to prosper. The rest are systematically denied access to the material conditions of success. The poor differ from the rest of us only in that they possess the least adaptable skills to meet the demands of the global economy. They are the least ready to go roaring and united into the twenty-first century. Only if they are unwilling to be responsible and to grab their opportunities do they then become a social burden. According to neo-liberals, schools fail to serve the economy, the government, and the individual. That is, schools are not equipped philosophically or financially to produce workers who are able to keep pace with the growing global economic competition. Employing functionalist logic to change schools in order to improve the skills of individual workers, neo-liberals call upon the federal government and philanthropic foundations to exert pressure upon school personnel to rise to this challenge. Both these social institutions have complied during the last fifteen years, but have been successful only in bringing the neo-liberal business agenda to the center of discussions about schooling in America. Clearly, with their willingness to use the needs of business as the primary criteria for political decisions, neo-liberals pursue a course in support of private democracy.

These successes began by selling the notion that schools are not serving the public; they continued through the identification of a reading crisis; and now they have settled in the struggle between business and the education bureaucracy to bethe savior of schools, children, and, ultimately, society. They have spawned such apparently disparate positions as Hirsch's cultural literacy, which attempts to specify exactly what should be known and when, and the IRA/NCTE Standards for English Language Arts, which does not. In between rests a variety of research studies and instructional practices that seek to find a general fix for a part or all of the reading crisis in order that all may be served better through schooling. Professional journals and magazines are replete with articles intended to effect the teaching of reading for all children, increasing their chances for academic and then economic success.

What pulls these attempts together is the unquestioned belief that America suffers from a reading crisis, the idea that it affects all Americans and threatens our economic welfare, and the notion that a national solution for it is not only warranted but possible. That solution, a fully literate society based on some set criteria, will bring economic and social prosperity to us all and raise the standard of living among the poor. The logic within the neo-liberal position may be sound, but the premises on which it is based are subject to much debate. Many charge that the reading crisis is largely a myth based on the wishful thinking that American businesses demand sophisticated literacy from their workers.

In *The Manufactured Crisis: Myth, Fraud, and the Attack on America's Public Schools*, Berliner and Biddle (1995) report that, according to the NAEP's own data, there has been virtually no decline in reading-test scores during the last generation.

Table 6–1 Neo-Liberals on Poverty: Definition, Causes, Commentators, and Reading Solution

NEO-LIBERAL
Income below the poverty line and lack of job-related skills.
Lack of opportunity to acquire well-paying job because general institutional structure is inadequate to meet demands of global economy. Too many people compete for poor-paying jobs.
Bill & Hillary Clinton Mark Tucker E. D. Hirsch Lauren Resnick P. David Pearson
High academic standards and state and national testing will force schools to improve general performance for all citizens. Even the poor will be able to compete for high-skill/high-wage jobs.

Moreover, scores for Hispanic and black students have increased significantly during that time, although they still lag behind white students. Rural and disadvantaged urban students also lag behind wealthier and suburban students in reading. When pushed, government officials concede this fact, but they still cling to the idea that the skills levels of a generation ago are not appropriate for today's jobs. Berliner and Biddle explain that reading tests, by design, are written so that only a low percentage of students will reach the proficient and advanced levels of scores. If too many respondents correctly answer questions requiring sophisticated reasoning, then the item is eliminated from the test as one that doesn't discriminate

effectively. Therefore, the low percentages of American students scoring in the higher levels of these tests are an anticipated artifact of the way in which such tests are written, not
necessarily an indication of respondents' literacy performance.
Finally, Berliner and Biddle suggest that the public should not
confuse in-school reasoning with out-of-school reasoning.

> Studies have appeared concerning second graders who sell chewing
> gum on the streets of lesser developed countries. These children
> estimate their market, determine markup, factor in inflation rates,
> determine sales prices, compute discount rates for big purchases,
> and make change for big bills. But the same children fail in
> standard tests because they do not know how to solve the in-school
> problems with approved in-school algorithms. Students with
> "street smart" mathematical skills often do poorly with some
> NAEP questions. (30)

Others argue that businesses do not use the literacy their
employees already possess. Hull (1993) challenges the popular
notion that workers are deficient in basic skills, which then
prevents them from performing well in their current jobs. By
visiting workers in their workplaces and interviewing them
about the literacy demands of their work, she found that most
job tasks require simple literacy skills of identification and
listing. She concluded that workers' literacy skills are, in fact,
under-utilized in factories, offices, and service institutions.
Noble (1994) used a National Center on Education and the
Economy report, *America's Choice: High Skills or Low
Wages*, against the neo-liberal argument about workers' inadequate literacy. "the National Center's Commission on Workforce Skills found that ninety-five percent of America's
employers still use Taylorist production methods requiring of
most workers less than an eighth-grade education and minimal training" (18). The Sandia Report (Carson, Huelskamp,
and Woodall 1991), which was commissioned and then
shelved by the Bush Administration, puts job-skill requirements in some perspective by listing the five most important
attributes mentioned by employers in two surveys. In Michigan, employers seek employees who don't abuse substances,
are honest, follow directions, respect others, and show up for
work. In Rochester, New York, employers changed only one
attribute: rather than honesty, they seek employees who

follow their safety rules. The least important attributes in both studies included mathematics, social sciences, natural sciences, computer programming, foreign languages, and art.

Without the reading crisis or demanding workplaces, the neo-liberal arguments lose much of their steam. In fact, given the opportunity, most Americans can communicate with one another, they can meet the daily demands on their literacy, and they are not holding back the American economy. This, of course, is not to say that every American can use language in the ways that the IRA or the NCTE propose; clearly, they cannot. But it is to say that the neo-liberal rationale for helping people in general to become literate is suspect. Helping everyone become more sophisticated in their uses of literacy will not save the economy from global competition. Moreover, the notion that general literacy solutions will aid the poor indirectly is dubious. They may, however, help the rich get richer as new skills blend with old advantages (Gee, Hull, and Lankshear 1996).

Using the presidency as a bully pulpit because the federal government has few legal rights concerning public education, President Clinton pressed his neo-liberal values into public policy. In the Glenbrook, Illinois, high school auditorium on January 22, 1997, President Clinton stated, "to pretend that somehow . . . agreeing that there has to be some uniform way of measuring [student performance] is giving up local control is just an excuse to avoid being held accountable." On February 14, 1997, during his State of the Union Address, President Clinton called for a national examination in reading for all students at the end of fourth grade. He recommended the NAEP as the designated test, making its rubric the default national curriculum for reading. However, federally mandated neo-liberal reading education will not deliver all of us roaring and united into the twenty-first century.

SEVEN

COME ON UP, I'VE GOT A LIFELINE
Reading Targeted Programs

In *When Work Disappears: The World of the New Urban Poor,* Harvard sociologist William Julius Wilson offers a stronger, liberal version of the restricted-opportunity explanation for poverty. According to this position, economic, social, and cultural structures of American life prevent the poor and other marginalized groups from equal participation in the negotiation of their life's possibilities. That is, biases based on race, class, and gender are encoded systematically in institutional policies, procedures, and practices that discriminate against members of racial and linguistic minorities, the poor, and women. In this way, general solutions to social crises cannot possibly alleviate the problems of the poor because they mask the effects of these biases and, at best, maintain current economic, social, and political inequalities. Liberals argue that general solutions often make things worse for the poor. For example, the Clinton Administration's attempts to improve the general economy in order to increase the incomes of the poor by balancing the federal budget through spending cuts have hurt rather than helped the poor. Although low income programs comprise only twenty-one percent of the federal budget, they have incurred sixty-seven percent of the cuts during his first administration.

> This retreat from public policy as a way to alleviate problems of social inequality will have profound negative consequences for the future of disadvantaged groups such as the ghetto poor. High levels of joblessness, growing wage inequality, and the related social problems discussed in this book are complex and have their sources in fundamental economic, social, and cultural changes. They therefore require bold, comprehensive, and thoughtful solutions, not simplistic and pious statements about the need for greater personal responsibility. Progressives who are concerned about the current social conditions of the have-nots and the future generation of have-nots not only have to fight against the current public-policy strategies, they also are morally obligated to offer alternative strategies designed to alleviate, not exacerbate, the plight of the poor, the jobless, and other disadvantaged citizens of America. (Wilson 1996, 209)

Addressing his liberal obligation to propose strategies to overcome effects of discrimination and poverty, Wilson provides long- and short-term solutions. Among the long-term ones—those that will take years to have a positive impact upon the poor—he applauds the neo-liberal interest in setting rigorous

academic standards that will prepare all students for the jobs of
the twenty-first century. However, he places this interest
within the current inequalities among schools across America.
He argues that if national academic standards are not going to
become one more way in which to measure the failures of poor
and working-class students, then schools that serve predomi-
nantly poor families will require additional support. Linda
Darling-Hammond, Dean of the School of Education at Co-
lumbia University, asks, "Can the mere issuance of standards
really propel improvements in schooling, or are there other
structural issues to contend with—issues such as funding,
teachers' knowledge and capacities, access to curriculum resources, and dysfunctional school structures?" (1994, 480). Wilson contends that such issues are more acute for inner-city and
rural schools. In a report given before a Senate subcommittee
on poverty, Rotberg and Harvey put it this way:

> More often than not, the "best" teachers, including experienced
> teachers, offered greater choice in school assignment because
> of their seniority, avoid high-poverty schools. As a result, low-
> income and minority students have less contact with the best
> qualified and more experienced teachers, the teachers most often
> likely to master the kinds of instructional strategies considered
> effective for all students. (1993, 52)

Rotberg and Harvey suggest that the most effective methods to
teach all students are already in place within schools serving
middle- and upper-class students. Lack of access to these effective methods keeps the poor from academic and, later, job
success. Although this position shares some common features
with that of neo-liberals—a standard solution for all, a
scientific and business-like orientation toward their concern,
and a faith in schooling to address social problems—Rotberg
and Harvey's argument centers on their belief that only the
poor lack sufficient literacy capabilities to make their way in
the world. Moreover, they imply that more should be done to
improve the chances of the poor to compete in and out of
school. They show their liberal stripes by first avoiding the
conservative temptation of blame the victim and then, second,
by pointing toward institutional shortcomings as the cause of
the isolated literacy problems. According to Rotberg and
Harvey, the poor don't learn to read well because schools do not
provide them with the same curriculum or instruction as they

do for their more well-to-do counterparts. They suggest that this failure is not because poor schools lack standards or policies equal to others, rather, they identify an inferior quality in human resources in poor schools as the problem.

SEARCHING FOR THE BEST METHOD TO TEACH THE POOR TO READ

The best method for teaching reading is a subject of much debate among liberal educators. That debate carries over into liberals' concern for how literacy can help the poor. For example, teachers and literacy researchers debate where to start their curriculum, whether to teach content directly, and what constitutes success. These struggles have caused a good bit of heat recently with featured articles in professional journals (e.g., *Education Week* and *Teacher*), popular magazines (e.g., *Atlantic Monthly* and *U.S. News and World Report*), and news media (e.g., *20/20* and *Los Angeles Times*). State legislatures debate regularly whether to mandate one particular method for all school classrooms—often overriding recommendations of the state's Department of Education (e.g., Ohio, Texas, and Arizona).

In *The Reading Crisis: Why Poor Children Fall Behind*, Chall, Jacobs, and Baldwin report their study to ascertain the causes of "the apparent slippage in lower-class students' academic progress as they pass through the elementary school grades" (1990, 8). They conclude that lower-class students rely too heavily on context when reading, writing, and using language, which prevents them from meeting the increased demands on oral and written language in later grades and the workplace. They offer four recommendations that would reestablish standard practices of teachers before the Second World War:

1. early teaching of systematic explicit phonics (149)
2. direct instruction in spelling, grammar, and punctuation (152)
3. the use of basal reading textbooks and workbooks (154–155)

4. that parents of lower-class students should spend time with their children, establish good relations with schools, and seek reading clinics when schools won't or don't help (158–160)

There are several variations on this general theme, ranging from Beriter and Englemann's *Distar* program, which begins with modified letters and symbols to convert English orthography into a completely alphabetic system, hand signals to elicit student response, and instructional scripts for teachers, to Clay's *Reading Recovery* program, which relies completely on a carefully trained teacher to make informed decisions during a standardized instructional routine with one student at a time. In between those extremes are several code-based programs targeted at the poor, or the currently acceptable euphemism for poverty, "at risk." These programs are interventions into the schooling and sometimes homes of students who are at risk of not learning to read sufficiently well to accomplish the tasks at school and, later, at work (Hiebert and Taylor 1994). Most advocates of these programs are careful not to appear to be proposing the conservative flawed-character explanation. "We are not suggesting that poor or minority children should be the focus of early reading interventions. Indeed, many children who are poor or from minority groups come to school with rich literacy backgrounds and high levels of literacy. What we are arguing for, however, is that all children, especially poor children who might have had insufficient access to high-quality early reading interventions in school, are in need of such help" (Hiebert and Taylor 1994, 4).

Attention to skills and direct instruction do not end with intervention into young children's schooling (Anderson 1989). To maintain the impact of the early interventions, poor and minority students require explicit help in learning the complexities of grammar, text organization, and style to enable them to master the power codes that middle- and upper-class students seem to acquire and use apart from school (Cope and Kalantzis 1993). This help takes the form of fixed strategies in which students learn when and how to find main ideas (e.g., Baumann 1984), to summarize the ideas of others (Brown and Day 1983), and to answer someone else's questions about a text (Raphael 1984). With these interventions, advocates believe that participants are no longer at risk of failure at school or work.

Not everyone agrees that learning to read starts with the alphabetic code. Dahl, Freppon, and Purcell-Gates collaborated on a series of studies that compare kindergarten and first-grade students' written language use and knowledge in classrooms that featured either a code-based or a meaning-centered orientation. They found a great number of similarities in learning outcomes among students experiencing either type of curricula, leading them to question Chall's and others' previous findings. Moreover, they found that students from meaning-centered classrooms "expressed extensive interest in themselves as literacy learners" (Dahl and Freppon 1995, 70), and they concluded that some children within the code-based programs "did not weave together the cloth of literacy" (Purcell-Gates and Dahl 1991, 21). Based on their investigations, they argue that uses of meaning and context do not injure or retard poor students' language or literacy learning or use, and they suggested that poor children who begin their schooling interested in books and who think of themselves as readers and writers, while mindful of their strengths and weaknesses, have better chances to persevere through the trials and tribulations of schooling and to make it in the world of work.

In the introduction to the book, *Engaging Children: Community and Chaos in the Lives of Young Literacy Learners,* Allen, Michalove, and Shockley (1994) name the meaning-centered approach and describe their hopes for its promise. They label their teaching "whole language" and express their interest in changing their and their students lives in their classrooms. "Teachers felt that in spite of efforts to help all children to be successful in the school's curriculum, many children were not succeeding to their fullest potential. . . . They felt the prime culprit was the inflexibility and inappropriateness of the reading and language-arts textbook curriculum, especially as commonly practiced in the district: Early ability grouping, basal-determined promotional guidelines, sequenced skills instruction, and little opportunity for reading and writing for meaningful purposes" (1994, 3). Rather, they based their reading program for poor children on seven principles:

1. When children are just getting started, they learn best by going from meaning to code.
2. When children are immersed in a community that values reading and writing, they will value reading and writing also.
3. All learning must make sense to and be purposeful for each student.
4. Children who "fail" in school also have been failed by the school.
5. Sufficient time must be allotted for reading, writing, and talking about both each day.
6. Children should be responsible for their own learning, particularly the ones who view themselves as failures.
7. Children must view themselves as valued members of a literate community if they are to take the necessary risks to learn to read and write at school.

Beyond the primary grades, students are encouraged to pose their own questions and to use reading to address them (Short, Harste, and Burke 1996). This inquiry method features the utility of reading by placing it in the service of the students' questions. By recognizing the various purposes for reading, the poor develop the same understanding of the power of literacy as their more well-to-do peers, while at the same time they work to control its complexities. Because the questions are their own, students become responsible for both the content and the depth of their learning. In this environment, the teacher helps students progress toward sophisticated reading practices by reacting to students' attempts to address their inquiries and to gain control over their reading. From this point of view, student-centered, meaning-based inquiries make students better learners at school and prepare them for the high-skill/high-wage jobs of the twenty-first century waiting for them in our post-industrial, information-based global economy.

Although advocates of both code-based and meaning-centered approaches share the liberal belief that (1) the best method is necessary for the poor to overcome institutional barriers to learning to read and write, and (2) scientific investigations will arbitrate among alternatives strategies, they disagree stridently over what constitutes science evidence and academic success.

Neither Delpit nor I denigrate the heritage or language of children from minority culture groups, nor do we deny the need for multicultural education in the truest sense (i.e., for members of all cultural groups within society). From different perspectives, we both are concerned about the inequality of leaving children from outside the mainstream to figure out what they need to know without some direct instruction. Marginalized children need public education even more than do mainstream children. Mainstream children, if they don't establish themselves through scholarship or hard work, can always get a job from "Uncle Frank." If poor children fail to develop the reading and writing skills that they need to be productive members of mainstream society, there is generally no "Uncle Frank" to give them a job. (Stahl 1994, 137)

Traditional approaches to literacy instruction can fetter students, not liberate them. Mastery of traditional literacy instruction sometimes permits access to certain societal resources. But these traditional curricula depend on one single interpretation of one prescribed text; the use of conventional Standard English as the only criterion for evaluation of writing; and the standardized, multiple-choice reading tests, which have only one right answer per item, as the passport to the next grade. Therefore, these literacy curricula inordinately favor speakers from middle and upper classes; from dominant groups who simply "acquire" Standard English at home, as contrasted with those who have to "learn" it deliberately in school. Prescribed texts and standard conventions tend to be seen as the only "true" texts and conventions, as "natural" rather than constructed or chosen. No wonder these curricula tend to maintain, rather than improve, the status of subordinate groups. Members of such groups are held behind "gates" in elementary grades, kept from graduating high school by "competency" tests, and reminded one last time (if they didn't understand before) when they score poorly on the standardized tests in adult basic education (ABE) classes, that they do not belong in the mainstream. . . . The choice between accepting and rejecting assimilation into the dominant culture is muffled in a Whole Language classroom, since the home cultures of all students are welcomed there. (Harman and Edelsky 1989, 393 and 395)

INTERVENTIONS AT SCHOOL AND IN HOMES

Because institutions have systematically discriminated against the poor in the past, liberals advocate proactive and reactive interventions to ensure that the poor have access to the best available methods of teaching reading. These interventions target pregnant women, infants and toddlers, preschoolers, schoolchildren of all ages, dropouts, adults, and their families. Some interventions require strict regimens to disrupt what is deemed damaging behavior; others seek to change basic patterns of behavior slowly over time. These interventions are legion. For example, the federal government sponsors no less than twenty such programs through six departments to help poor children enter school on an equal social and intellectual footing with their middle- and upper-class peers.

U.S. Department of Agriculture
1. Special Supplemental Nutrition Programs for Women, Infants, and Children
2. Food Stamps
3. Child and Adult Care Food Programs
4. Food Safety Inspection
5. National Extension Parent Education Model
6. Forest Service in Inner Cities
7. Child Youth Family Education and Research Network

U.S. Department of Justice
1. Operation Weed and Seed
2. Public and Private Partnerships Against Violence
3. Title V Delinquency Prevention
4. Race Against Drugs

U.S. Department of Defense
1. Sure Start
2. Families and Schools Together
3. Immunization Programs
4. Family Advocacy New Parent Support Program

U.S. Department of Education
1. Even Start Family Literacy
2. Title I (ESEA)
3. Bilingual Program, Program Development Implementation Grants

U.S. Department of Housing and Urban Development
1. Family Investment Centers
2. Public Housing Preschool Programs (Head Start)

U.S. Department of Health and Family Services
1. Head Start

Beyond providing some measure of food, shelter, and safety, these federal interventions attempt to rectify past inequalities in service to the poor by helping families acquire the skills necessary for school, parenting, and job success. The programs are clearly focused on family life.

> It has become increasingly clear that any family's stability and pro-
> ductivity are linked not only to employment and employability, but
> also to the education levels of family members. Some early-
> childhood programs like Head Start and Even Start were designed to
> "break the cycle" before it began. Current family-literacy research
> and practices focus attention on the proposition that the cycle of
> deprivation and distress that so often accompanies lower levels of
> literacy skills could at the very least be mitigated by effective inter-
> vention. (U.S. Department of Education, Office of Education
> Research and Improvement 1996, 1)

Head Start and Project Follow Through offer the longest running debate about the most effective intervention. In 1964,
Head Start programs were designed to better prepare poor children for elementary school. At their outset, they were summer
programs, six to eight weeks in duration, which were expected
to permanently raise the IQs of participants. During its second
year, the Head Start format became a year-round endeavor. The
initial legislation established controlled competitions among
models to decide objectively which model was the best. These
competitions were conducted concerning immediate impact
and to follow graduates of Head Start programs through their
early elementary years. Using a series of measures of academic,
social, and health indicators, these studies suggested that code-
based programs had the greatest initial impact on poor children's academic readiness for traditional school (Becker 1977).
However, these advantages disappeared as poor children who
had not attended a Head Start program caught up during elementary school years. Child-centered and meaning-based programs claimed important positive effects on socialization
among the poor concerning criminality, family structure, and
career success (Schweinhart, Barnes, and Weikart 1993). Results of these studies are unequivocal only on the issue of
health. Graduates of Head Start programs, regardless of the
model, have better health, immunization rates, nutrition, and
socioemotional characteristics (Zigler and Styfco 1994).

The absence of dramatic, permanent academic effects
from school-based programs has redirected educators' attention toward family environments and their conduciveness to
continuously support children's development. Head Start programs now have compulsory home-visit programs in which
parents must become their children's first teacher and devote

time each day helping them learn. To accomplish this, Project Even Start linked adult academic training with preschool education to enable parents to fill the role as first teacher. Senator John Chafee from Rhode Island provided the rationale for this new intervention at a Senate Hearing in 1986:

The Even Start Act is based on the belief that illiteracy, like many of our society's worst problems, begins in the home. Most illiterate adults are not being reached by existing adult education programs and many of them inadvertently are passing on illiteracy to their children. Raised in houses in which reading is never done, the children of illiterates often begin school at a disadvantage, quickly fall behind their classmates, and cannot turn to their parents for help because their parents can't read. (Hearing before the Committee on Education and Labor, 99th Congress, HR. 25–35 1986, 6)

The initial Even Start grants were awarded to expanded Head Start programs that sometimes made tenuous connections with adult literacy programs. For example, during 1989, Ola Even Start Project in Arkansas simply enhanced the home-instruction elements of their Head Start program to include twenty minutes of reading aloud to children during their regular home visits. Yet most others arranged networks between several adult and preschool programs. Lost Creek/West Milford Even Start program in West Virginia combined a school-based adult-education program that met four hours each day in an elementary school with a child-centered, meaning-based preschool program in the same building. The school-based instruction was continued through twice weekly home service during the summer months. Similar Even Start projects developed in Minnesota, Texas, Washington, and across the United States, many of them based on the Kenan Trust Model developed at the National Center for Family Literacy in Kentucky.

The National Center for Family Literacy began as a state-sponsored program for adult education during the 1980s. A large grant from the Kenan Trust Foundation enabled the Center to conduct a study to "break the cycles of illiteracy and poverty" by intervening in the lives of poor families. Members of the Center were and are convinced that

1. If literacy is to be increased and poverty reduced among the current generation of families, it is necessary to increase the educational skills of the parents.

2. If literacy is to be increased and poverty reduced among the next generation of families, it is necessary to increase the educational skills of the children beginning at an early age.

3. To increase education and reduce poverty for this generation and those that follow it, it is necessary to approach illiteracy as a family issue. (The National Center for Family Literacy 1994, 2)

Accordingly, the Center developed a model for family literacy training based on elements of early-childhood education, adult literacy training, parental support programs, and interaction therapy. The Kenan Trust Model required parents and children to visit a center to work with trained staff separately to acquire appropriate academic and social skills, and then to practice those skills with each other under the observation of staff members. Children's programs include traditional preschool curricula—following rules, segmenting the day by time, as well as early literacy activities of listening to stories, identifying letters and words, and choral reading. Parents were counseled, asked to work on their academic skills, and required to play with their children under staff supervision to facilitate school-like interactions later at home. Results of the study demonstrated success in helping adults with their academic skills, children with scores on school-readiness tests, and both groups with persistence in the program.

Despite these successes with poor families, the Center seems to worry about its ability to attract sufficient support from the general public to continue its programs. With remarkable candor, it plays to the self-interests of the middle and upper classes to garner this support through its promotional literature.

Twenty-five years from now, the baby-boom generation will be reaching retirement age. It will then be left to today's declining pool of young workers—an increasing proportion from poor and minority backgrounds—to drive the economy and create the wealth necessary to maintain America's prosperity and support the rest of us in our retirement. (The National Center for Family Literacy 1989, 5)

Denny Taylor, founder of the Progressive Center for Literacy Research, suggests that this pandering to self-interest is not just an attempt to open the purses of the middle and upper classes. Rather, she suggests that the Center's programs seem based, at least in part, on a conservative flawed-character, deficit model of both poverty and literacy. Following the liberal tradition, Taylor argues that the poor do not make their own poverty; rather, they are systematically denied access to sufficient services, jobs, and incomes to enable them to reach the working and middle classes. Moreover, she writes, "sixteen years of ethnographic research in families and communities have taught me that sex, race, economic status, and setting cannot be used as significant correlates of literacy" (Taylor 1993, 551). To increase educational opportunities for families, Taylor suggests that educators learn more about their students' family and community life and bring the lessons they learn into the elementary schools with them. To accomplish this, Taylor advocates for interventions that favor student-centered, meaning-based approaches to reading in preschool and elementary school classrooms—ones that also show more commitment to a restricted opportunity explanation of poverty than the National Center for Family Literacy currently demonstrates.

A QUESTION OF CULTURE

A second set of liberal research and programs within the stronger version of restricted opportunity suggests that characterizations of the poor and definitions of literacy have made the poor appear incapable of sophisticated thoughts or actions and, therefore, different from Americans of other social classes. Advocates of this position suggest that our impulse to intervene in the lives of the poor, whether to correct their flawed characters or to provide them with better services, has obscured our vision of poor peoples' capabilities and the viability of their literacy practices in the world.

Without a focus on social relationships and persons-in-activities, it is very easy for outsiders (educators) to under-estimate the wealth of funds of knowledge available in working-class households. Funds of knowledge are available regardless of families' years of formal schooling or prominence assigned to literacy. (Moll and Greenberg 1991, 327)

Heath (1992) demonstrates how poor, rural Southeastern families and communities construct and pass on knowledge and
literacy practices in order to meet the demands and opportunities of their lives. By examining the lives of white and black
working- and middle-class families, she points to the ways in
which language patterns form around the opportunities available to each group. Socialization of the young with family and
community patterns affords them the advantages of group
membership and opportunities for influence within those settings, but also constricts their chances to cross the borders
between social groups.

In a first set of examples, Heath describes how three communities construct rules of communication, a sense of time
and place, and conceptions of stories that differ from one another in important ways. These rules, social practices, and conceptions work well to make the young valued members of local
communities, but they serve the groups differently when children arrive at school. Schools seem to value only one set of
rules, one sense of time and place, and one view of stories.
Teachers rank social groups according to the number and size
of the differences from their implicit but largely consistent
standards.

White and black middle-class students fair much better in
school because their community socialization is the basis for
school practices. White working-class children seemed to
have the deportment of their middle-class counterparts, but
lacked the cognitive flexibility of the middle-class youth.
Black working-class youth bring the opposite socialization
with them to elementary school. They appear to be flexible
and fluent but unprepared for the expected behaviors. At
school, the differences in socialization are often understood as
deficits and become reasons for segregating groups to help
them close the gap between themselves and their middle-class
peers. At the end of *Ways with Words*, Heath (1983) suggests
that understanding difference through the study of various
ways of using language, time, space, and story would change
the class-based relationships in school classrooms, affording
the poor a more valued and equitable place to learn.

In a second set of examples from rural and urban socialization patterns within black communities, Heath demonstrates
how the rural communal patterns of language use prepares
them well for the new management schemes of group projects

and decision-making. That is, the reported language practices of high-skill/high-wage jobs that businesses seek—collaboration about meaning, compromise in turn-taking, creativity in form and response—are already standard among rural black community members. The very practices that elementary schools denigrate and then remediate to extinction are the ones that all students are expected to master in order to assume the high-skill/high-wage jobs that the neo-liberals believe will be available in quantities during the twenty-first century.

The irony of this outcome is not lost on others. Taylor and Dorsey-Gaines (1988) found sophisticated literacies among the homeless, unemployed, under-employed, and single-parent families in cities of the Northeast. Moll (1993) locates traditional ways in which knowledge of the world, work, and word are passed back and forth among generations in the Southwest. Both describe how teachers, schools, and educational bureaucracies often misunderstand and discount these strengths among the poor. Brodkey (1992) illustrates how traditional schooling, which privileges abstracted knowledge and skills above all others, separates teachers and poor students from one another at all levels. Because the poor display their knowledge, support for others, and literacies in culturally specific and socially contextualized ways, they are considered empty vessels at best or vessels filled with the wrong types of human capital at worst. In these ways, the accepted definitions of literacy and schooling are complicit in discrimination against the poor.

Rather than proposing further interventions into the lives of the poor, these and other researchers and educators work to find ways that the lives of the poor can intervene in the day-to-day practices of schooling. They begin with contextualized notions of literacy practices (Solskin 1993)—abandoning the abstract singular definitions of literacy that kept the poor from full participation in schoolwork. With broader parameters for acceptable practices, schools accommodate the funds of knowledge of the poor and extend those funds with knowledge and literacies of other social groups. For example, Au's work (1993) with Hawaiian children offers a balance-of-rights model for classroom practices, which alter the interaction patterns between teachers and students to encourage greater student participation. Lee (1995) reports how African American adolescents' patterns of using language expressively can be tied directly to their understanding of and responding to literature.

Many researchers and educators provide ways to bring gender and social class to the center of literacy and school curricula through reading and writing about students' lives (e.g., Cherland 1994; Christian-Smith 1993; Finders 1996).

Far from being retreats from the standards and rigors of traditional classrooms, these reverse interventions attempt to interrupt traditional teaching assumptions and practices in order to challenge discrimination within literacy education and provide unrestricted opportunities for academic success in school and employment. For if schools can become inviting and effective places in which the poor feel valued and learn, then they are more likely to engage students in the new activities and events sponsored at school. In turn, those engagements would increase the human capital of the poor, improving their chances for later employment in beyond poverty-level wages. The liberal intent of these new culturally sensitive programs remains the same even when the sponsored activities and events change—unrestrictive schools and literacy programs are still expected to add sufficient value to individuals in order to end their poverty.

LIBERAL LITERACY

Liberals provide a broad array of alternatives to help the poor overcome discrimination—from skill interventions into home life to tightly sequenced skill programs at school to meaning-based programs and reverse interventions—to bring students' everyday literacy practices into classrooms. Despite the apparent variety, virtually all liberals subscribe to a similar set of values. For example, liberals accept many neo-liberal assumptions about the future: our lives are changing at greater rates of speed, certainties of the past are no longer secure, and competition seems more harsh than before. Yet liberals and neo-liberals read the present with different lenses, leading them to derive different meaning from various social texts. Neo-liberals seem willing to sacrifice all for the general advance of the American economy and national unity around that goal. Accordingly, neo-liberals can support the end of the federal guaranteed income for poor children because of its expense; capital-gains taxes can be cut for amounts over $600,000 because the government won't use the money to improve the economy; and affirmative action can be curtailed because it interferes with business efficiency. Liberals cannot support these actions, however, and they focus on the consequences of these new realities for those who have been dealt with harshly in the past. Liberals cast a more humane eye upon the poor, recognizing how past injustices have isolated them from the rest of society, impeding their ability to prepare themselves

Table 7–1 Liberals on Poverty: Definition, Causes, Commentators, and Reading Solution

LIBERAL
Income below the poverty line and social and psychological malaise.
Institutional, social, and private discrimination based on race, class, and
gender restricts the poor's life opportunities.
Rebecca Blank William Julius Wilson Linda Darling-Hammond Jeanne Chall Ken Goodman
Targeting the best practices of teaching reading at the poor. Schools can prepare the poor to compete for well-paying jobs when anti-discrimination policies in employment are enforced.

for the future. Following the functionalist traditions of the New Deal and the Great Society, liberals seek to ameliorate these inequalities through government and private interventions so that all Americans may compete for success on a more equal footing. For all their efforts to help the poor, they do not move beyond the limits of private democracy.

A brief history of Title I educational intervention of the ESEA, the largest federal education program, offers a view of the political nature of reading policies directed toward the poor. Title I programs were created in 1965 as a main thrust of President Johnson's liberal War on Poverty. They were intended to improve school services to children living in poverty and, ultimately, to end the culture of poverty. True to the conservative project to reverse social legislation of the 1960s, Ronald Reagan reduced funding for Title I and "drastically pared" the restrictions on the use of Title I funds during his first term in office (Johnston 1994, 41). The newly named Chapter One failed to close the learning gap between poor and middle-class students. "The test scores in high-poverty schools started lower than in low-poverty schools and the gap increased slightly over the next five years" (Hoff 1997b, 53). Moreover, substantial amounts of Chapter One funds found their way into wealthy communities. For example, more than $138 million was allocated to the twenty richest counties in America (Hoff 1997a, 37).

In 1994, during its assault on the "Reagan Revolution," the Clinton Administration revised the rules of the ESEA apparently redirecting it toward its original purpose. Undersecretary of Education Marshall Smith stated, "Our sense was Title I stood for support of the disadvantaged, and the change to Chapter One stripped that away" (as quoted in Johnston 1994, 41). However, the Clinton Administration has stamped its own neo-liberal imprint on the newly retitled Title I intervention. The new Title I discourages pulling individual students out of classrooms to provide remediation. Rather, it encourages schools to use the funds to provide a general upgrading of their reading programs in regular classrooms. In schools with poverty rates of more than fifty percent, administrators may use Title I funds exclusively to raise the general achievement of the student body. In fact, program evaluation now will focus on the effectiveness of school reform rather than on individual achievement. In these ways, Title I interventions have been redirected toward the general reading crisis, targeting the skills of all students to prepare them for the global economy.

Although the current iteration of Title I blurs its focus on the poor, the program retains the liberal assumption that the best instructional practices will raise reading-test scores and improve educational prospects of targeted individuals. The zealous pursuit of higher scores implies that liberal educators and policymakers take higher test scores among the poor as a direct indication that the income gap between classes will close. Each new challenger for the crown of "best practice" must prove its mettle by demonstrating how it can raise the test scores of the poor higher and faster. For example, in 1996, because students' test scores fell to the bottom in state-by-state comparisons, the California Department of Instruction reversed its ten-year curricular project to promote and employ its version of meaning-based instruction by mandated systematic skills instruction (Honig 1996). These lower scores plunged California liberals back into an acrimonious debate over best practices in teaching reading, undercutting their authority with the public as, once again, they do not have consensus about a reading program to meet the country's needs.

Lost in the din of such arguments is the questionable assumption on which most of the liberal position is based— that science will decide what ought to be our response to poverty. Frankly, if test scores were truly predictive of later economic success, then women could expect to earn more than men. Certainly, their reading scores are higher throughout most of their schooling. There is nothing scientific about the social practices of women being paid seventy percent of men's salaries. While liberals have identified institutionalized discrimination as a primary cause of poverty, they seem reluctant to consider structural changes to those institutions. They appear willing to accept the cultural and economic inequalities endemic to the American economic and political systems. For example, rather than reconsider what schools and reading education are for, in schools they examine methods of instruction. To consider these changes, liberals must explore their moral convictions about what they value most in America, and then work to bring those convictions to bear on their everyday lives.

EIGHT

EVERYBODY LOOK WHAT'S GOIN' DOWN

Reading Educational Functionalism and Rereading Poverty in America

Despite the apparent differences among the various expressions of possible relationships between reading and poverty, most follow the same functionalist logic. Regardless of their political position, most theorize reading as a tool for school and, later, economic success. Although many qualify their equation with variables such as literary appreciation, lifelong learning, teacher and student accountability, and even discrimination, most still end up with a pretty straight line between literacy and employment and the maintenance of the economic, cultural, and political status quo. Accordingly, the rationale for reading education, just like the general rationales for aid to the poor, is clear—increased funding for reading programs will reduce the long-term costs of social services, increase per capita productivity, and improve lives.

Conservatives offer a natural explanation for poverty based on genetically fixed intelligence and tempered with notions that people respond to incentives and disincentives, they are not inherently hardworking or moral, and they must be held accountable. Although genetic endowments cannot be altered and, therefore, economic positions cannot be changed, reading programs can be organized to meet the relative intellectual and social needs of all individuals. In this way, individuals' knowledge of their place in the world and of how to be satisfied within that place can be taught to them during reading education at school. As Bloom suggested, there are literacies for the intellectual elite that should not be mediated by the popular culture of the masses (Bloom 1987). If they are to become leaders in economic and cultural life, then these intelligent individuals must be taught to judge others according to the cultural standards of previous elites. Individuals with middle and lower intellectual capacities can be taught to value elite culture and to add their own cultural contributions, although their economic compensation for these acts may be meager. During these lessons, the less able must also learn to put forth their best efforts at their jobs and in their communities regardless of extrinsic rewards. Toward those ends, the content and form of reading education can be fit to any intellectual capacity so that all will be prepared to take their places in the American economy.

Neo-conservatives begin from a somewhat different set of assumptions and offer a different solution through reading education. Although poverty is still assumed to be the result of

flaws in an individual's makeup, it is not considered a consequence of nature. Rather, individuals are poor because they
have flawed characters, not necessarily flawed minds. These
character flaws—laziness, responsibility, lust, indulgence—are
learned behaviors in cultures of poverty that misshape the
poor's behavior. Within corrected environments, however, the
poor can overcome these flaws and work their way out of poverty by taking and persisting in the jobs made available to
them. Reading education is a primary means by which this
culture of poverty, what Bennett refers to as moral poverty, can
be corrected one individual at a time. Through a steady diet of
purposefully selected texts and carefully led discussions of
what these texts mean, the morally, economically poor can be
helped to become productive, model citizens. Because the
moral poverty begot the economic poverty, the virtuous reader
is transformed simultaneously into the virtuous worker.

Neo-liberals reject the character-flaw explanations of poverty, and maintain a position that poverty results from
restricted opportunities to succeed economically. They place
poverty in a social context in which all Americans face several
crises, which must be prioritized and addressed in proper
sequence. Two crises are at the top of their list. First, Americans are unprepared to triumph in the dazzling competition of
a global economy. If not corrected, this lack of preparation
will continue to reduce all Americans' standard of living. To
address this crisis, Americans must remake all schools in the
image of the projected business organizations of the future—
organizations that are flexible to meet the demands of ever-
changing markets. In these remade schools, according to
Emig, Pearson, Myers, and others, all students will be taught
according to the same high standards and will be tested to
ensure that they have mastered them. Mastery will enable all
individuals, even the poor, to compete for and perform at the
high-skill/high-wage jobs that await them as America tri-
umphs in the economy of the twenty-first century. Reading
education, then, is identified as the linchpin to enable this
restructuring process to start and succeed. The second crisis
facing America is a national identity and spirit that will
empower us to tackle the first crisis. Accordingly, President
Clinton asks all Americans to Stand for Children and to Volunteer for America to ensure that all children can read a book
by the end of second grade.

Table 8–1 Private Democratic Political Ideologies on Poverty

	CONSERVATIVE	NEO-CONSERVATIVE	NEO-LIBERAL	LIBERAL
What is poverty?	Low income without achieving personal satisfaction through civic involvement.	Inability to be responsible for self or family. Poor life choices lead to low incomes.	Income below the poverty line and lack of job-related skills.	Income below the poverty line and social and psychological malaise.
What is its cause?	Low intelligence because of poor genetic endowment inhibits ability to compete for adequate income. Government policy to ameliorate problems exacerbates them.	Lack of moral character prevents poor from making good (middle-class) choices for behavior. With inappropriate morals, can't compete for jobs with sufficient incomes.	Lack of opportunity to acquire well-paying job because general institutional structure is inadequate to meet demands of global economy. Too many people compete for poor-paying jobs.	Institutional, social, and private discrimination based on race, class, and gender restricts poor's life opportunities.
Who advocates this stance?	Richard Herrnstein Charles Murray Thomas Sowell Lawrence Mead Allan Bloom	Joe Klein James Q. Wilson Glenn Loury William Bennett Mark Gerson	Bill & Hillary Clinton Mark Tucker E. D. Hirsch Lauren Resnick P. David Pearson	Rebecca Blank William Julius Wilson Linda Darling-Hammond Jeanne Chall Ken Goodman

Table 8–1 Private Democratic Political Ideologies on Poverty (continued)

	CONSERVATIVE	NEO-CONSERVATIVE	NEO-LIBERAL	LIBERAL
How is reading education involved in solution?	By tracking reading education to IQ of individual, all can prepare properly to perform role consonant with genetic endowment. Content of texts will teach the poor to value ascribed stations in life.	Reading education for moral literacy will correct moral poverty in America, which in turn will end all social problems and correct economic poverty.	High academic standards and state and national testing will force schools to improve general performance for all citizens. Even the poor will be able to compete for high-skill/high-wage jobs.	Targeting the best practices of teaching reading at the poor. Schools can prepare the poor to compete for well-paying jobs when anti-discrimination policies in employment are enforced.

Liberals acknowledge the restricted opportunities as the cause of poverty, but they recognize the limits of the "something for everyone" solutions to poverty that neo-liberals propose. In fact, Blank and other liberals question the authenticity of neo-liberals' concern for the poor (Blank 1997). To help the poor, liberals argue that the federal government must intervene to reduce if not eliminate discriminatory institutional practices that limit economic possibilities of the poor. According to Wilson, strict enforcement of laws and policy against racism, sexism, and classism must be coupled with programs that target the poor to receive equal opportunities as their more well-to-do peers (Wilson 1996). In many instances, this means that programs must compensate for past discrimination to enable the poor to take advantage of current economic opportunities. According to Chall, Goodman, and others, fundamental to these compensation projects is the effort to make the best practices of teaching reading available to the poor. These practices will enable the poor to learn to read and to succeed at school and, when accompanied by the enforcement of anti-discrimination laws, they will empower the poor to enter the job market on an equal footing with other Americans.

Ignoring the fact that most of the poor already work, conservative, neo-conservative, neo-liberal, and liberal solutions to poverty are based on the assumption that there are jobs waiting for the intelligent, virtuous, and skilled poor to acquire (Hornbeck and Solomon 1991). Moreover, they assume that these jobs will pay sufficiently well to enable poor individuals and their families to work their way above the official poverty line. According to this line of reasoning, without the availability of good jobs, literacy and schooling lose all functional value for the society and the poor. That is, if a surplus of well-paying jobs is not available in the American economy, the poor cannot change their economic status regardless of their intelligence, character, literacy skills, or schooling. Without well-paying jobs, it doesn't matter in which ways advocates of functionalist solutions rearrange existing social institutions. Studies of school dropouts suggest that some social groups have already received this message (e.g., Fine 1991).

Despite government rhetoric to the contrary, the U.S. economy is not producing enough good jobs to end poverty. Moreover, the majority of new jobs do not pay enough to enable the poor to crawl over the poverty line permanently.

Even a former U.S. Secretary of Labor holds this to be true; Robert Reich has "a profound sense that economic forces are out of control—that neither hard work nor general economic improvement will lead to higher incomes" (as quoted in Freidman 1995, E9). Government policies, such as the exchange of workfare for welfare and the North Atlantic Free Trade Agreement, do not offer the poor much assistance in their plight and appear to sacrifice their future for the benefit of business. If all this is true, where does it leave the poor? And if jobs are not waiting, where does it leave schooling and reading education? To consider these questions, however, we must first gain some understanding of the jobs available and the income distribution in America. We must reread poverty without the private democratic lens that conservative, neo-conservatives, neo-liberals, and liberals offer us in order to limit the scope of our gaze. Without a clear-eyed reading, we cannot fully identify the limits of current definitions and solutions, and we cannot begin to develop radical, democratic alternatives.

GET A JOB

The most significant economic problem in America is not the drain social programs place on the economy; rather, it is the inability of the economy to produce enough good jobs to sustain even the current social structure. And it's not just the poor who face fewer good jobs, lower incomes, and governmental neglect—working- and middle-class Americans do as well. Recently, the spread of unemployment and under-employment has caught the attention of the media. For example, Bartlett and Steele (1996), investigative reporters for the *Philadelphia Inquirer*, and the editors (1996) of the *New York Times* published a series of articles entitled "America: Who Stole the Dream" and "The Downsizing of America." The *New York Times* editorial from March 10, 1996, declares:

As the economist Joseph Schumpeter observed long ago, capitalism embodies a process of "creative destruction" in which outdated enterprises must give way. But there is something new and disturbing about current economic afflictions. The middle and upper classes—the very groups benefiting most from the education and training that have for decades been the path upward—are experiencing massive losses of jobs for the first time. Most of these victims have to accept diminished pay and benefits in less secure jobs. The spread of layoffs in relatively good times and among companies with strong profits has created a searing climate of insecurity as employees accept less, contributing to the leveling off and even decline of wages in the last two decades. (As quoted in the *New York Times* 1996, 223–224)

Currently, the employment problems that the poor have always faced—the absence of secure employment at living wages—have spread to classes of people who thought that their incomes would rise forever and they would never become the poor "other." The titles of other popular books portray the seriousness of this problem: *When Work Disappears* (Wilson 1997), *The End of Work* (Rifkin 1995), *The Jobless Future* (Aronowitz and DiFazio 1994), and *Chaos or Community* (Sklar 1995).

Since the 1980s, presidential candidates of both parties have based their campaigns in part on the assumption that "old solutions" such as the expansion of the welfare state must be abandoned in favor of fiscal policies to stimulate economic growth in the private sector. This growth would, in turn, increase the number of jobs available in all sectors of the economy, thereby providing the opportunity for all to work and bidding up the wages for each job. Such growth is credited for the considerable reduction of poverty during the 1960s (Reich 1991). This assumption was and is used as a rationale for President Reagan's supply-side economics, President Bush's capital-gains tax cuts for the wealthy, and President Clinton's expansion of the North American Fair Trade Agreement. Each policy was expected to increase the capital available for corporate investment, which in turn would enable businesses to increase production, creating enough new jobs to overwhelm the problems of poverty. Through continuous economic growth, advocates assume that America will enjoy a full-employment economy reducing joblessness, poverty, and public assistance to short propositions.

These functionalist assumptions are, simply, straightforward and wrong. As economist Blank admits:

In 1986, I had published an article with my colleague at Princeton, Alan Blinder, in which we documented the effect of economic growth on poverty. Using historical data through the early 1980s, we showed that when jobs expanded and unemployment fell, poverty also declined sharply. We predicted a steep decline in poverty over the 1980s, as the United States economy recovered from the severe recession at the beginning of that decade. I *knew* that economic growth reduced poverty. I didn't have a clue why it hadn't worked in 1988.

The apparent problem has become worse over the years. In fact, in November 1994, when the government released its official statistics documenting income and poverty changes over the previous year, it showed a historically unprecedented result: In 1993, when the rate of aggregate economic growth (after inflation) was three percent—a very healthy growth rate indeed—the proportion of Americans who were poor in that year actually *rose* at the same time the aggregate economy was expanding. Behind these dry statistics lies one of the most discouraging facts for American social policy: an expanding economy no longer guarantees a decline in poverty. (Blank 1997, 54)

In part, this new reality has been created by the changing nature of American jobs. First, there is the feminization of the workforce. Since the 1950s, women have increased their participation in the workforce and men have worked fewer hours. Women's participation is often credited with keeping many working-class families above the poverty line as living expenses outstrip many men's incomes even in prosperous times. During the 1990s, however, women's rate of increase has slowed and men's has continued to decline (Economic Report of the President 1995, 315). Because women are paid less than men—on average less than seventy percent of male salaries—this feminization of the workforce and its recent dip in hours worked has reduced household incomes significantly. President Clinton acknowledged this fact during his Wyandotte campaign address when he suggested that families working "two and three jobs" have little time left to read to their children. During the 1990s, even combined incomes of many two-parent families have started to decline.

Second, over the same period, the ratio of manufacturing, service, and agricultural jobs has changed. In the 1980s, the United States lost nearly six million factory jobs when businesses moved their production to other countries; another 2.5 million were moved in the early 1990s (Aronowitz 1994). Agricultural jobs now constitute less than three percent of the American workforce, with service work providing seventy-five percent. The U.S. Bureau of Labor Statistics "The American

Workforce: 1992–2005" (1993) predicts employment growth in the following occupations (listed in descending order):

Fastest Growing by Rate	Occupations with Most New Jobs
home health aides	retail sales
human services workers	registered nurse
home care aides	cashier
computer engineers	general office clerk
systems analysts	truckdriver
physical therapy aides	waiter
physical therapists	nursing aide
paralegals	janitor
special education teachers	food preparation worker
medical assistants	systems analyst

With all the rhetoric about the creation of new jobs, it is important not to confuse the occupations with high growth rates with occupations creating the largest number of jobs. Some high-paying jobs have high rates of growth, but do not and will not employ many Americans (e.g., physical therapists and special education teachers). Conversely, many low-paying jobs have low growth rates, but employ large numbers of people (e.g., janitors and food preparation workers). Over half of the total job growth projected in the 1992–2005 period will be in occupations that require only a high-school education. President Clinton's call for extending free public schooling to two years of post-secondary education seems destined to promote under-employment. According to a 1992 Labor Department study, thirty percent of each new class of college "graduates between now and 2005 will march straight into the ranks of the jobless or the under-employed" (Greenwald 1993, 36). We are an over-educated workforce in many respects, not the under-educated one that neo-liberals would have us believe.

During the last twenty years, the number of involuntary part-time positions has more than doubled, and temporary employment has increased by 211 percent (Callaghan and Hartmann 1991). Manpower, Inc., is now the largest employer in the United States (Tilly 1991). Often referred to as "contingent workers," these employees provide temporary, contract, leased, or part-time service. Their numbers are up sharply since the 1980s; they now total a third of all American workers. By the turn of the century, contingent workers are expected to outnumber permanent full-time employees. Except for a few who actually choose to accept this type of employment permanently, contingent workers have little hope of promotion, regular benefits, pensions, or paid vacations. The United Parcel Service strike during the summer of 1997 was called precisely to challenge the rapid increase in these employment trends (Greenhouse 1997). Moreover, contingent workers face decreased job security, no unemployment insurance, and the permanent juggling of long hours at multiple, changing jobs. In *Time Magazine*, Castro (1993) summed up the advantages for employers as no benefit costs, no costly training, no lawsuits for unlawful termination, no unions, and no scheduling problems. "Long-term commitments of all kinds are anathema to the modern corporations" (44).

In the pages of the *Wall Street Journal*, Jensen and Fagan, from the Harvard Business School, argue that current economic realities of job loss, declining wages, and contingency work are part of the natural cycle in the triumph of capitalism over communism. Their opinion editorial of March 29, 1996, entitled "Capitalism Isn't Broken" acknowledges these temporary hardships for some, but portrays them as necessary preludes to general growth and prosperity for all. Moreover, they forecast the upswing for jobs and greater income parity for the early part of the twenty-first century. They argue if capitalism isn't broken, then the government should not tamper with it. Any adjustments to ameliorate the hardships will simply prolong them, stall the economy, and plunge more people into poverty.

Rifkin (1995) does not foresee the expected upswing or upside of the current economic and job condition. Rather, he explains the current realities as natural consequences of capitalism in which technology has been used to conquer labor costs and concerns in manufacturing, government, and now service industries. Jensen and Fagan's Third Industrial Revolution, Rifkin argues, will treat social classes more harshly and differently than the last. Moreover, the harshness will not end without political and social adjustments. According to Rifkin, some few will amass enormous wealth, while many will lose their well-paying jobs or not find employment sufficient to keep a family above the poverty line. Most workers will be forced into a third sector of the economy, the civic sector, which currently comprises more than 1.4 million nonprofit organizations from schools to youth organizations, hospitals, theaters, and art galleries. "The opportunity now exists to create millions of new jobs in the third sector. Freeing up the labor and talent of men and women no longer needed in the market and government sectors to create 'social capital' in neighborhoods and communities will cost money" (33). Rifkin assumes that those with employment in the first two sectors—business and government—will recognize that employment for the displaced and new workers is in their own best interest and will act rationally by parting with increased taxes to accomplish this task.

The hardships and the opportunities for reemployment in the civic sector are not spread evenly over the American population. Wilson (1997) explains that, for the first time in the twentieth century, most adults in many inner-city ghetto neighborhoods are not working for wages during a typical week. Although poverty has been historically concentrated in cities, he maintains that the new absence of jobs is cause for great alarm. "A neighborhood in which people are poor but employed is different from a neighborhood in which people are poor and jobless. Many of today's problems in the inner-city ghetto neighborhoods—crime, family dissolution, welfare, low levels of social organization, and so on—are fundamentally a consequence of the disappearance of work" (xiii). Although fewer poor people now live in small towns or rural areas then when Harrington discussed their invisibility during the 1960s, lack of employment opportunities are still severe (Levitan, Gallo, and Shapiro 1993). The poorest counties in the United States are rural counties and unemployment rates are often higher than those of cities. The decline in agricultural jobs and the historic lack of manufacturing in rural areas leave the prospects of well-paying jobs bleak.

A LOT OF MONEY—THAT'S WHAT I WANT

Many of those Americans who have jobs find that their incomes are diminishing. From 1973 to 1993, incomes for the poor, working, and middle classes (sixty percent of the population) have decreased. Incomes for the poor have dropped 0.78 percent annually; the working class lost 0.33 percent each

year, and the middle class has had to tighten its belt also, as
Cassidy (1995) explains:

The prototypical middle-class American worked for the better part
of two decades, during which he or she saw communism collapse,
four presidents occupy the White House, and five San Francisco
49ers teams win Super Bowl rings. He or she collected eight hundred and thirty-two weekly paychecks, the last one for an amount
twenty-three dollars less than the first one. (114)

The declines have been most steep among the young (Children's Defense Fund 1992a). Forty percent of all children in
families headed by someone younger than thirty were
officially living in poverty in 1990. Adjusting for inflation, the
median income of these families plunged thrity-two percent
between 1973 and 1990 (Ellwood 1988). Incomes dropped 12.8
percent for married couples and 27.2 percent for female-
headed, single-parent families. Young black families' incomes
were nearly cut in half during that time. Schooling mediated,
but did not redirect, these losses. The incomes of young families whose main wage-earners had dropped out of high school
decreased 45 percent, and the family incomes of wage-earners
who completed some college also decreased nearly 15 percent.
Only young families with college graduates increased their
incomes by 2.5 percent in twenty years.
    The jobs and wages available to many less-skilled workers
(i.e., high-school graduates, those with an equivalent amount
of education, and high-school dropouts) are not sufficient for
them to earn enough to escape poverty unless some form of
income assistance is available. Blank (1997) argues that only
thirty percent of single mothers with two children earn
enough from their jobs to pass the poverty line. If they require
even modest child care (i.e., $2,000 annually or $40 dollars a
week), only twenty-two percent earn enough. One-quarter of
married couples with two children did not earn enough to
escape, even when assuming one parent worked full time
while the other worked twenty hours a week at minimum
wage. Only sixty percent of the single, less-skilled workers
earn enough to cross the poverty line without some form of
income assistance. In *Making Ends Meet*, Edin (1997) argues
that working single mothers are worse off in the job market
than they were on welfare because their extra income is con-
sumed by work-related expenses such as child care, clothes,

and transportation. Therefore, the logic behind the recent efforts to cut welfare costs by forcing more recipients to find work disregards the low wages for such work and the increased hardships for families that will follow.

Citing a 1993 report from the Inspector General of the U.S. Department of Labor, Barlett and Steele (1996) report that the prospects are not much better for the working and middle classes. Not only are their incomes decreasing, but their chances to remain employed are diminishing. Reemployment, as it is called, often means a permanent drop in income. In the recent past, federal and state programs to assist skilled workers who lost their jobs because of foreign economic competition have not helped the majority to regain their economic standing.

Just five of every ten displaced workers who were eligible to attend retraining courses did so.

Of those five workers who completed retraining, only two found work in their new field.

And only one of the five retrained workers found a job in the new field "that paid or had the potential to pay suitable wages" (i.e., at least, eighty percent of their previous wage).

The median weekly wage of workers in their new jobs was down twenty-five percent from the jobs they lost.

The more money workers made in the jobs they lost, the less likely they were to earn as much or more in their new jobs. (187)

Simply put, well-paying jobs are not sufficiently available to form the putative cornerstones of the bootstrap programs of the Reagan and Bush Administrations, the end-of-moral-poverty programs of Bennett and the neo-conservatives, and the workfare and reemployment initiatives of the Clinton Administration. There are not enough jobs to raise all the poor above the poverty line, or even to keep the working and middle classes at income levels they once enjoyed. The systematic withdrawal of the social safety net in order to subject labor to the chaos of the marketplace has left at least sixty percent of us searching for the American Dream. And families in the upper-middle classes—the twenty percent of households with incomes between $45,000 and $65,000—are not as secure as they once were.

Moreover, despite the rhetoric of recent attacks on affirmative action, job loss and low wages are unequally distributed across races, ages, and gender. Racial and ethnic minorities are more likely to be hired for service work than better-paying managerial jobs (U.S. Bureau of Labor Statistics 1994a). Their wages have declined relative to their white counterparts during the last fifteen years (U.S. Bureau of Labor Statistics 1993). Their unemployment rates run two to three times higher than those of whites. Entry-level wages for high-school graduates have dropped twenty-five percent during the last twenty years and have declined by seven percent for university graduates during that period (Lopez 1993). Unemployment rates for workers under twenty-five years of age vary from ten to forty percent, depending on race and geographic region (U.S. Bureau of Labor Statistics 1994b). Although more women are entering the workforce and have made gains in finding professional employment, they still are often employed in pink ghettos (U.S. Bureau of Labor Statistics 1993), earn less than seventy percent of male peers' salaries and wages (Current Population Report 1992), and carry most of the responsibility for raising children (Shelton 1992). Last to be hired, people of color, the young, and women are the first to be "downsized" from better-paying jobs and then to be hired again for low-paying service work.

During the same twenty years from 1973 to 1993, however, upper-middle-class income rose 0.5 percent annually, and incomes of the rich rose 1.13 percent on average, with the richest twentieth of the U.S. population increasing two percent and the richest hundredth rising five percent *each year*. In fact, since 1980, the incomes of the rich have increased at a rate unparalleled in American history (Schiller 1995). In the *Cost of Talent* (1993), Derek Bok, former President of Harvard University, identifies the most extreme case of the different trajectories of incomes among classes when he examines the incomes of chief executive officers from top American businesses. Compensation for CEOs far outstrips the increases of any other category of workers, except perhaps a few sports and entertainment stars. For example, in 1995, the CEO of General Electric received $5,250,000, 133 times the income of the median family income in America. Michael Eisner, then CEO of Disney, reported earnings of more than $280,000,000. In America, it is true that the rich get richer while the rest of us get poorer.

The U.S. Bureau of Census practice of reporting the distribution of annual income in quintiles covers up this fact. Quintiles appear to be benign and a useful way to distinguish among economic classes. Yet these categories suggest that the relative differences among economic groups is a normal condition and that the distribution of income from salaries and wages among these groups shows that the top quintile averages little more than ten times that of the bottom. Although a factor of ten may appear outrageous to some, it is merely the tip of the iceberg. These annual reports mask the differences among the total wealth of these groups. Bartlett and Steele (1996) attempt to make these concealed differences concrete by offering a metaphor of a small three-hundred-family town, which they call "Inequalityville," to represent the distribution of wealth in America. Bartlett and Steele offer only three classes of families: The very rich, three among the three hundred families, who own houses worth more than $5 million and thirty percent of all town assets; the well off, twenty-seven families (or nine percent), who enjoy $750,000-houses and thirty-seven percent of the town's wealth; and the rest, 270 families who have houses worth $67,000 and control thirty-three percent of the town's wealth.

Behind the U.S. Bureau of Census lies the fact that ten percent of American families own sixty-seven percent of America's wealth. According to the Center for Popular Economics (Folbre 1995), this ten percent owns eighty percent of all nonresidential real estate, ninety-one percent of all business assets, eighty-five percent of all stocks, and ninety-four percent of all bonds. The other ninety percent of Americans owns twenty percent or less in each category of capital. Of course, important distinctions can be made concerning the relative wealth among this ninety percent of American families. However, those distinctions may seem less alarming when it is acknowledged that only one-third of the American pie is being considered during such analyses. To this way of thinking about the distribution of wealth and income in the United States, the poor, working, middle, and even upper-middle classes have more in common economically with each other than they do with the rich.

WITH A LITTLE HELP FROM MY FRIENDS

Although it is within the nature of capitalism for the economic prospects of upper and lower classes to pull away from each other (Castells 1980), these differences in fortune are not solely due to nature. Federal and state governments have interfered often with the invisible hand of capitalism, and often in favor of the well-to-do. For example, federal income taxes, which are labeled progressive (i.e., taxing Americans according to their abilities to pay), are in fact leveling off. As Table 8–2 demonstrates, the income tax cut of 1986 initiated a sliding scale to provide incentives for Americans to invest in America. The rich received between sixty and five thousand times the savings as did the poor or near-poor. This is a form of government redistribution that does not receive much attention in the media or other publics.

Table 8–2 Distribution of Tax Cut and Income in 1989

Income	Size of Cut	Average Savings
1. $0 to $16,952	9%	$50
2. $16,953 to $29,999	11%	$300
3. $30,000 to $45,000	13%	$800
4. $45,001 to $66,794	16%	$1,520
5. $66,795 to $100,000	18%	$3,030
6. $100,001 to $500,000	24%	$17,800
7. $500,001 to $1,000,000	34%	$86,080
8. $1,000,001 and over	31%	$281,030

Citizens for Tax Justice 1991.

For the last decade at least, Congress has debated and passed various cuts in taxes on capital gains (i.e., income derived from the sale of stocks, bonds, commodities, and other assets) and inheritance taxes. In 1989, capital gains on tax returns totaled $150.2 billion. Of that sum, $108.2 billion—or seventy-two percent—was reported by 7.2 million tax filers who had incomes under $100,000. Ninety-three percent of American taxpayers claimed no capital-gains taxes and received no benefit from capital-gains tax cuts (Bartlett and Steele 1992). Currently, estate inheritances under $600,000 are exempt from taxation. In 1997, the Clinton Administration accepted as part of federal-budget negotiations a proposal to raise that threshold to $1,200,000. Only thirty thousand Americans paid estate taxes last year, leaving nine out of ten taxpayers unaided by this reform. Legislative efforts to cut these taxes, which are tenets in most congressional and presidential candidates' platforms, amount to nothing more than welfare for the rich.

According to its own accounts, the federal government is not as generous with people at the other end of the economic spectrum. For example, in 1992, the government spent about $464 billion on entitlements that people receive regardless of their income level—Social Security, Medicare, veteran's pensions and retirement, and unemployment insurance benefits—ten times as much as on AFDC and Food Stamps during the same year. Tax exemptions for the value of employer-sponsored health insurance in 1992 amounted to $20 billion more than was spent on Medicaid. Mortgage-interest deductions from income taxes were nearly three times the budget for low-income housing assistance and low-rent public housing (Albelda and Folbre 1996). The end of the federal guaranteed income through welfare reform is indicative of the transfer of public funds to private business. State control of welfare programs without federal constraints on how block-grant funds can be used has resulted in heated competitions among private businesses and agencies to deliver welfare services to the poor at a profit for the state and the company (Bernstein 1996; Conniff 1997; Pear 1996). If allowed to continue, the increased hardships of the working poor will translate into increased stock dividends for the rich.

The Board of Governors of the Federal Reserve System controls the prime interest rate at which bank members can borrow money. The Board is a group of bankers who are appointed by the president to fourteen-year terms to steer the economy, raising interest rates to induce recessions when the economy is growing too fast, causing inflation, and lowering them to encourage economic growth when the economy is sluggish. Interest rates influence not only decisions about borrowing, but also decisions about bond investments and savings. When the rates are high, those with the means already in their possession are likely to invest in them; when they are low, return rates decline. This fact puts the Board in direct conflict with workers. High interest rates yield high return for investors, but discourage economic growth. The rich benefit from higher returns on their bonds, but workers do not have more jobs from which to choose or higher wages to attract them to those jobs. Rising wages mean that costs and prices

rise also, leading to inflation, which decreases
banks because each dollar paid in interest is wo
interest rates reduce returns on bonds, but typica
wages will rise. Despite recent economic grov
inflation, Alan Greenspan, Chairman of the Boar
eral Reserve System, has kept the prime rate higher tnan necessary to guard against inflation, choosing to aid banks and
bondholders over workers. Just to underscore Greenspan's
power, Reich (1997) suggests that a single sentence from
Greenspan that national health insurance would hinder economic expansion of the early 1990s was enough to persuade
President Clinton that his health plan was inappropriate.

WHAT'S GOIN' ON

Within these economic conditions, the assumed functionalist
relationships between poverty and literacy are not accurate
and should not seem too compelling to three-fourths of the
U.S. population. When those individuals look at the future,
they do not see the high-tech/high-wage jobs that the government and business say are waiting for them to grab, if only
they will act responsibly and become literate. Rather, they see
high levels of unemployment, job insecurity, and low-wage
service- or civil-sector jobs staring them in the face in an
economy that even a Secretary of Labor says is "out of control." Moreover, they see educational systems that can't
deliver on the prosperity they promise, a media that ignores
their problems while exploiting their desires, and governments that seem, on the whole, openly hostile to their well-
being. Traditional moral training, general school reform,
debates over methods of teaching the poor, or even cultural
adaptation within reading programs will not reconnect the
functionalist lines between reading education and the end of
poverty in America. Each policy may bring relief to some individuals among the poor and near-poor, but our economy will
not allow three-quarters of the American population to dream.

The changing nature of American jobs has disrupted
Americans' certainty about their economic position and, perhaps, themselves. Employment is not stable, if available, and
the wages will not keep pace with the cost of living. No longer

can working- and middle-class Americans look at the poor as facing unique problems. To varying degrees, seventy-five percent or more of American workers face similar futures. The poor are us. Instability of work and declining wages blur boundaries. Workers with high IQ scores are losing their jobs or finding ones that do not pay well. The moral challenges of idleness face Americans of all ages and many economic classes as media tabloids are eager to remind us. Highly skilled college graduates cannot find work in their professions or vocations despite their technical expertise. While these facts have long been the case for women and minority workers, during the 1990s, white males well up into the middle- and upper-middle classes must face them as well.

Accepting conservative, neo-conservative, neo-liberal, or even liberal conceptions of poverty and their suggested solutions, we follow the functionalist logic to continue the unjust status quo, which works against the interests of seventy-five percent of America. When we track learners toward their "proper" place in society, offer carefully selected moral training for everyone, accept business practices as the measure of human worth, or argue endlessly over which methods will raise test scores the most, we work toward a private democracy in which protection of property (theirs more than ours) is paramount. If we read the formal and tacit policies that arise from these seemingly different but ultimately similar private democratic political views, we can begin to identify how these political, cultural, and economic values keep that seventy-five percent of Americans separated into small powerless groups—Democrats and Republicans, men and women, blacks and whites, middle class and poor—offered to us as if they were natural, benign, and our own social categories.

As Aronowitz suggests, "if the job culture proves to have been a historically situated way of measuring value, then the ethical basis of contemporary life requires reexamination and, with it, the goals and purpose of schools" (1994, 141). Like it or not, we stand at the center of this ethical dilemma. We need new theories of poverty that encourage public democracy and new nonfunctionalist rationales for schooling and reading instruction.

NINE

LISTEN HERE PEOPLE, LISTEN TO ME, I DON'T WANNA BE MISTREATED BY NO BOURGEOISIE

Reading the Road Ahead

I came to Washington thinking the answer was simply to provide people in the bottom half with access to the education and skills they need to qualify for better jobs. But it's more than that. Without power, they can't get the resources for good schools and affordable higher education or training. Powerless, they can't even guarantee safe workplaces, maintain a livable minimum wage, or prevent sweatshops from reemerging. Without power, they can't force highly profitable companies to share the profits with them. Powerless, they're as expendable as old pieces of machinery.

(Reich 1997, 17) ◆◆

As Widemann (1995) explains, when politicians talk to us about relationships between crime and society, we assume that the prison system they suggest meets the general needs of society and that tinkering will make it even more efficient. However, when we step back and look beyond our immediate fear of criminals—a social group who, we are told, are not like us—we realize that the prison system removes the human objects of our fears from our sight, thoughts, and civic lives, but it deals only with the results of criminal behavior, not its causes. Dealing only with symptoms and consequences requires continuous tinkering and reification of socially constructed distinctions between us and them. If in what passes for the public debate about crime, we allow ourselves to be limited to discussions of punishment and deterrence, we accept the position that criminals are not like us, and we lose opportunities to explore its causes, its consequences, and our relationships to both.

In a similar way, Robert Reich, Secretary of Labor during the first Clinton Administration, acknowledges that the political debate about poverty has been limited. By starting with the functionalist assumptions that the social and economic status quo are the best we can hope for and work toward, we "do good" by giving the poor, who are not like us, the tools to possibly work their way out of abject poverty into dire hardships. As Reich implies, we do this without altering the fundamental relationships of power that brought about poverty in the first place. When we step back from these efforts, as Reich apparently has started to do, we can recognize the limits of functionalism in a society where power and wealth are so unequally distributed, and we can see that we must develop other options for addressing the possible relationships of poverty in society—ones that take into account economic realities of our times.

During this century, Communists have carried the struggle to bring power to the bottom half in capitalist societies. Yet with the collapse of the Soviet Union, we are said to be living in a post-Communist world—one in which the dictatorship of the proletariat and the withering away of the state seem impossible. In such a world, we experience the colliding forces of global economics in which national borders become porous and less meaningful; labor is increasingly abandoned to the logic of the market; various social groups struggle for recognition of their histories, cultures, and values; and individuals search for some control, stability, and freedom in their lives. These forces pull the bottom half (which I have argued is really three-fourths) of the U.S. population apart from one another, decreasing their chances to obtain power to protect themselves in the ways that Reich imagines and to enhance democratic prospects for the future in ways that he does not. In radical democratic retheorizing of poverty and the poor, we must find ways to develop solidarity among this majority, while avoiding the past problems of Leftist politics—that is, if we intend to enhance the prospects of public democracy. Reading can play a role in this search.

PROBLEMS OF THE PAST

Tradionally, leftists have subordinated cultural issues to those of class. In the late twentieth century, the struggle for recognition has surpassed the struggle for socioeconomic redistribution as the chief medium for political mobilization against injustice. Under the banners of nationality, race, gender, and sexuality, social groups have sought cultural and legal recognition of difference rather than the reallocation of economic resources as the primary means to correct social injustices. New political visions exploring issues of identity, difference, and cultural domination have supplanted traditional Leftist concerns of interests, exploitation, and commodification. "To many groups, the economic emphasis of socialism has become an insufficient explanation for problems like ethnic-cleansing, gay-bashing, or sexual harassment. A more encompassing paradigm is needed" (Trend 1996, 2). With cultural domination as the fundamental injustice, groups can point their accusing fingers toward both the political Right and Left. While the subordination of cultural issues in the Right's political agenda is perhaps understandable, if not defensible, the Left's suppression of issues of gender, race, and sexuality within concerns for social class was and is inexcusable and incomprehensible outside the logic of Marxism.

Many on the Left seem prepared to acknowledge past oppressions within movements conducted in the name of the oppressed. For example, while arguing for a positive role of the

Left in American history, Aronowitz (1996) admits that internal politics that kept young white males in positions of power and limited conceptions of injustice to issues of class splintered the New Left into feminist-, racial-, and gay-rights groups. In *Hegemony and Socialist Strategy*, Laclau and Mouffe (1985) reformulate the Leftist project of redistribution in terms of a radical and plural democracy, in which democratic ideals of liberty and equality are extended to more and more areas of social life. Such a strategy requires abandoning the notion of "the people" as a homogeneous and unified entity with a single general will. Even some unrepentant Socialists call for a broader radical democratic framework.

Rejecting the idea that culture is the main arena of struggle and that subversion lies at the margins of society does not have to mean going back to the authoritarian structures of the Communist movement or the domination of social movements by white men. An updated social-democratic politics would have to be internally democratic. It would have to address questions of whose agendas are to be included, who will shape the coalitions and frame demands. It would have to find forms that would enable full expression for all of the overlapping groups that form the potential basis for a progressive politics: working-class people, groups of color, women, sexual, and other cultural minorities. It would have to find ways of incorporating the recognition that none of these groups speaks with one voice. Such a movement would also have to be majoritarian: whites, men as well as women, would have to have a legitimate place. (Epstein 1996, 136)

Cultural injustices are rooted in social patterns of representation, interpretation, and communication. Without the power to represent themselves in public and private discourses, women and people of color often find themselves maligned or disparaged in stereotypic cultural representations and every-day interactions. Patterns of interpretations often render their cultural practices invisible or relegate them to the realm of the exotic or vulgar. Forms of communication set exclusive norms that are often alien or hostile to those of subordinate groups. These means of oppression, not always overt and seldom explicit any longer, nonetheless imprison groups and individuals in a false, distorted, reduced mode of being (Taylor 1992). "Beyond simple lack of respect, it can inflict a grievous wound, saddling people with crippling self-hatred. Due recognition is not just a courtesy, but a vital human need" (25).

These struggles for recognition occur in a world of increasing material inequality. As I have tried to point out in this book, inequalities exist and are increasing not only in terms of income, wealth, access to work, education, and leisure time, but also in caloric intake, health care, and exposure to toxic environments. Although these inequalities often have cultural manifestations and entailments, they also are rooted in the political and economic structure of society. They stem from exploitation in which others accrue profits from one's labor; economic marginalization of some groups to poorly paid or undesirable employment, while finding "biologic," "cultural," or "divine" rationales for these exclusions; and systemic deprivation of an adequate material standard of living to many in society. From a radical democratic viewpoint, virtually every struggle against injustice implies demands for both redistribution and recognition.

Several writers have discussed the limits of "identity politics" as a singular solution to social injustice. For example, Reed (1997) discusses the questionable assumption that membership within a group gives access to a shared perspective and an intuitive understanding of that group's collective interests. He suggests that the appointment and confirmation of the Supreme Court Justice, Clarence Thomas, should be evidence enough to the fallacy of that premise. "There's no such thing as authenticity; it's only a marketing ploy. No coherent group perspectives are decreed automatically by nature or by social and economic 'laws,' and this applies to class consciousness as well as identity politics" (19). Congressman Jesse Jackson, Jr. (1997) asks if it is possible to achieve racial justice in the context of economic injustice. Although he answers that racial injustice is not the same as economic injustice—there would still be racism in a full-employment economy—he argues that systematic and steady progress on racial issues can only be made to the degree that people of color make progress on basic economic issues. Declaring that freedom is the ultimate goal of movements for social justice, June Jordan states:

What the new emerging majority of these United States holds in common, at its core, is a need for freedom to exist equally and a need to become the most knowledgeable, happy, productive, interconnected, and healthy men and women we can. Ours is a need for freedom that does not omit any racial, gender, ethnic, sexual, or physical identity from its protection. But unless we will, each of us, reach around all of these identities and embrace them even as we cherish our own, no one's freedom will be assumed. (1993, 18)

RECOGNITION AND REDISTRIBUTION

Yet, as Fraser (1995) explains, the goals of recognition and redistribution pull in opposite directions. Success of recognition is to valorize a group's specificity through revaluing of cultural and symbolic forms and practices. However, the logic of redistribution is to erase group specificity through the political and economic restructuring of income redistribution, reorganization of labor, and democraticization of investment decision-making. The means to address this dilemma is not to be found in currently popular political ideologies within the United States that work in various ways to preserve the principles and realities of private democracy. Although conservative groups often decry the savagery of subordinate cultural groups, their views of poverty work to separate groups along whatever lines appear at hand to maintain what they consider the natural order in the social world. Neo-conservatives acknowledge differences among groups and even, grudgingly, offer an economic safety net to those in dire need. Yet they deplore multiculturalism as a national metaphor, and they cling to moral absolutes that favor the established cultural and economic order. Neo-liberals subject everything to the logic of the marketplace. Cultural and economic injustices that impede the abilities of American businesses to triumph in the global economy are to be challenged, but those that do not interfere are ignored.

Roma Pizzeria in Washington, D.C., the example that begins this book, demonstrates how neo-liberal solutions to recognition and redistribution work—or rather do not work— toward empowerment. The professional class—lawyer Domenici—defines the problems facing (inner-city) youth as ones of training and self-esteem. Although the neo-conservative charge of irresponsibility lurks in the background, Domenici translates it into a restricted-opportunity hypothesis that links education and morality to the marketplace. Domenici selects poor minority adolescents to shape their intellectual, social, and moral education, producing minimum wage-level workers for service industries. At Roma, economic inequalities are addressed through the movement of individuals from predicted places in welfare lines or crime to possible spots among the working poor. Cultural inequalities are engaged through the production of counter-examples to the stereotypes of urban youth. Federal funds are saved and some individuals consider themselves better off. However, in both parts, the model for combating poverty does little to further Reich's project to empower the bottom half of society.

Although Reich discovered the differences between the neo-liberal and liberal position on the dilemma of recognition and redistribution while in office, he does not adequately address the issues of power, poverty, and discrimination. Reich proposes what Fraser calls "affirmative remedies for injustice," which are "aimed at correcting inequitable outcomes of social arrangements without disturbing the underlying framework that generates them" (Fraser 1995, 82). For example, to overcome discrimination based on race or gender, Reich offers affirmative action in school admissions, contract bidding, job training, and employment. All things being equal, people of color and women should get preference over white males. This redresses some cultural injustices by revaluing previously devalued group identities, but without changing the cultural and political pathologies that caused the original devaluing. Ultimately, such policies increase the distance among cultural groups by creating the illusion that society is just and any problems reside within the individuals who must rely on affirmative benefits.

Redistribution for liberals historically has been associated with the welfare state. Social Security and compensation programs are offered to safeguard the employed, and direct and indirect aid programs provide some income, food, shelter, and health care to some of those who can prove their desperate need. While these policies increase the consumption share of the poor, they do not significantly restructure the economic and political systems. By creating this two-pronged program, liberals emphasize the division between the employed and the unemployed, shifting attention away from capitalists and capitalism altogether. Along with the aid, the poor must endure the antagonisms of members of other economic classes, who see the poor receiving undeserved privileges. Because these

liberal remedies do not address the systems that cause economic disadvantage, allocations of aid must be adjusted again
and again to meet increased prices and costs. These apparently
continuous adjustments mark the poor as inherently deficient
and insatiable. The current backlash against affirmative
action and welfare among the working and middle classes can
be read as a (perhaps unanticipated) consequence of self-
contradictory practices of American liberalism—a political
perspective that simultaneously seeks and fears power within
the bottom half of the population.

Hope Meadows, Eheart's planned community for adolescents flooding the foster care and adoption facilities in Chicago, represents an appealing example of liberal affirmative
remedies for redistribution and recognition. Again, a white
professional names both the problem and the solution for a
group that is defined as unable to fend for themselves. Redistribution is accomplished through relocating both adolescents
and adoptive families to a suburban setting. Eighteen thousand dollars is given to each family to enable one parent to be
home and available at all times for these children. Senior citizens are offered reduced rent in exchange for tutoring the
adolescents. At Hope Meadows, recognition is addressed
through the construction of a multicultural community (i.e.,
multiple age groups, races, incomes, gender balance, and
single- and two-parent families) in which representation of
difference is a primary focus. Within the community, there
may be significant reallocation of existing goods and respect
that make the lives of members more secure and rich.

Yet power relationships have not changed for these individuals and groups. Eheart defined the problem, organized the
community, and effectively removed the foster children from
society without addressing the structural issues that create
the need for foster care. Without addressing causes, the rate of
children entering the foster-care system will not decrease and
the constant need to duplicate and adjust Hope Meadows will
continue without apparent end. Continuous adjustments
eventually will cause the same social resentments as welfare
programs, stemming from the illusion that this group is a
drain on society. The causes of the impoverishment of the
lives of these adolescents remain the same and the stigma of
their circumstances remains as well. The political, economic,
and valuing structures are left unchanged and power relationships have not been altered.

FINESSING THE DILEMMA

Fraser suggests that "our best efforts to redress these injustices via the combination of the liberal welfare state plus mainstream multiculturalism are generating perverse effects. Only by looking to alternative conceptions of redistribution and recognition can we meet the requirements of justice for all" (1997, 33). To address the problems of powerlessness among the majority of Americans while avoiding the pitfalls of affirmative remedies within struggles for justice, radical democrats recommend transformative strategies that would couple recognition with redistribution. Transformative remedies for cultural injustices seek to significantly change current patterns and structures of cultural valuation. Attempts to destabilize existing group identities are intended not only to raise the self-esteem of members of currently disadvantaged groups, but also to change everyone's sense of belonging, affiliation, and self. Transformative cultural action is expected to deconstruct the socially constructed black/white, rich/poor, woman/man dichotomies that function as axes on which cultural injustices turn. Such action is intended to make problematic all pretensions of fixed identities in order to affirm the multiple, fluid, and shifting identities we all possess and employ according to social circumstances. I have endeavored throughout much of this book to deconstruct the fixed identities of economic classes to increase the possibilities of broader coalitions among all groups struggling against injustice.

Transformative remedies for economic inequalities historically have been associated with socialism. Unjust distribution of income and wealth is addressed through the underlying political-economic system. Transformative actions typically combine social-welfare programs, steeply progressive taxation, macroeconomic policies to achieve full employment, public ownership, and democratic decision-making about economic priorities. Fundamental to these actions is the intent to uncouple issues of well-being from employment. In this way, basic necessities of life—food, shelter, health care, and minimum income—become basic human rights for which the federal government is responsible. These basic rights blur the distinction among social groups, decreasing the possibilities that recipients are stigmatized as beneficiaries of special treatment and increasing the possibilities that social groups can find common goals in struggles against inequalities. Unlike liberal affirmative solutions, transformative radical democratic acts toward recognition and redistribution compliment one another. The blurring of group differentiation and the recognition of a need for structural changes within our political and economic systems in order to bring about social justice create the conditions for the empowerment of the bottom three-fourths of the American population.

The Dudley Street Neighborhood Initiative (DSNI) stands in stark contrast to the affirmative models and policies projected from Roma Pizzeria and Hope Meadows. The Dudley Street community is among the poorest in Boston. Suffering from thirty years of disinvestment policies that decreased its tax base and increased its physical decline, this community has united to redirect its future. From its beginning, community members in the DSNI struggled to keep local control of physical, human, and economic development of its area. Although it has not always been easy or efficient, the democratic process the DSNI chose for its deliberations has produced lasting results that successfully finess some of the dilemma of recognition and redistribution. Because the organizers valued the cultural diversity of the community, early in its development the DSNI took pains to ensure ethnic, racial, and gender balance among its leadership and to build an organization that brought people of differing classes and political power together as equals. Right from the start, this commitment to difference enabled a small core group to begin organizing across the various neighborhoods within the community. The careful recognition of each group and its members facilitated the DSNI's mobilization of large numbers of community members to accomplish its goals.

Community members hold the power to set goals of a better life for themselves. The DSNI sought physical development without displacement of current residents, human development that would build upon the skills that the community already possessed and transfer the skills for which they intially contracted, and economic development with people in mind. The community has been remarkably successful in pursuit of its goals for physical development—illegal dumping has stopped; vacant lots were claimed by DSNI through eminent domain for development into housing, parks, and businesses; low-income housing has retained community architecture and enabled low-income families to remain; and all the streets are paved. "You can build all the doggone houses, condominiums, whatever you want. But if you're not trying to touch people's lives and help them improve their lives, you're just putting up bricks and mortar" (Che Madyun, President of DSNI, as quoted in Medoff and Sklar 1994, 169). Touching people's lives does not mean doing things for them. Rather, in the Dudley Street community, it meant helping them learn intellectual, communicative, and technical skills so that they can take ownership of whatever changes they sought within the community. Along with this development has come the power to critique as well as to perform, and the DSNI leadership has shown great courage in its willingness to decenter its authority.

To this point, economic development has not advanced greatly in the Dudley Street community. Companies with significant numbers of employees are rarely managed locally, and they are subject to the same global demands that have caused many communities across the United States to lose jobs as factories close. For example, in 1993, the Stride Rite and Digital Equipment corporations closed their Dudley Street plants, causing 340 employees to lose their jobs. These businesses accounted for seventeen percent of the district's manufacturing jobs. To its credit, the DSNI has not jumped at the quick-fix offers of many companies who require subtantial government and community concessions in return for locating businesses in a particular spot. The DSNI seeks small businesses that are in keeping with its community orientation. Yet it realizes that without a more aggressive and successful economic plan—one that signficantly raises the community's average income above the poverty line—residents may be displaced by the more well-to-do as the community's reputation and future brightens.

In 1993, the DSNI published a declaration of community rights statement to project its goals for recognition and redistribution in a transformed cultural and economic system.

We—the youth, adults, and seniors of African, Latin American, Caribbean, Native American, Asian, and European ancestry—are the Dudley Street community. Nine years ago, we were Boston's dumping ground and forgotten neighborhood. Today, we are on the rise! We are reclaiming our dignity, rebuilding housing, and reknitting the fabric of our communities. Tomorrow, we realize our vision of a vibrant, culturally diverse neighborhood, where everyone is valued for their talents and contributions to the larger community. We, the residents of the Dudley Street area, dedicate and declare ourselves to the following:

1. We have the right to shape the *development of all plans, programs, and policies* likely to affect the quality of our lives as neighborhood residents.
2. We have the right to quality, affordable *health care* that is both accessible to all neighborhood residents and culturally sensitive.
3. We have the right to control the *development* of neighborhood land in ways that ensure adequate *open space* for parks, gardens, tot lots, and a range of recreational uses.
4. We have the right to live in a hazard-free *environment* that promotes the health and safety of our families.
5. We have the right to celebrate the vibrant cultural diversity of the neighborhood through all *artistic forms of expression.*
6. We have the right to *education and training* that will encourage our children, youth, adults, and elders to meet their maximum potential.
7. We have the right to a share in the *jobs and prosperity* created by economic development initiatives in metro-Boston generally and in our neighborhood specifically.
8. We have the right to quality and affordable *housing* in the neighborhood as both tenants and homeowners.
9. We have the right to quality and affordable *child care* responsive to the district's needs of the child and family, as well as available in a home or center-based setting.
10. We have the right to safe and accessible *public transportation* serving the neighborhood.
11. We have the right to enjoy quality *goods and services*, made available through an active, neighborhood-based commercial district.
12. We have the right to enjoy full *spiritual and religious life* in appropriate places of worship.
13. We have the right to *safety and security* in our homes and in our neighborhoods.

Note the radical democratic tone of recognition and power and the call for redistribution within this declaration. All groups are recognized and acknowledged for their separate contribution and for their common goal of a sustainable community. Control is reserved for the community as they negotiate with the world outside its boundaries. Advocacy groups, government agencies, and philanthropic organizations are partners with the community, not administrative experts who decide what's good for the neighborhood and control the processes of redevelopment. The DSNI claims its share of economic development and seeks to redistribute the wealth created in and around its community.

Through the Declaration of Community Rights, the DSNI states its intention to bring about a transformed community within a transformed country. Group identities are simultaneously celebrated and blurred as each member is asked to recognize the multiple memberships in the community as contextual demands on individuals and groups change over time. Issues of well-being are uncoupled from employment as they become basic community rights. Although current actions for redistribution rest on the community's ability to negotiate with government agencies, its tenacious efforts to apply democratic principles to development and economic decisions suggest a vision of restructuring the economic and political systems that sent Dudley Street into decline in the first place. Medoff and Sklar's *Streets of Hope: The Fall and Rise of an Urban Neighborhood* (1994) portrays the genius and courage of people who are often represented as the negative sum of their needs and "risks." They also chronicle the missteps, the fragile alliances, and the frustrations with an economy that will not keep people in mind. (See Stein's "Yoland Rivera, Dream Maker," 1997, and Cooper's "A Town Betrayed," 1997, for other examples of poor and middle-class communities struggling for democratic decision-making about economic priorities.)

The DSNI created public spaces in which community members can exercise certain types of power, and worked to have those spaces and that power recognized inside and outside of its geographic and political area. Dudley Street residents acquired the power to name themselves, their rights, their problems, their competence, their solutions. They forged the power to unite around and across cultural differences for common purposes. They wrestled the power to represent themselves from the newspapers, the city, and the social agencies. They practiced the power to act on their own terms in partnership with others. They are developing the power to become what they desire to be. At the same time, certain types of power that affect their daily lives elude their grasp. For example, they do not have power to control information or capital. That is, media representations of urban life, cultural differences, and political and economic systems in general impede their visions of what alternatives to their current thoughts, beliefs, and actions might be possible. Although community members do not control economic capital in and around their area, their declaration of community rights suggest that they are vying for the political control to negotiate the problematic issues that Reich seeks for America's bottom half—good schools and training, safe workplaces and environments, good jobs, and a share of the profits.

A PLACE FOR READING

Within the Dudley Street example are some indications of how reading education can be productively employed in radical democratic struggles over social justice and power within the United States and in social movements to advance public deomocracy. Clearly, the functionalist logic that appropriate reading instruction leads directly to school and later work success was not operational in the Dudley Street community before the 1980s. Populated exclusively by people who many educators refer to as "at risk," even the best that Boston schools had to offer (and I am not suggesting that this is what Dudley Street students received) could not create a prosperous community against the social, political, and economic problems causing urban decay. Academic tracks, moral literacy, national standards and testing, or even targeted programs have not and, I have argued, cannot produce a community of academic and economic success on Dudley Street. Yet many Dudley Street residents were and are able to employ sophisticated literacies to take control of their community's development. This was not accomplished by only a few individuals who planned and wrote what other community members would read, follow, and say during negotiations. Although there were and are leaders in the DSNI, many members of the Dudley Street community were intimately involved in the indentification of concerns, the development of goals and plans, and the articulation of policies and practices in cleaning up the environment, securing land, designing streets and housing, and continuous negotiating with government officials.

The DSNI was and is successful in helping individuals learn to use sophisticated literacies when schools were not because they had a new (or perhaps renewed) answer to the question, Why read? Rather than the rhetoric of future academic or economic benefit, the Dudley Street movement offered immediate opportunities to participate actively in community life. That participation was and is not contrived or simulated; rather, it had immediate and substantial consequences for their well-being. Questions such as Who (not what) makes up our community? How should we be represented? What are our needs? How do we wish to live together? and What should be done? were asked, discussed, and tentatively answered by community members of all ages, races, genders, and languages. At the outset, community members were thought to possess the capabilities to participate in the civic life of their community without preliminary instructions on "how to do it properly." Members found some common ground during their early interactions on issues of cultural, social, and economic justice and were successful in their negotiations with each other, social agencies, and city departments to gain some small successes. Faith in their abilities, opportunity to participate actively in civic life, and small successes toward their goals of social justice enabled this "at risk" population to recognize and to develop reading as a weapon of critique and as a tool for building new lives for themselves and others for whom they care.

This is not to say that faith, opportunity, and small successes transformed Dudley Street community members into professionals with a fully developed repertoire of sophisticated literacies. However, it is to say that the Dudley Street movement enabled community members to act as their more well-to-do peers do outside their communities. Whether these peers were considered dull, average, or bright at school had little consequence for their subsequent literacy development. Rather than teaching them sophisticated literacies, their school lessons—both explicit and tacit—taught them that they had the right to be in environments that demand sophisticated literacy and that once there, they were relatively likely to be successful (Neilson 1989). They did not learn sophisticated literacies at school—they didn't need to—rather, they learned that they were part of society's "haves." As haves, they have the right, the opportunity to, and the requisite mental attitude for learning sophisticated literacy from already capable individuals who have enjoyed such benefits previously. The DSNI extends those lessons to society's "have-nots" in ways that put these sophisticated literacies in service of social justice.

The scope of the community rights that the DSNI members declared for themselves demonstrates the breadth of their opportunities to participate in Dudley Street civic life. Health care, environment, art, jobs, housing, child care, public transportation, commercial life, spirituality, and safety are all deemed rights worthy of serious consideration and support. Democratic participation in the community is the only clearly superordinate goal, and that promotes the likelihood of neophytes connecting with experienced mentors in all these fields. In the words of DSNI's 1993 *Framework for a Human Development Agenda:*

> Our community has a gold mine of natural assets and resources. . . .
> They take many forms: human, institutional, and physical. Our
> community-rebuilding strategy must be anchored in the power and
> strength of our people and our neighborhood. . . . We know the
> process of rebuilding and reknitting our community back together
> is as important as the goal itself. Among our richest resources
> are our young people. . . . As adults, we must assure them of the
> gifts they hold and of the gifts they are. (As quoted in Medoff and
> Sklar 1994, 171)

The Dudley Street community's commitment to youth seems genuine and complex. For example, the development of designs for a community center was placed in the hands of community youth. With support from the DSNI and a local architect working without pay, a committee of forty-five preteens and teenagers set about the task of developing plans. All of the information about community concerns and interests in the project, the site development, and the building-code requirements were conducted by youth. A subset of committee members was elected and selected to comprise Dudley's Young Architects and Planners to oversee the preparation of a final design. Architect Gail Sullivan reported that several of the youths "couldn't add three plus six when we started doing the measuring. They had to count with their fingers. Some of them had creative and unique systems for figuring out square footage. They found a way to make the math work for them" (as quoted in Medoff and Sklar 1994, 222). Although the community-center project waits on a list of priorities, the youth who participated in its design in the early 1990s still use the literacies that they learned in the process and, as Sullivan wrote in her report to DSNI, "Dudley's young people refuse to accept as their inheritance disinvestment, neglect, and despair" (225).

RADICAL DEMOCRATIC LITERACY

Others have called for apprenticeship models for reading education. For example, Lauren Resnick, professor of psychology at the University of Pittsburgh and Codirector of the neoliberal New Standards Project, argues that apprenticeships would enable experts to support learners' efforts in authentic ways in which teachers cannot. In *The End of Work*, Rifkin (1995) suggests that schools should prepare the young for the third sector of the economy, the civic sector, which must be cultivated if a majority of American citizens are to find work at all in the twenty-first century. Even President Clinton suggests that service work in impoverished communities would be spiritually uplifting for the volunteers and beneficial for those that receive services. The Dudley Street example differs primarily in the way community members answer the question, Why read? Resnick, Rifkin, and Clinton continue the functionalist logic to support the status quo among society's institutions; on Dudley Street, they seek transformations that will redirect power in small and large ways, from the twenty to twenty-five percent of Americans who are secure and prospering under past and current political, cultural, and economic conditions, to the seventy-five percent who are insecure and floundering. On Dudley Street, they read and learn to use sophisticated literacies in order to participate actively in their community life as equals to all others. They read to establish, protect, and extend their community and human rights. They seek a public democracy through their reading.

Table 9–1 Public Democratic Political Ideology on Poverty

PUBLIC DEMOCRACY
RADICAL DEMOCRATS
Lack of control and security of circumstances of well-being. Subject to loss of jobs, health care, housing, etc., without much recourse or governmental support.
Imbalance of power favoring the wealthiest 20% of the American population. Inability of the poor to recognize their multiple identities and to form conditions to address mutual goals.
Holly Sklar Francis Fox Pivens Herbert Gans Jonathan Kozol Henry Giroux
Reading education based on active engagement in civic life can help individuals participate in transformative struggles for recognition of difference and redistribution of cultural and economic capital.

During the last two decades, advocates of two approaches to reading education have offered alternatives within radical democratic tradition. Despite their differences, Freirian and systemetic linguistic approaches share the aim of increasing readers' power in society (Luke 1993). Both models make broad assumptions about the sociological effects and consequences of reading. Freirians argue that literacy brings people forced to society's margins to voice, which they use to articulate their interests through their readings of the world. Freirian literacy enables individuals to learn about themselves—their culture and history—to make connections between themselves and others with various social structures, and to act on the new knowledge that they create in these processes. In contrast, advocates of systemic linguistic approaches to literacy education assume that mastery of powerful textual structures can lead to enhanced social access and mobility. These approaches stress explicit instruction concerning the mastery and awareness of those linguistic structures and forms that appear to be prerequisites to gain access to dominant polities, economies, and cultures (Cope and Kalantzis 1993). Both Freirians and advocates of systemic linguistic approaches boast that their preferred literate practices necessarily generate power for the masses.

The argument for systemic linguistic approaches to teaching reading rests on five core assumptions (Cope, Kalantzis, Kress, and Martin 1995). First, lack of access to valued knowledge leads to unequal educational outcomes and, later, economic inequalities. This self-fulfilling prophecy—low educational outcomes reduce opportunities for advanced instruction—hides the institutional nature of this inequality as marginalized individuals and groups are denied further access because of "inherent" deficits. Second, valued knowledge is encoded in the linguistic structures and forms (genre) that experts use in academic disciplines. Third, those genre are clearly definable and are independent of one another (Wignell 1994). Fourth, genres can be taught directly without the necessity of apprenticeship. Five, choice and control of the linguistic forms of disciplinary knowledge will enhance individuals' agency within mainstream institutions and lead to social mobility through credentialed access to better-paying jobs (Halliday and Martin 1993). These assumptions, which seem affirmative at best, are limited in several ways. Overall, they do not include a critique of the inequalities advocates seek to end. Nothing inherent to these approaches leads literate citizens to question their cultural, economic, and political positions in society. Although power may appear to reside in the genres themselves, not all individuals who can choose and control these genres are powerful in society.

There is no guarantee that they will become empowered: the goalposts may shift, as many women and those from ethnic minorities and working-class backgrounds have discovered in the USA and UK, where statistics show that women and people of color who have university degrees cannot obtain the kinds of jobs achieved by white men with comparable qualifications. If the markers of separation are indeed often trivial, then it is not very difficult for those in power to change them as new cohorts of "outsiders" learn the spelling, grammar, and phonology of the dominant group. (Street 1995, 139–140)

Critical Language Awareness (CLA), an offshoot of systemic linguistics, avoids some of the problems with genre approaches to reading education. Often associated with the work of Fairclough (1989, 1992), CLA begins with the premise that the main objective of schooling should be to develop a critical awareness of the world and of the possibilities of changing it. Rather than assert that language necessarily carries power as the genre advocates claim, advocates of CLA attempt to demonstrate the ways language and text shape peoples' understanding, literacy practices, and values. Taking a view that all texts are social constructions, CLA advocates question the apparent transparency and self-evidence of text by reconstructing the generally forgotten processes that underlie it and give it value. Toward that end, learners' language experiences become the curriculum as they develop technical linguistic skills and a critical view of their lives in order to interrogate the origins of their and others' thoughts, values, and actions. They examine texts from their daily experience to investigate how writers describe what is going on in terms of participants, topics, and agency; how the writers indicate attitudes of self, subject, and reader through mood and word choices; and how the contents are organized by theme, voice, and cohesion (Wallace 1995). They also seek to expose the ways in which language and texts are used to create new workers in the neo-liberal mode (Gee, Hull, and Lankshear 1996). In these ways, CLA focuses on developing collective language capabilities of dominated groups "through what Freire calls the conscientization of existing language practices and what enables and constrains them" (Clark, Fairclough, Ivanic, and Martin-Jones 1991, 48).

Freirian approaches to reading education flow from the work of Paulo Freire, a Brazilian educator, who synthesized a pedagogy of the oppressed out of critical theory, liberation theology, and existentialist psychology (Freire 1970). Freirians begin from the assumption that the social world (history) is negotiated among people with differing amounts of power and, consequently, social benefits are owned and distributed accordingly. The historical legacy of these negotiations silences, oppresses, and colonizes the less powerful, who come to see themselves as beneath culture, incapable of managing their own lives, and objects of the "natural" fates that befall them. These conceptions of themselves and their values are presented and represented to the less-powerful daily in the media, through the curricula and practices of schooling, and the policies and regulations of law and other social institutions. Learning to read these messages, imbuing them with authority, and accepting them at face value domesticates and stupefies the less-powerful and reduces the possibilities of public democracy (Macedo 1994). Through literacy education broadly defined, Freirians work to change these historical conditions of inequality and injustice by becoming aware of their own and others' locations in negotiations of the social world, by recognizing the ways in which interests and power act in those negotiations, and by engaging in democratic action based on these new understandings.

What is important to recognize here is the need to reconstitute a radical view of literacy that revolves around the importance of naming and transforming those ideological and social conditions that undermine the possibility for forms of community and public life organized around imperatives of a critical democracy. This is not merely a problem associated with the poor or minority groups; it is also a problem associated with the middle and upper classes who have withdrawn from public life in a world of privatization, pessimism, and greed. (Giroux 1988, 151)

Central to Freirian literacy projects are the complementary goals of helping the powerless to understand the human basis of the social world and history, and to recognize that they have and can play active roles in these constructions. By examining their everyday experiences to determine how social interests are encoded in them, learners begin to understand that laws, policies, even institutions are human artifacts and, therefore, are changeable. In this way, reading to name history gives way to the recognition that the literate can remake history with themselves as active subjects this time. Reading, then, becomes "not just walking on the words, nor flying over the words either" (Freire, as quoted in Shor and Freire 1988, 10). Rather, reading becomes a means to discover connections between a text and its immediate context, and between that immediate text/context and past and present negotiations of the social world. For Freirians, reading is not a technical matter (although techniques are involved); rather, it is an intellectual *and* activist endeavor through which the powerless can grasp the complexities of the social world, evalute them, and actively negotiate and renegotiate them in their community life. (For examples of teachers appropriating Freire, see the essays in Edelsky in press; Shannon 1992; and Shor 1988.)

To develop radical democratic pedagogies consistent with their principles, Freirians attempt to remake the roles of authority, rigor, and context in their teaching. Acknowledging the different knowledges between and among teacher and students, Freirians explore the tension between authority and authoritarianism. That is, they attempt to teach by demonstrating what it means to learn—enabling their learners' knowledge to contribute to the new understanding they develop. Rigor becomes the level to which participants engage the topic at hand—what types of questions are asked, how consequential they are in the participants' lives, how learners are changed by the process. The context for Freirians has at least two dimensions. All words, thoughts, and texts are situated in social, economic, and cultural spaces worthy of exploration. But they are also set in time, which must be examined. Although Freirians do not follow a single orthodoxy, Shor (1988) outlined eight values of Freirian pedagogy.

Reading instruction should be:

1. **Participatory:** Learners must be subjects, not objects, in the development of curricula and the processes of learning.
2. **Critical:** The nature of the curricula leads to analysis and questioning of the sociopolitical and economic realities that shape our lives.
3. **Situated:** The entrance to that analysis and questioning is through learners' daily experiences.
4. **Dialogic:** The processes of learning are inquiries that engage both learners and teachers in the construction of new knowledge through discussion and conversation.
5. **Desocializing:** The curricula and processes of learning seek to identify and explore the effects of society on each learner and teacher.

6. **Democratic:** Although authority cannot be shared equally among learners and teacher, hierarchial relations are reduced by the other pedagogical values, and meanings are socially negotiated.

7. **Interdisciplinary:** Situated experiences of the curricula across academic subject areas and dialogic analyses encourage broad and deep thinking from those areas.

8. **Activist:** Consciousness-raising and skill development are put in service to transformative projects of recognition and redistribution.

Although Freirian approaches to reading education are not widespread in the United States (Shannon 1990), several examples are in practice. Perhaps the most widely known public-school example is the Rethinking Schools group, an organization of teachers who work toward developing transformative solutions to cultural and economic injustices in and out of schools. The organization began in 1986 when a small group of Milwaukee teachers took up the problems of textbook-dominated school curricula and standardized testing. At present, they publish a bimonthly newspaper with a distribution in all fifty states, all Canadian provinces, and many English-speaking countries around the world. In *Rethinking Our Classrooms: Teaching for Equity and Justice*, they offer their statement of purpose:

Brazilian educator Paul Freire writes that teachers should attempt to "live part of their dreams within their educational space." Rethinking Schools believes that classrooms can be places of hope, where students and teachers gain glimpses of the kind of society we could live in and where students learn the academic and critical skills needed to make that vision a reality. (Rethinking Schools 1994, 4)

Often the *Rethinking Schools* newspaper offers classroom teachers' stories about their curriculum and pedagogy in urban schools. For example, Linda Christensen (1992), a high-school English teacher from Portland, Oregon, describes how her students explore issue of race, class, and gender in fairy tales and children's films. Their discussion spread from texts to film to video games to popular music, and ended in the students preparing a pamphlet for parents of school-age children that evaluated these artifacts of popular culture and graded them from A to F based on their help in struggles for cultural and economic understanding and justice. Rita Tenerio, a grade-school teacher from Milwaukee, writes about her efforts to help children learn about each other. "Dealing with issues of race is perhaps the most complicated problem I have encountered as a kindergarten teacher" (1991, 1). This work led to a school-wide policy on antibiased education, in which the complexities of difference become a central element of the school curriculum. Stan Karp, an English teacher from Patterson, New Jersey, encourages teachers to look beyond their classrooms when they think about working for justice. "Critical teaching should not merely be an academic formula for classroom experimentation. It should be a strategy for educational organizing that changes lives, including our own" (1992, 15). He offers a list of ways in which teachers can participate more actively in public life.

Ten Things You Can Do Beyond Your Classroom

1. Serve on a local school council.
2. Become active in your union.
3. Breathe new life into a standing union/school committee.
4. Organize a teachers' study or discussion group.
5. Join the National Coalition of Education Activists.
6. Help distribute *Rethinking Schools*.
7. Join a community organization with an interest in schools.
8. Investigate and publicize trading policies in your school.
9. Flood your faculty room with provocative materials about critical teaching.
10. Investigate and publicize education-funding policies in your state (Karp 1992, 16).

Guiding this work is Rethinking Schools' commitment to transformation. "Schools are integral not only to preparing all children to be full participants in society, but also to be full participants in this country's ever-tenuous experiment in democracy. That this vision has yet to be fully realized does not mean it should be abandoned. . . . We believe teachers, parents, and students are essential to building a movement to go fetch a better future: in our classrooms, in our schools, and in the larger society" (Rethinking Schools 1994, 5).

Other examples of Freirian approaches to reading education include Bizzell's (1992) and Shor's (1992) separate works on pedagogy for transformative recognition and redistribution on university campuses. In *Pedagogies of the Non-Poor*, Alice Evans, Robert Evans, and William Kennedy (1990) offer case studies of privileged learners exploring their location in cultural and economic systems in order to confront their complicity in perpetuating oppression. My *text, lies, & videotape* (Shannon 1995) offers Freirian reading and theorizing of the stories of everyday life. Walsh (1991) describes her work with young Puerto Rican students in New York City struggling to make sense out of and to fashion a voice from the multiple and often contradictory realities that comprise their daily lives. *Writing Permitted in Designated Areas Only* (1992) presents Brodkey's ongoing struggle to infuse Freirian principles into adult literacy courses. Working from a set of letters between adults enrolled in a basic literacy course and learners studying with Brodkey to become teachers in such programs, she offers this Freirian reminder: "Functional literacy requires them to learn to read what we write—our tropes, our worlds, our politics. The letters remind us that in our eagerness to instruct others, we forget that 'illiterate' others also have tropes for literacy. Dialogic literacy would require us to learn to read the unfamiliar tropes in which they write their lives" (87).

Although pointing us toward radical deomocratic practices, Freirian approaches to reading education are not without problems. Freire's personal example worked from a generative set of themes from which labels for important concepts were analyzed according to syllabic rules (Freire 1973). This later aspect has been challenged on two fronts. Edelsky (1991) argues that language cannot be built from the mechanical addition of sounds as Freire claims and that English in particular is not phonically regular. Street (1995) contends that in many attempts to emulate Freire's method, the attention to word-building displaces or postpones attention to meaning-centered work. The use of Freirian methods in mass literacy campaigns has led to charges of cultural insensitivity because generative themes selected by central administrators are not relevant or appropriate for all social subgroups (e.g., Freeland

1990) and because they have not considered the history of oppression in specific historical contexts (e.g., Gibson 1994). Ellsworth (1989) charges that many Freirians assume a greater homogeneity of interests among social groups than actually exists and ease of leveling authority than is possible in a North American context. Freirians contend that power necessarily results from opening the curriculum to provide space in which marginalized people can articulate their interests and develop an analysis of the world. In a sense, this equates power with voice as if words can substitute for material demonstrations of opposition to injustice. While Freirian literacy can help us name and understand cultural and economic injustices, literacy alone won't transform cultural and economic systems. Literacy can help us to see ourselves as agents of history, understand and critique our current conditions, and visualize a better world, but these cerebral tasks must be followed by action to bring about material changes.

Literacy in these terms is not the equivalent of emancipation; it is in a more limited but essential way the precondition for engaging in struggles around both relations of meaning and relations of power. To be literate is *not* to be free; it is to be present and active in the struggle for reclaiming one's voice, history, and future. (Giroux 1988, 155)

READING FOR PUBLIC DEMOCRACY

Throughout this book, I have endeavored to expose the myths of private democracies by demonstrating that seventy-five percent of Americans face the same problem—we do not have sufficient power to gain or maintain security over our well-being. No matter how smart we are, how ethically we behave, or which skills we possess, we are fundamentally vulnerable to a market economy that will not keep people in mind and a government that protects capital, but not us. Our incomes may range from $7,000 to $70,000, but we are similarly subjected to economic, political, and cultural decisions that appear beyond our comprehension or control. Rather than intervene to bring stability to our lives, the federal government has retreated from its modest guarantee to citizens ready to work, reversed its stand on income redistribution through taxes, and wavered on its commitment to citizens who can no longer work. Rather than offering national health insurance, child care, or housing programs, the federal government supports health maintenance organizations, lectures on family values, helps first-time home buyers, and volunteers us to read to children. The divide-and-conquer strategies of conservatives and liberals alike have proved successful in keeping the focus of concern in these matters on individuals and off the transformation of systems based on inequalities. Although these strategies seem to valorize social groups, they have intensified racial, gender, and class antagonisms by apparently favoring some groups over others.

Functionalist views of reading are designed to maintain the cultural, political, and economic unequal status quo—they cannot bring prosperity. Tracked reading by "ability," moral literacy, national standards, and targeted programs attempt to smooth over some rough spots as few of us go "roaring and united into the twenty-first century," as President Clinton says often. His America Reads project borrows neo-conservative and liberal elements to shore up his neo-liberal national standards of every child reading a book independently by third grade and his national examination three times during a school career. Moreover, his criteria for citizenship in "our America" echoes the values of private democracy—be responsible for your own well-being, believe in property rights over all others, and seize the opportunities the global markets make available to us. Schooled with functionalist literacies, many of us are unprepared to look behind the image of two young children reading aloud on library steps or beyond the promise of wealth trickling down from Wall Street. Functionalist reading does not prepare us to see the social in our personal troubles or to recognize the importance of publics in our constructions of common good.

The turning point against private democracy is the current economic context in which the economy can no longer grow its way out of the social problems it causes. This is not just an economic turning point, but an educational one as well because the traditional rationales for schooling and reading education are no longer viable, and we must rethink both; that is, unless we are willing to consciously serve cultural and economic injustices. Under these conditions, issues of recognition and redistribution that have been heretofore unthinkable now deserve our attention, careful consideration, and action. We must develop new ways of thinking about poverty, schooling, and ourselves. Moreover, we must build new partnerships for doing that thinking to garner enough power to transform structures, as well as help individuals.

These facts should not make us pessimistic or render us inactive in public life. Rather, the values expressed in transformational theories and practices present us with opportunities and methods to engage in struggles for cultural and economic justice that will mediate or end poverty. One role for us in these struggles is to read poverty and to help others do so as well, while struggling for public democracies within our classrooms, schools, and communities. To begin, we must find ways to help our students, our colleagues, and ourselves to understand the implications of embracing a relative definition of poverty—one that connects our lives with those of all others. To acknowledge these connections is to grasp a basic tenet of sociological imagination that embeds personal troubles within the problems of social institutions and mores within a private democracy. When poverty is the primary focus, this imagination helps us understand that most Americans face a similar future. That shared future will be a bleak one if we continue to allow ourselves to be isolated as individuals or rigid social groups. It should be more promising if we find ways to embrace our differences and band together to derail the logic of the marketplace from issues of peoples' cultural and economic well-being in our efforts to establish new parameters about what we consider basic human rights.

This is the road that lies ahead. It's not well lit, has many twists and turns, and offers few comfort stops along the way. Certainly, our current location is not a place of rest for most of us. We cannot go back to previous stops, when middle and working classes felt comfortable and the poor did not. Our new knowledge and moral values will not let us pursue that route, even if it were possible. We must go forward because we have visions of a better place that lies along that road. Reading poverty helps us plan our trip. Our efforts in reading education can help more of us deliberate and decide where we shall stop and stay. The time has come to begin. Together we must start walking.

POSTSCRIPT

When You Walk That Walk

When we travel over physical distances, we often have maps or advice to help us along the way. Traveling great distances, we allow an airline, Amtrak, or a bus line to navigate our paths. If we drive ourselves, we call the American Automobile Association for a detailed travel packet that offers us a few options other than times of departure along the way. Locally, we ask someone who's been there before for street names or landmarks to help us find our way. At some level, I wish I had a detailed map to direct all of our paths toward transformative struggles for recognition and redistribution that seek to end poverty as we have come to understand it. Perhaps it would be easiest if I or someone else could simply tell us how to get there. However, I have not drawn nor can I point to a map for all of us to follow, and I see several dangers in a quick grab for directions before the majority of Americans engage actively in public deliberations over issues of poverty.

First, the act of following on public matters is a hallmark of private not public democracy. As I have tried to explain, poverty is not someone else's problem, and it is not a problem that someone else can solve without our input and help. Poverty is our problem that confronts us in general and specific ways in our daily lives. Like it or not, we must engage in

◆◆

203

efforts to name the problems of poverty and to deliberate on what we should do about them. Poverty won't go away and, in fact, it will get worse without our interventions. As the conservative, neo-conservative, neo-liberal, and liberal maps have demonstrated, someone else's map won't take us very far toward cultural and economic justice in America.

Second, although radical democratic principles, the DSNI, and CLA are landmarks for us on our paths, they are not destinations that can be transported across historical, cultural, and geographic boundaries without significant adaptation. Different contexts require negotiations of the meaning and value assigned to the particulars of these landmarks within the specific interests and goals of the coalitions of people engaged in the struggle at hand. Moreover, these landmarks are not complete themselves. They are evolving, even as we consider their possible value, because each new group who takes them up changes them both subtly and profoundly, depending on our perspective. At best (and I do think they are the best), these landmarks and others that I mentioned in this book become topics of public conversation and deliberation as we walk toward equality, security, and freedom.

Third, some of the allure of a ready-made map is in its timesaving. Many of us do not see ourselves as having the luxury of time to probe the dialectics of destination and mode/process of travel. Time is at a premium for many of us as we struggle to find or maintain some security for ourselves and our families in an economy that cannot profit from our well-being. In subtle and not-so-subtle ways, our time becomes less under our control as we work harder and longer at our jobs and at home, just to keep ourselves from falling more abruptly. The forced march of the many works to advance the positions of the few because we have less and less time to consider the underlying causes of our rush to stay still or to contemplate alternatives. With our jobs, our families, and our few social commitments, how could we find the time to travel without a map?

We must face our action humbly, acknowledging that we are capable of only a small part of the actions needed to transform barriers to cultural and economic justice. Without being immodest, but rather believing in transactional reading theory, I believe that we are changed by reading poverty. For some, this change may be inconsequential because, despite my best efforts, they have reaffirmed their commitments to private democracy, property, and inequality while they read this book. In others, however, this change may be substantial as you recognize the futility of continuing conservative, neo-conservative, neo-liberal, or liberal practices of reading education as efforts to serve most of the American people. Within that recognition, you acknowledge your multiple and changing identities and your relationships to poverty. Perhaps you see yourself as facing a dilemma: How do we act on our principles and still keep our jobs?

Because reading poverty exposes the private democratic interests of much of governmental policy, institutional structure, and everyday school practices, we have many levels upon which to direct our actions. Our identities as teachers, workers, community members, and citizens might help us choose to act on one level or proceed on several simultaneously. At any level, we must understand ourselves as part of an ongoing movement and seek fellow travelers who can inform us and whom we can inform. This means establishing ourselves as trusted and supportive members of a group or several groups with whom we share common purposes and goals within particular contexts.

I do not offer the following suggestions lightly because I recognize the difficulties of attempting to change personal practices and the risks of being an agent of change in environments structured to maintain the status quo within the chaos surrounding the current rhetoric of crisis and reform. As teachers, we can develop a more critical praxis within our classrooms as we help others to read poverty also. Such action might take the subtle forms of shifts in our understanding of poor performance and resistance from our students. We now understand IQ, standardized tests, curricular standards, and compensatory programs differently than before we began to read poverty. They cannot be assigned the same explanatory powers as before. The stories offered to convince us of irresponsibility, neglect, and other moral failures of other families now tell us more about the tellers than the told. Even when forced by direct, bureaucratic, and technical forms of power to track, test, and manage our students, we will now find ways to communicate to them that we are not the same as we were

before. The stories we tell, the voices we listen to and consider in our classrooms, and the ways in which we respond to
their efforts will show this to our students.

Changes in our teaching might take less subtle forms also.
We might help students evaluate the official knowledge of our
textbooks and media to investigate what they have to say
about the poverty, the poor, and the possibilities of citizenship. Or perhaps we might seek multiple perspectives on the
stories told, read, written, and watched in our classrooms to
recognize difference, to explore the origins of those differences, to investigate ways in which those differences are val-
orized in the classroom and the world, and to develop ways in
which we might learn to live together with differences. Finding teachers who have pedagogical or unfocused concerns
about the current policies, organization, and practices of
schools, we might consider ways to dissent from the policies
and practices that direct us to teach against minorities and to
work against the majority. In this way, we can provide leadership in helping our peers read poverty, elevating the substance
of our critique, forming new coalitions, and offering new possibilities for real changes to occur.

Some of our energy should be devoted to organizing support for saving the idea of public schooling from conservative
and neo-conservative initiatives to privatize education
through vouchers and regressive school-choice schemes or
neo-liberal projects to reduce schooling to training for business. Schools are among the last public places where the
majority of Americans meet together—or at least have the
opportunity to meet together if geographic isolation does not
allow racial and class segregation. As an established public,
which admittedly has not served that function for a long time
in many communities, public schools offer us a place and an
issue to begin our work toward justice. The possibilities for
discussion of differences, economic realities, and our future
together are built into the daily life of public schooling. For
too long, we have followed someone else's map about the
potential of public schools to serve the majority. Because of
their location in every community, public schools offer us
opportunities to embed our efforts within the material circumstances and interests of our school communities.

Such action requires that we become part of the communities in which we work, as well as the ones in which we live.

In times of school redistricting, mobile populations, and (let me be honest) fear of the other, we often don't live in the same communities in which we teach. That fact should not preclude us from coming to know our students, their families, and other community members as citizens, workers, church members—as people like us. Walking the streets of the communities surrounding the schools in which we teach, attending community meetings apart from school, and inviting community members into your curriculum through oral histories and expert lessons can help many recognize the roles that public schools could play in community life. If nothing else, schools are probably the largest public space in any neighborhood. They can become the largest site for organizing community engagement in civic, cultural, and political action. As teachers interested in cultural and economic justice, we must find ways to make our schools places where the community comes to deliberate and engage in public democracy, and not just a place to send their children and to come to vote in a private one.

As workers, we might find ways to join efforts with others outside our daily workplace to increase workers' control over their own and their families' well-being. Despite the term *teaching profession,* we are service workers who are not easily included in discussion of productive capacity or profit. We provide services on several levels to individuals and society. We are clearly among the seventy-five percent of Americans who have seen their incomes drop, their security wane, and their control over their lives fade. Like the production workers at General Motors, service workers at United Parcel, and federal employees across the country, we have seen our work become subcontracted to decrease costs, negotiated contracts that establish a tiered system of employment and benefits among teachers, and terms of employment that become more and more contingent on our employers' wishes. Although teachers are the most unionized employment in the United States, we rarely demonstrate solidarity with other unions and groups attempting to gain better control of their present and future. We can show individual support for such actions in the future with our time and money. If we find ways to make our example lead to union, or broader support among teachers, for workers' rights, then we can rightfully expect other workers and their families to support us when our interests intersect.

As community members, we can join church groups, private charities, and civic organizations in their efforts to help individuals and families find enough to eat, a safe place to stay, and decent medical care. With various levels of government retreating from these responsibilities, these groups find themselves overwhelmed by the demand for their services. We should do what we can, but we must be clear that these efforts do little to alleviate the causes of poverty, and they do not stop the widening gap between the rich and the rest of us. They do not redistribute power in society in order to democratize the control over personal well-being. Being a community member is being a citizen, and we must fight not just to prevent conservative attempts to blame inequalities upon us or to restore the liberal affirmative programs that give with one hand and take away with the other. Rather, we must find ways to insert our reading of poverty in the current public spaces available to us in our schools and in our unions, and to create new publics that bring broader audiences together to converse, deliberate, and debate issues of cultural and economic justice in America.

Ultimately, our work in and out of schools should be to help the majority read poverty—to develop their voices, learn to use them in multiple contexts to express their interests, explore differences to find ways to form fluid coalitions based on collective goals, and act in the world to help us all walk toward justice. This is a worthy new rationale for schooling and reading education.

REFERENCES

Adler, M. 1982. *The Paideia Proposal: An Educational Manifesto.* New York: Macmillan.

Albelda, R., and N. Folbre. 1996. *The War on the Poor: A Defense Manual.* New York: The New Press.

Allen, J., B. Michalove, and B. Shockley. 1994. *Engaging Children: Community and Chaos in the Lives of Young Literary Learners.* Portsmouth, NH: Heinemann.

Allington, R., and S. Walmsley. 1995. *No Quick Fix: Rethinking Literacy Programs in America's Elementary Schools.* New York: Teachers College Press.

Anderson, R. 1989. *Becoming a Nation of Readers.* Washington, DC: National Institute for Education.

Aronowitz, S. 1994. "A Different Perspective on Educational Inequality." *Review of Educational Research,* 14, 135–142.

————. 1996. "Toward Radicalism: The Death and Rebirth of the American Left." In D. Trend (ed.), *Radical Democracy: Identity, Citizenship, and the State.* New York: Routledge.

Aronowitz, S., and W. DiFazio. 1994. *The Jobless Future: Sci-Tech and the Dogma of Work.* Minneapolis, MN: University of Minnesota Press.

Aronowitz, S., and H. Giroux. 1985. *Education Under Siege.* South Hadley, MA: Bergin and Garvey.

Au, K. 1993. *Literacy Insturction in Multicultural Settings.* Fort Worth, TX: Harcourt Brace.

Baker, E. 1994. "Researchers and Assessment Policy Development: A Cautionary Tale." *American Journal of Education,* 102, 450–477.

◆◆

Ball, S. 1990. *Politics and Policy-making in Education: Explorations in Policy Sociology.* New York: Routledge.

Bartlett, D., and J. Steele. 1992. *America: What Went Wrong?* Kansas City, MO: Andrews and McMeel.

Bartlett, D., and R. Steele. 1996. *America: Who Stole the Dream?* Kansas City, MO: Andrews and McMeel.

Baumann, J. 1984. "The Effectiveness of a Direct Instruction Paradigm for Teaching Main Idea Comprehension." *Reading Research Quarterly,* 20, 93–115.

Becker, W. 1977. "Teaching Reading and Language to the Disadvantaged—What We Have Learned from Field Research." *Harvard Educational Review,* 47, 518–543.

Bennett, W. 1984. *What Works: Research About Teaching and Learning.* Washington, DC: Government Printing Office.

————. 1986. *First Lessons: A Report on Elementary Education in America.* Washington, DC: Government Printing Office.

————. 1988. *James Madison Elementary School: A Curriculum for American Schools.* Washington, DC: Government Printing Office.

————. (ed.) 1994a. *The Book of Virtues: A Treasury of Great Moral Stories.* New York: Simon & Schuster.

————. 1994b. *The Index of Leading Cultural Indicators: Facts and Figures of the State of American Society.* New York: Touchstone.

————. (ed.) 1995a. *The Moral Compass.* New York: Simon & Schuster.

————. (ed.) 1995b. *The Children's Book of Virtues.* New York: Simon & Schuster.

————. 1996. *Body Count: Moral Poverty and How to Win America's War Against Crime and Drugs.* New York: Simon & Schuster.

Berliner, D., and B. Biddle. 1995. *The Manufactured Crisis: Myths, Fraud, and the Attack on America's Public Schools.* Reading, MA: Addison Wesley.

Bernstein, N. 1996. "Giant Companies Entering Race to Run State Welfare Programs: Powers Like Lockheed Explore New Profit Area." *New York Times,* (15 September,) A1, 26.

Besharov, D. 1995. "A Moral Imperative." In R. Jacoby and N. Glauberman (eds.). *The Bell Curve Debate: History, Documents, Opinions.* New York: Times Books.

Bizzell, P. 1992. *Academic Discourse and Critical Consciousness.* Pittsburgh, PA: University of Pittsburgh.

Blackburn, M. 1994. "International Comparisons of Poverty." *American Economic Review,* 4, 371–374.

Blank, R. 1997. *It Takes a Nation: A New Agenda for Fighting Poverty.* Princeton, NJ: Princeton University Press.

Bloom, A. 1987. *The Closing of the American Mind.* New York: Simon & Schuster.

Bok, D. 1993. *The Cost of Talent: How Executives and Professionals Are Paid and How It Affects America.* New York: Free Press.

Boston Globe. 1996. Editorial. "A consensus of hope." (19 May,) 70.

Brimelow, P. 1994. "For Whom the Bell Tolls." *Forbes,* (24 October,) 37–41.

Brodkey, L. 1992. *Writing Permitted in Designated Areas Only.* Minneapolis, MN: University of Minnesota.

Brown, A., and C. Day. 1983. "The Development of Plans for Summarizing Texts." *Child Development,* 54, 968–79.

Brown, H. 1997. "Brenda Eheart." *Ms.* (January/February) 44–47.

Burke, E. 1949. *Selected Writings and Speeches on Reform, Revolution and War.* J. S. Ross (ed.) New York: Knopf.

Burtless, G. 1996. *Does Money Matter: The Effect of School Resources on Student Achievement and Adult Success.* Washington DC: Brookings Institution Press.

CBS/*New York Times.* 1995, April 1–4. "Public's Opinion on Government Spending." Conducted by Roper Center for Public Opinion Research.

CSR. 1985, June. *The Impact of Head Start on Children, Families, and Communities.* (Contract No. 105-81-C-26). Washington, DC: CSR Publishing.

Calfee, R., and P. Drum. 1979. *Teaching Reading in Compensatory Classes.* Newark, DE: International Reading Association.

Callaghan, P., and H. Hartmann. 1991. *Contingent Work.* Washington DC: Economy Policy Institute.

Cancian, M., and L. Gordon. Fall 1996. "Making Mothers 'Work'." *Dissent,* 73–75.

Carnegie Forum on Education and the Economy. 1986. *A Nation Prepared: Teachers for the Twenty-first Century.* New York: Carnegie Foundation.

Carson, C., R. Huelskamp, and T. Woodall. 1991. *Perspectives on Education in America: Annotated Briefing—Third Draft.* Albuquerque, NM: Sandia Laboratories.

Carville, J. 1996. *We're Right, They're Wrong: A Handbook for Spirited Progressives.* New York: Random House.

Cassidy, J. 1995. "Who Killed the Middle Class?" *The New Yorker,* (16 October,) 68, 113–124.

Castells, M. 1980. *The Economic Crisis and American Society.* Princeton, NJ: Princeton University Press.

Castro, J. 1993. "Disposable Workers." *Time,* (29 March,) 57–59.

Celebreeze, A. 1965. *Aid to Elementary and Secondary Education: Hearings Before the General Subcommittee on Education of the Committee on Education and Labor,* 89th Congress, 1st session. Washington, DC: Government Printing Office.

Chall, J., V. Jacobs, and L. Baldwin. 1990. *The Reading Crisis: Why Poor Children Fall Behind.* Cambridge, MA: Harvard University Press.

Cherland, M. 1994. *Private Practices: Girls Reading Fiction and Constructing Identity.* Bristol, PA: Falmer.

Children's Defense Fund. 1992. *The State of America's Children.* Washington, DC: Children's Defense Fund.

————. 1992. *Vanishing Dreams: The Economic Plight of Young Families.* Washington, DC: Children's Defense Fund.

Christensen, L. 1992. "Unlearning the Myths That Bind Us: Critiquing Fairy Tales and Films." *Rethinking Schools,* 5, 1, 9–10.

Christian-Smith, L. 1993. *Texts of Desire: Essays on Fiction, Femininity, and Schooling.* Bristol, PA: Falmer.

Citizens for Tax Justice. 1991. *Inequality and the Federal Budget Deficit.* Washington, DC: Citizens for Tax Justice.

Clark, R., N. Fairclough, R. Ivanic, and M. Martin-Jones. 1991. "Critical Language Awareness: Towards Critical Alternatives." *Language and Education,* 5, 41–54.

Clinton, W. 1996. Wyandotte Speech. (27 August) Washington, DC: Democratic Party Press Release.

Congressional Record. 1995. (February 8,) E301.

Conniff, R. 1997. "Girding for Disaster: Local Officials and Private Charities Brace Themselves for Welfare Reform." *Progressive,* (March) 61, 22–25.

Coontz, S. 1992. "Testimony Before the House Select Committee on Children, Youth, and Families July 23, 1992." In K. de Koster (ed.), *Poverty: Opposing Viewpoints.* San Diego, CA: Greenhaven Press.

Cooper, M. 1997. "A Town Betrayed: Oil and Greed in Lima Ohio." *Nation,* (14 July,) 265, 11–14.

Cope, B., and M. Kalantzis (ed.) 1993. *The Literacies of Power and the Powers of Literacies.* Philadelphia, PA: Falmer Press.

Cope, B., M. Kalantzis, G. Kress, and J. Martin. 1995. "Developing the Theory and Practice of Genre-based Literacy." In B. Cope and

M. Kalantzis, eds. *The Power of Literacy*. Philadelphia, PA: Falmer Press.

Cremin, L. 1988. *American Education: The Metropolitan Experience 1876–1980*. New York: Harper and Row.

Current Population Report. 1992. *Money Income of Households, Families, and Persons in the U.S.*, 184, 13–37.

Dahl, K., and P. Freepon. 1995. "A Comparison of Inner City Children's Interpretations of Reading and Writing Instruction in the Early Grades in Skills-based and Whole Language Classrooms." *Reading Research Quarterly*, 30, 50–75.

Danziger, S., and P. Gottschalk. 1995. "Hardly Making It: The Increase in Low Earnings and What to Do About It." In T. Schwartz and K. Weigirt (eds.), *America's Working Poor*. South Bend, IN: Notre Dame University.

Danziger, S., and D. Lehman, 1994. "Jobs Available to the Poor." In S. Danziger, G. Sandefur, and D. Weinberg (eds.) *Confronting Poverty: Prescriptions for Change*. Cambridge, MA: Harvard University Press.

Darling-Hammond, L. 1994. "National Standards and Assessments: Will They Improve Education?" *American Journal of Education*, 102, 478–510.

Davis, P. 1995. *If You Came This Way: A Journey Through the Lives of the Underclass*. New York: John Wiley and Sons.

Delpit, L. 1995. *Other People's Children*. New York: New Press.

Deutsch, M. 1963. "The Disadvantaged Child and the Learning Process." In A. H. Passow (ed.), *Education in Depressed Areas*. New York: Teachers College Press.

Diegmueller, K. 1994. "Ehlich Group Loses Funding for Standards." *Education Week*, (30 March,) 14, 1, 9.

Dreyfuss, R. 1996. "The End of Social Security as We Know It?" *Mother Jones*, (November/December) 20, 50–58.

Easton, D. 1953. *The Political System: An Inquiry into the State of Political Change*. NewYork: Knopf.

Economic Report to the President. 1995. Washington, DC: Government Printing Office.

Edelsky, C. 1991. *With Literacy and Justice for All: Rethinking the Social in Language and Education*. Philadelphia, PA: Falmer Press.

———. (in press). *Critical Literacy in the Classroom*. Urbana, IL: National Council of Teachers of English.

Edin, K. 1997. *Making Ends Meet*. New York: Russell Sage Foundation.

Ellsworth, E. 1989. "Why Doesn't This Feel Empowering? Working Through the Repressive Myths of Critical Pedagogy." *Harvard Educational Review*, 59, 297–324.

Ellwood, D. 1988. *Poor Support: Poverty in the American Family.* New York: Basic Books.

Elson, J. 1994. "History, the Sequel." *Time*, (7 November,) 64.

Emig, J. 1993. "Curricular Standards: Federal or National." *Reading Today*, 11, 40.

Epstein, B. 1996. "Radical Democracy and Cultural Politics: What About Class? What About Political Power?" In D. Trend, ed., *Radical Democracy.* New York: Routledge.

Evans, A., R. Evans, and W. Kennedy. 1990. *Pedagogies of the Non-Poor.* New York: Orbis Books.

Fairclough, N. 1989. *Language and Power.* New York: Longman.

Fairclough, N. 1992. *Discourse and Change.* Cambridge, England: Polity Press.

Family Research Council. 1994. *Welfare and Families.* Washington, DC: Family Research Council.

Finders, M. 1996. *Just Girls: Hidden Literacies and Life in Junior High.* New York: Teachers College Press.

Fine, M. 1991. *Framing School Dropouts: Notes on the Politics of an Urban Public High School.* Albany, NY: SUNY Press.

Folbre, N. 1995. *The New Field Guide to the U.S. Economy.* New York: New Press.

Fowler, F. 1995. "The Neo-liberal Value Shift and Its Implications for Federal Education Policy Under Clinton." *Educational Administration Quarterly*, 31, 38–60.

Fraser, N. 1995. "From Redistribution to Recognition? Dilemmas of Justice in a 'Post Socialist' Age." *New Left Review*, 212, 68–93.

——— . 1997. *Justice Interruptus: Critical Reflections on the "Post-Socialist" Condition.* New York: Routledge.

Fraser, S. (ed.) 1995. *The Bell Curve Wars: Race, Intelligence, and the Future of America.* New York: Basic Books.

Freeland, J. 1990. *The Atlantic Coast in the Nicaraguan Revolution.* New York: Blackwell.

Freidman, J. 1995. "Buchanan for President." *New York Times*, (24 December,) E9.

Freire, P. 1970. *Pedagogy of the Oppressed.* New York: Seabury.

——— . 1973. *Education for Critical Consciousness.* New York: Seabury.

Fulwood, S. 1990. "Working and Poor." *Los Angeles Times*, (9 February,) D1.

Gailbraith, J. K. 1992. *The Culture of Contentment.* Boston, MA: Houghton Mifflin.

Gans, H. 1995. *The War Against the Poor.* New York: Basic Books.

Gardner, H. 1994. "Cracking Open the IQ Box." *The American Prospect,* (Winter) 121–126.

Gee, J. P., G. Hull, and C. Lankshear. 1996. *The New Work Order: Behind the Language of the New Capitalism.* Boulder, CO: Westview Press.

Gerson, M. 1996. *The Neo-conservative Vision: From the Cold War to the Culture Wars.* Lanham, MD: Madison Books.

————. 1997. *In the Classroom: Dispatches from an Inner-city School That Works.* New York: Free Press.

Gibson, R. 1994. *Promethean Literacy: Paulo Freire's Pedagogy of Reading, Praxis, and Liberation.* An unpublished doctoral thesis, Penn State University.

Gilder, G. 1981. *Wealth and Poverty.* New York: Basic Books.

Gillette, M. 1996. *Launching the War on Poverty: An Oral History.* New York: Twayne Publishers.

Giroux, H. 1988. *Schooling and the Struggle for Public Life: Critical Pedagogy in the Modern Age.* Minneapolis, MN: University of Minnesota Press.

Glazer, N. 1994. "Is Intelligence Fixed?" *National Review,* (5 December,) 62–63.

Goldberg, D. T. 1990. *Anatomy of Racism.* Minneapolis, MN: University of Minnesota Press.

Goodman, J. 1996. "Student Pizzeria Still Delivering Second Chances." *Washington Post,* (28 November,) C1, 3.

Goodman, K. 1996. *On Reading.* Portsmouth, NH: Heinemann.

Gordon, D. 1996. *Fat and Mean: The Corporate Squeeze of Working Americans and the Myth of Managerial Downsizing.* New York: Free Press.

Gould, S. J. 1994. "Curveball." *The New Yorker,* (28 November,) 24–29.

Greenhouse, S. 1997. "UPS Strike Over Trends in Employment." *New York Times,* (14 August,) A1, A22.

Greenwald, J. 1993. "Bellboys with BAs." *Time,* (22 November,) 36.

Greer, C., and H. Kohl. (eds.) 1995. *A Call to Character: A Family Treasure.* New York: Harper Collins.

Halliday, M., and J. Martin. 1993. *Writing Science.* Philadelphia, PA: Falmer.

Harman, S., and C. Edelsky. 1989. "The Risks of Whole Language Literacy: Alienation and Connection." *Language Arts, 66,* 392–406.

Harrington, M. 1962. *The Other America: Poverty in the United States.* New York: Macmillan.

———. 1984. *The New American Poverty.* New York: Holt, Rinehart & Winston.

Heath, S. B. 1983. *Ways with Words.* New York: Cambridge University Press.

———. 1992. "Oral and Literate Traditions Among Black Americans Living in Poverty." In P. Shannon (ed.), *Becoming Political.* Portsmouth, NH: Heinemann.

Heilbronner, R., and L. Thurow. 1982. *Economics Explained.* Englewood Cliffs, NJ: Prentice-Hall.

Heller, W. 1964. "The Problem of Poverty in America." In *The Annual Report of the Council of Economic Advisors.* Washington, DC: Government Printing Office.

Herrnstein, R. 1971. "IQ." *Atlantic Monthly,* (September) 43–64.

Herrnstein, R., and C. Murray. 1994. *The Bell Curve: Intelligence and Class Structure in American Life.* New York: Free Press.

Hiebert, E., and B. Taylor. 1994. *Getting Reading Right From the Start.* Boston: Allyn & Bacon.

Hirsch, E. D. 1987. *Cultural Literacy: What Every American Needs to Know.* Boston, MA: Houghton Mifflin.

———. 1993. *The Dictionary of Cultural Literacy. 2nd Edition.* Boston, MA: Houghton Mifflin.

———. 1996. "Reality's Revenge: Research and Ideology." *American Educator,* (Fall) 19, 4–6, 31–47.

Hoff, D. 1997a. "Title I Quirks Pit Well-to-do, Poor Schools." *Education Week,* (5 February,) 14.

———. 1997b. "Chapter One Aid Failed to Close Learning Gap." *Education Week,* (12 April,) 12.

Honig, B. 1996. *Teaching Our Children to Read: The Role of Skills in a Comprehensive Reading Program.* San Francisco: Corwin.

Hornbeck, D., and L. Solomon. 1991. *Human Capital and America's Future.* Baltimore, MD: Johns Hopkins University.

House, E. 1978. "Evaluation as Scientific Management in U.S. School Reform." *Comparative Education Review, 22,* 388–401.

Hull, G. 1993. "Hearing Other Voices: A Critical Assessment of Popular Voices on Literacy and Work." *Harvard Educational Review, 63,* 20–47.

Hunter, C. St. John, and D. Harman. 1979. *Adult Illiteracy in the United States: A Report to the Ford Foundation.* New York: McGraw-Hill.

Jackson, Jr., J. 1997. "Why Race Dialogue Stutters." *Nation,* (31 March,) 264, 22–24.

Jacoby, R., and N. Glauberman. (eds.) 1994. *The Bell Curve Debate: History, Documents, Opinions.* New York: Times Books.

Jendryka, B. 1993. "Failing Grade for Federal Aid." *Policy Review,* 66, 77–81.

Jensen, A. 1969. "How Much Can We Boost IQ and Scholastic Achievement?" *Harvard Educational Review,* 39, 1–123.

———. 1994. "Paroxysms of Denial." *National Review,* (5 December,) 37.

Jensen, M., and P. Fagan. 1996. "Capitalism Isn't Broken." *The Wall Street Journal.* (29 March,) A1.

Johnston, R. 1994. "By Any Other Name, Chapter One Program Will Still Aid Children." *Education Week,* (12 October,) 14.

Jordan, J. 1993. "Freedom Time." *The Progressive,* (November) 57, 18–20.

Kaestle, C., and M. Smith. 1982. "The Federal Role in Elementary and Secondary Education, 1940–1980." *Harvard Educational Review,* 52, 384–408.

Kantor, H., and R. Lowe. 1994. "Class, Race, and the Emergence of Federal Education Policy: From the New Deal to the Great Society." *Educational Researcher,* 24, 4–11.

Karp, S. 1992. "Why We Need to Go Beyond the Classroom." *Rethinking Schools,* 5, 1, 5, 6.

Katz, M. B. 1989. *The Undeserving Poor: From the War on Poverty to the War on Welfare.* New York: Pantheon Books.

Kennickell, A., and J. Shack-Marquez. 1992. "Changes in Family Finances from 1983 to 1989." *Federal Reserve Bulletin,* 78, 1–18.

Keppel, F. 1965. *Aid to Elementary and Secondary Education: Hearings Before the General Subcommittee on Education of the Committee on Education and Labor, 89th Congress, 1st Session.* Washington, DC: Government Printing Office.

Kincheloe, J., S. Steinberg, and A. Gresson. 1996. *Measured Lies: The Bell Curve Examined.* New York: St. Martin's Press.

Klein, J. 1993. "How About a Good Swift Kick?" *Newsweek,* (23 July,) 30.

Knoblauch, S., and L. Brannon. 1993. *Critical Teaching and the Idea of Literacy.* Portsmouth, NH: Boynton/Cook.

Kozol, J. 1985. *Illiterate America.* New York: Anchor.

————. 1991. *Savage Inequalities: Children in America's Schools.* New York: Crown.

————. 1995. *Amazing Grace: The Lives of Children and the Conscience of a Nation.* New York: Crown.

Laclau, E., and C. Mouffe. 1985. *Hegemony and Socialist Strategy: Toward a Radical Democratic Politics.* London: Verso.

Lee, C. 1995. "A Culturally-based Cognitive Apprenticeship." *Reading Research Quarterly,* 30, 608–631.

Leo, J. 1996. "Shakespeare vs. Spiderman." *U.S. News and World Report.* (1 April,) 37.

LeTendre, M. J. 1991. "The Continuing Evolution of a Federal Role in Compensatory Education." *Educational Evaluation and Policy Analysis,* 13, 328–334.

Levitan, S., F. Gallo, and I. Shapiro. 1993. *Working but Poor: America's Contradiction.* Baltimore, MD: Johns Hopkins University.

Lewis, O. 1966. "The Culture of Poverty." *Scientific American,* 215, 19–26.

Lopez, J. 1993. "College Class of '93 Learns Hard Lesson." *The Wall Street Journal,* (20 May,) B10.

Loupe, D. 1997. "Literacy in Georgia: An Interview with our First Lady." *Atlanta Constitution,* (26 February,) C4.

Loury, G. 1994. "Dispirited." *National Review.* (5 December,) 42–43.

Lowery, G. 1996. "A Dissent from the Incentive Approaches to Reducing Poverty." In M. Darby (ed.), *Reducing Poverty in America.* Thousand Oaks, CA: Sage Publications.

Luke, A. 1993. "Genres of Power? Literacy Education and the Production of Capital." In Freebody and A. Welsh (eds.), *Knowledge, Culture, and Power.* London: Falmer.

Macedo, D. 1994. *Literacies of Power: What Americans Are Not Allowed to Know.* Boulder, CO: Westview.

Magnet, M. 1993. *The Dream and the Nightmare: The Sixties' Legacy to the Underclass.* New York: William Morrow and Co.

————. 1994. "A Lack of Moral Values Created the Underclass." In K. de Koster (ed.), *Poverty: Opposing Viewpoints.* San Diego, CA: Greenhaven Press.

Mann, H. 1848. "Twelfth Annual Report of the State of Schools in Massachussetts." In L. Cremin (ed.), 1957, *The Republic and the School.* New York: Teachers College Press.

Marshall, R., and M. Tucker. 1992. *Thinking for a Living: Work, Skills, and the Future of the American Economy.* New York: Basic Books.

Massey, D. and N. Denton. 1993. *American Apartheid: Segregation and the Making of the Underclass.* Cambridge, MA: Harvard University Press.

McCollum-Clark, K. 1995. *National Council of Teachers of English, Corporate Philanthropy, and National Education Standards: Challenging the Ideologies of English Education Reform.* An unpublished dissertation, The Pennsylvania State University.

McGill-Franzen, A. 1987. "Failure to Learn to Read: Formulating a Policy Problem." *Reading Research Quarterly*, 22, 475–490.

———. 1993. *Shaping the Preschool Agenda: Early Literacy, Public Policy, and Professional Beliefs.* Albany, NY: SUNY Press.

McLaughlin, M. 1975. *Evaluation and Reform.* Cambridge, MA: Ballinger.

Mead, L. 1992. *The New Politics of Poverty: The Nonworking Poor in America.* New York: Basic Books.

———. 1996. "Raising Work Levels Among the Poor." In M. Darby (ed.), *Reducing Poverty in America.* Thousand Oaks, CA: Sage Publications.

Medoff, P., and H. Sklar. 1994. *Streets of Hope: The Fall and Rise of an Urban Neighborhood.* Boston, MA: South End Press.

Meisler, S. 1990. "Reading the Signs of Crisis." *Los Angeles Times,* (11 May,) A1, 18.

Merton, T. 1967. *Social Theory and Social Structure.* New York: Free Press.

Mills, C. W. 1959. *The Sociological Imagination.* New York: Oxford University Press.

Moll, L. 1993. "Bilingual Classroom Studies and Community Analysis." *Educational Reseracher*, 21, 20–24.

Moll, L., and J. Greenberg. 1991. "Creating Zones of Possibility." In L. Moll (ed.), *Vygotsky and Education.* New York: Cambridge University Press.

Murray, C. 1984. *Losing Ground: American Social Policy 1950–1980.* New York: Basic Books.

———. 1996. "Reducing Poverty and Reducing the Underclass: Different Problems, Different Solutions." In M. Darby (ed.), *Reducing Poverty in America.* San Diego, CA: Sage Publications.

Myers, M. 1993. "Work Worth Doing." *The Council Chronicle,* (June) 2.

———. 1994. "Problems and Issues Facing the National Standards Project in English." *Education and Urban Society*, 26, 141–157.

———. 1995. "National Standards Movement and CCCC: Why Participate?" *College Composition and Communication*, 46, 438–440.

Myrdal, G. 1944. *An American Dilemma: The Negro Problem and Modern Democracy.* New York: Harper & Row.

National Assessment of Educational Progress. 1996. *NAEP 1994 Reading Report Card.* Princeton, NJ: Educational Testing Service.

National Center for Education Statistics. 1993. *Adult Literacy in America.* Washington, DC: U.S. Department of Education.

National Center for Family Literacy. 1989. *Breaking the Cycle of Illiteracy.* Louisville, KY: Kenan Charitable Trust.

———. 1994. *The Power of Family Literacy.* Louisville, KY: National Center for Family Literacy.

National Commission on Excellence in Education. 1983. *A Nation at Risk.* Washington, DC: U.S. Department of Education.

National Council of Education Standards and Testing. 1991. *Raising National Standards for American Education.* Washington, DC: U.S. Government Office of Printing.

National Council of Teachers of English and International Reading Association. 1996. *Standards for the English Language Arts,* (March) Urbana, IL: NCTE/IRA.

"NCTE/IRA Say Standards Effort Will Continue." 1994. *The Council Chronicle.* (June) 24.

Neilsen, L. 1989. *Literacy and Living: The Literate Lives of Three Adults.* Portsmouth, NH: Heinemann.

New York Times. 1995. Editorial. "How Our Money is Spent." (13 June,) A21.

———. 1996. *The Downsizing of America.* New York: Times Books.

———. 1996. "How Not to Write English." Editorial. (14 March,) A22.

Noble, D. 1994. "Let Them Eat Skills." *The Review of Education/ Pedagogy/ Cultural Studies,* 16, 15–29.

Nussbaum, M. C. 1994. "Divided We Stand." *The New Republic,* (10 and 17 January,) 38–42.

Oakes, J. 1985. *Keeping Track: How Schools Structure Inequality.* New Haven, CT: Yale University Press.

Olszewski, L. 1993. "U.S. Strains to Cope with Literacy Crisis." *San Francisco Chronicle,* (17 September,) A1, 13.

Parsons, T. 1959. "The School Class as a Social System." *Harvard Educational Review,* 29, 297–319.

Pear, R. 1996. "States' Authority on Welfare Money Is Being Disputed." *New York Times,* (29 December,) A1.

Pearson, P. D. 1993. "Standards for the English Language Arts: A Policy Review." *Journal of Reading Behavior,* 25, 457–475.

Phillips, K. 1990. *The Politics of Rich and Poor*. New York: Random House.

Piper, W. 1984. *The Little Engine That Could*. New York: Platt & Munk.

Piven, F., and R. Cloward. 1971. *Regulating the Poor: The Function of Public Welfare*. New York: Vintage.

Postman, N. 1996. *The End of Education: Redefining the Value of School*. New York: Knopf.

Proulx, A. 1993. "X Marks the Shame of Illiteracy." *Chicago Tribune*, (28 September,) A21.

Prunty, J. 1985. "Signposts for a Critical Policy Analysis." *Australian Journal of Education*, 29, 133–140.

Purcell-Gates, V., and K. Dahl. 1991. "Low-SES Children's Success and Failure at Early Literacy in Skills-based Classrooms." *Journal of Reading Behavior*, 23, 1–34.

Raphael, T. 1984. "Teaching Learners About Sources of Information for Answering Comprehension Questions." *Journal of Reading*, 27, 303–311.

Reed, Jr., A. 1994. "Intellectual Brown Shirts." *The Progressive*, (December) 58, 18–21.

————. 1997. "Token Equality." *The Progressive*, (February) 61, 18–19.

Reich, R. 1991. *The Work of Nations*. New York: Vintage.

————. 1997. *Locked in the Cabinent*. New York: Knopf.

Rethinking Schools. 1994. *Rethinking Our Classrooms: Teaching for Equity and Justice*. Milwaukee, WI: Rethinking Schools.

Rifkin, J. 1995. *The End of Work: The Decline of the Global Labor Force and the Dawn of the Post-market Era*. New York: Thacker Putnam.

Roper, R. 1994. "Income survey." *The American Enterprise*, 4, 9–10.

Rotberg, I. and J. Harvey. 1993. Federal Policy Options for Improving the Education of Low-Income Students. Santa Monica, CA: Rand Corporation.

Sanchez, R. 1996. "Reading Standards Criticized." *Washington Post*, (13 March,) A3.

Sapon-Shevin, M. 1995. *Playing Favorites: Gifted Education and the Disruption of Community*. Albany, NY: SUNY Press.

Schiller, B. 1995. *The Economics of Poverty and Discrimination*. Englewood Cliffs, NJ: Prentice-Hall.

Schwartz, J., and T. Volgey. 1992. *The Forgotten Americans*. New York: W. W. Norton.

Schweinhart, L., H. Barnes, and D. Weikart. 1993. *Significant Benefits: The High Scope Perry Preschool Study Through Age 27.* Ypsilanti, MI: High/Scope Press.

Schweinhart, L., D. Weikart, and M. Larner. 1986. "Consequences of Three Preschool Curriculum Models Through Age 15." *Early Childhood Research Quarterly,* 1, 15–45.

Sedgwick, J. 1994. "The Mentality Bunker." *GQ,* (November) 78–83.

Sehr, D. 1996. *Education for Public Democracy.* New York: SUNY Press.

Shannon, P. 1990. *The Struggle to Continue: Progressive Reading Instruction in the United States.* Portsmouth, NH: Heinemann.

———. 1992. *Becoming Political: Readings and Writings on the Politics of Literacy.* Portsmouth, NH: Heinemann.

———. 1995. *text, lies, & videotape: Stories About Life, Literacy and Learning.* Portsmouth, NH: Heinemann.

———. 1996. "Mad as Hell." *Language Arts,* 73, 14–18.

Shelton, B. 1992. *Women, Men, and Time: Gender Differences in Paid Work, Housework, and Leisure.* Westport, CT: Greenwood.

Sherman, A. 1994. *Wasting America's Future: The Children's Defense Fund Report on the Cost of Child Poverty.* Boston, MA: Beacon.

Shor, I. 1988. *Working Hands and Critical Minds: A Paulo Freire Model for Job Training.* Chicago, IL: Alternative School Network.

———. 1992. *Empowering Education: Critical Teaching for Social Change.* Chicago, IL: University of Chicago Press.

Shor, I., and P. Freire. 1988. *A Pedagogy for Liberation: Dialogues on Transforming Education.* Westport, CT: Bergin and Garvey.

Short, K., J. Harste, and C. Burke. 1996. *Creating Classrooms for Authors and Inquirers.* Portsmouth, NH: Heinemann.

Sklar, H. 1995. *Chaos or Community? Seeking Solutions, Not Scapegoats, for Bad Economics.* Boston, MA: South End Press.

Slavin, R. 1991. "Chapter I: A Vision for the Next Quarter Century." *Phi Delta Kappan,* 69, 586–589.

Smith, M., and B. Scoll. 1995. "The Clinton Human Capital Agenda." *Teacher College Record,* 96, 389–404.

Smith, R., and B. Vavrichek. 1987. "The Minimum Wage: Its Relation to Income and Poverty." *Monthly Labor Review,* 41, 21–42.

Solskin, J. 1993. *Literacy, Gender, and Work in Families and in School.* Norwood, NJ: Ablex.

Sowell, T. 1993. *Is Reality Optional?* Stanford, CA: Hoover Institution Press.

Spodek, B. (ed.) 1986. *Today's Kindergarten: Exploring the Knowledge Base, Expanding the Curriculum.* New York: Teachers College Press.

Stahl, S. 1994. "The Real Thing: Advertisements and Research in the Debate About Whole Language." In C. Smith (ed.), *Whole Language: The Debate* Bloomington, IN: ERIC Press.

Stein, M. 1997. "Yolanda Rivera, Dream Maker." *Ms.,* (July/August) 8, 30–33.

Street, B. 1995. *Social Literacies: Critical Approaches to Literacy in Development, Ethnography, and Education.* New York: Longman.

Stuckey, J. E. 1991. *The Violence of Literacy.* Portsmouth, NH: Boynton/Cook.

Tabor, M. 1996. "New Guidelines on English: A Sketch, Not a Blueprint." *New York Times,* (12 March,) A12.

Taylor, C. 1992. *Multiculturalism and The Politics of Recognition.* Princeton, NJ: Princeton University Press.

Taylor, D. 1993. "Family Literacy: Resisting Deficit Models." *TESOL Quarterly,* 27, 550–553.

———. 1996. *Toxic Literacies: Exposing the Injustice of Bureaucratic Texts.* Portsmouth, NH: Heinemann.

Taylor D., and C. Dorsey-Gaines. 1988. *Growing Up Literate.* Portsmouth, NH: Heinemann.

Tenerio, R. 1991. "Race and Respect Among Small Children." *Rethinking Schools,* 4, 3, 5–6.

Tilly, C. 1991. "Reasons for the Continuing Growth of Part-time Employment." *Monthly Labor Review,* 76, 10–18.

Trausch, S. 1993. "The ABCs of Illiteracy." *Boston Globe,* (15 September,) A13.

Trend, D. (ed.) 1996. *Radical Democracy: Identity, Citizenship, and the State.* New York: Routledge.

Twentieth Century Fund. 1983. *Report of the Task Force for Federal and Elementary and Secondary Policy.* New York: Twentieth Century Fund.

U.S. Bureau of Census. 1993. *Household Wealth and Asset Ownership,* 34, 70, vii.

U.S. Bureau of Labor Statistics. 1993, November 24. *The American Workforce: 1992–2005.* Washington, DC: Government Printing Office.

———. 1993. *Employment and Earnings,* 40(1), 79.

———. 1994a. *Employment and Earnings,* 41(1), 22.

———. 1994b. *Employment and Earnings,* 41(10), 18.

U.S. Department of Education. Office of Education Research and Improvement. 1996. *Directions in Research and Implications for Practice.* (January) Washington, DC: U.S. Government Printing Office.

U.S. General Accounting Office. 1985. *An Evaluation of the 1981 AFDC Changes: Final Report.* Washington, DC: U.S. Government Printing Office.

Vaughan, D. 1993. "Exploring the Use of the Public's View to Set Income Poverty Thresholds and Adjust Them Over Time." *Social Security Bulletin,* 55, 22–46.

Verdugo, R. 1992. "Earning Differentials Between Black, Mexican-American, and Non-Hispanic White Male Workers." *Social Science Quarterly,* 73, 663–674.

Wagner, D. 1995. "To Read or Not to Read." *Education Week,* (25 October,) 79.

Wallace, C. 1995. "Critical Literacy Awareness in the EFL Classroom." In N. Fairclough (ed.), *Critical Language Awareness.* New York: Longman.

Wallis, J. 1996. "A Crisis of Civility." *Sojourners,* (September/October) 32, 10–12.

Walljasper, J. 1997. "When Activists Win: The Renaissance of Dudley St." *Nation,* (3 March,) 264, 11–18.

Walsh, C. 1991. *Pedagogy and the Struggle for Voice: Issues of Language, Power, and Schooling for Puerto Ricans.* Westport, CT: Bergin and Garvey.

Walt, K. 1996. "The Crisis at Hand." *Houston Chronicle,* (1 February,) A1, 22.

White, B. 1996. "Student Goals Unveiled Today." *Atlanta Constitution,* (12 March,) C3.

Widemann, J. 1995. "Doing Time, Marking Race." *Nation,* (30 October,) 261, 502–505.

Wignell, P. 1994. "Genre Across the Curriculum." *Linguistics and Education,* 6, 355–372.

Willis, E. 1994. "The Median Is the Message." *Village Voice,* (15 November,) 26, 31.

Wilson, J. Q. 1983. *Thinking About Crime.* New York: Basic Books.

———. 1993. *The Moral Sense.* New York: Free Press.

———. 1994. "Tales of Virtue." *Commentary,* (April) 97, 30–35.

———. 1995. *On Character.* Washington, DC: American Enterprise Institute Press.

———. 1996. "Cultural Aspects of Poverty." In M. Darby (ed.), *Reducing Poverty in America.* Thousand Oaks, CA: Sage Publications.

Wilson, W. J. 1987. *The Truly Disadvantaged: The Inner City, the Underclass and Public Policy.* Chicago: University of Chicago Press.

———. 1997. *When Work Disappears: The World of the New Urban Poor.* New York: Knopf.

Woo, E. 1996. "National Standards Offered to English Teachers." *Los Angeles Times,* (12 March,) A1, 17.

York, R. 1992. Elderly Americans. Testimony Before the Select Committee on Aging, House of Representatives. June 24. Washington, DC: U.S. Government Printing Office. 72.

Zigler, E., and S. Muenchow. 1992. *Head Start.* New York: Basic Books.

Zigler, E., and S. Styfco. 1994. "Criticisms in a Constructive Context." *American Psychologist,* 49, 127–132.

INDEX

◆◆